Moving Millions

How Coyote Capitalism Fuels Global Immigration

JEFFREY KAYE

WILEY

John Wiley & Sons, Inc.

Published by John Wiley & Sons, Inc., Hoboken, New Jersey
Published simultaneously in Canada

For general information about our other products and services, please contact our Customer Care Department within the United States at (800) 762-2974, outside the United States at (317) 572-3993 or fax (317) 572-4002.

Wiley also publishes its books in a variety of electronic formats. Some content that appears in print may not be available in electronic books. For more information about Wiley products, visit our web site at www.wiley.com.

Library of Congress Cataloging-in-Publication Data:

Kaye, Jeffrey.
    Moving millions : how coyote capitalism fuels global immigration / Jeffrey Kaye.
       p. cm.
    Includes bibliographical references and index.
    ISBN 978-0-470-42334-9 (cloth)
       1. Emigration and immigration—Economic aspects.   2. Emigration and immigration—Social aspects.   3. Emigration and immigration—Government policy.   4. Foreign workers. I. Title.
    JV6217.K39 2010
    325—dc22

                                                                          2009034173

Printed in the United States of America

10 9 8 7 6 5 4 3 2 1

To the memory of my parents, Harry and Rebecca.
To my sister, Judith.
To my wife and best friend, Deborah.
And to my children, Sara and Sophie: May your own life voyages be
ones of fulfillment, compassion, love, and joy.

CONTENTS

ACKNOWLEDGMENTS

As an immigrant, a journalist, and a longtime resident of Los Angeles, I have found the subject of immigration to be an abiding and recurring theme. So this book is a product of not only my personal history, but also of a career in which I've tried to understand and explain the forces that spur people to uproot themselves, leave families, and cross borders.

I spent the first thirteen years of my life in London. My mother and father were born in England right after World War I to parents who had been part of the great westward-moving wave of Eastern Europeans. As a result, my family life was imbued with a hybrid culture —that spanned two worlds—an older, Yiddish-speaking generation, and that of my parents, a bridge between the Old World and the New.

As a thirteen-year-old, I had only a vague understanding of why my parents, Harry and Rebecca, decided to leave England with my sister Judith and me to journey to a quintessential destination for immigrants, Southern California. Living in *El Pueblo de Nuestra Señora la Reina de los Ángeles de Porciúncula*, I have often felt as if the world were arriving on my doorstep.

As I came to learn why people move, I realized that beyond the obvious personal calculations were factors beyond the control of migrants themselves. In that sense, some of the influences on my parents' immigration decision undoubtedly had parallels with those of my grandparents, Avram and Yetta Richtiger and Jakob and Sarah Krakovsky (later Kosky, then Kaye).

So, in a book that examines some of the mega-issues involved in migration, I need to acknowledge not only migrant ancestors and contemporary influences, but Alexander III Alexandrovich and Maurice Harold Macmillan, respectively the tsar of Russia (1881–1894) and the prime minister of the United Kingdom (1957–1963). If it were not for them, I would not be where I am today. Their policies and actions propelled my family to cross continents and oceans. In the case of the Russian emperor, anti-Jewish pogroms combined with economic hardships pushed my great-grandparents to England. In the early 1960s, high taxes imposed by the Macmillan government on jewelry, which my father—an artist and craftsman—made by hand, prompted my parents' decision to immigrate to the United States.

More directly, I thank my colleagues at the *PBS NewsHour* for providing twenty-five years' worth of rewarding assignments and opportunities that allowed me to expand my horizons and knowledge. In particular, Jim Lehrer, Les Crystal, Linda Winslow, Mike Mosettig, and Gregg Ramshaw supported reporting ventures that took me around the world. I am especially grateful for the wisdom and kindness of Patti Parson of the *NewsHour*, not only for her guidance and insights but for a wonderful friendship. *Moving Millions* also drew on reporting for HDNet's *World Report*, where I have been fortunate to work with the late Dave Green and, more recently, with Dennis O'Brien and Kathy Gettings.

My agent, Heather Schroder at ICM, guided and championed this project from the beginning. The team at John Wiley & Sons was enthusiastic and supportive. Thanks to Senior Editor Eric Nelson and Associate Editor Connie Santisteban, who asked tough questions, pushing me in the direction of clarity and focus; to Senior Production Editor John Simko and Copy Editor William D. Drennan for their smarts and attention to detail; to Editorial Assistant Ellen Wright for helping to keep things on track; and to cover designer Wendy Mount.

This book could not have been written without the assistance of collaborators who helped me find my way in travels around the world. Special thanks to Saul Gonzalez, my friend and former colleague at the *NewsHour*. The dirty little secret of traveling journalists is the extent to which we rely on "fixers" for local expertise, translation, and crosscultural guidance. In that respect, I am indebted to Hicham Houdaïfa in Morocco; Magdalena Sánchez and Liliana Lemus in Lindsay, California; Diego Reyes in Monterrey, Mexico; Jezmín Fuentes for her assistance in Tijuana, Mexico; Girlie Linao in the Philippines; Mamadou Bodian and Mahmoud Diallo in Senegal; Marynia Kruk in Poland; Ulrika Engström in Sweden; Bernard Goldbach in Ireland; Younus Mohamed in the United Arab Emirates; and Nguyen Huy Quang and Dang Nguyen Anh in Vietnam. Thanks also to Jeremy Green and Ruth Schamroth for their hospitality in London; and to Los Angeles immigration lawyer Rajkrishna S. Iyer.

In addition to those who have helped me directly, I have bene-fitted greatly from scholars and experts on immigration whose work I have followed and admired. These include Jorge Bustamante, Stephen Castles, Wayne Cornelius, Jorge Durand, Philip Martin, Douglas S. Massey, and Peter Stalker. I am also grateful for the wealth of resources available on the Web sites maintained by the Migration Policy Institute (www.migrationpolicy.org) and by attorney Daniel M. Kowalski (www.bibdaily.com).

I owe special thanks to a network of friends and to my family for their encouragement and support. I am particularly indebted to Hershl Hartman for imparting intellectual rigor and historical insights; to my cousin Lawrence Collin for his good humor and knowledge of family lore; to my sister Judith for her encouragement and feedback; and to my darling daughters, Sophie and Sara, who patiently listened to me and put up with my occasional absences over the years. Finally, to Deborah—my in-house editor-in-chief, reviewer, touchstone, and wife—thank you for your patience, inspiration, and enduring love.

Introduction

When I walk to the supermarket close to my house, my attention is often drawn to what is usually an unremarkable dot on the urban landscape: a manhole cover. What distinguishes the fairly ordinary-looking, brownish cast-iron covering is not so much its overall appearance. It is just a sewer lid. But what I find almost captivating is the noteworthy juxtaposition of twin phrases cast into its design. On one side, a semicircle of capital letters says: CITY OF L.A. Opposite, three words in the shape of a happy-face smile complete the circle, offering a perspective probably not intended by the designers or the makers of the sewer lid: MADE IN MEXICO.

I love it. Not just for the discovery of meaning, intended or otherwise, in a mundane, public utility fitting, but also for the unadorned statement it makes about connections in a city in which 40 percent of the residents (myself included) were born abroad, at a time when so much attention and public debate revolve around where we're from and what borders we've crossed.

For me, immigration has been an abiding interest, both professionally and personally. My grandparents and great-grandparents migrated from Russian-occupied Poland to England in the late eighteen hundreds and just after the beginning of the twentieth century. Decades later, my family's global odyssey continued when my parents left London and brought my sister and me to the United States. Our four generations migrated for the same reason most people move—the search for a

1

better life. My mother was a legal secretary. My father was a jeweler, a craftsman, who, because of high luxury taxes imposed by the British government, had difficulty selling his goods to retailers. Inspired by cousins who were moving to Los Angeles, in 1962 he wrote forty letters to jewelers asking for work. One offered to help. We moved in 1963 and I've lived here ever since.

My immigration story is somewhat typical in the way it involves family, risk, and the hope of a better life.

Of course, there's more to my story than that, and there's more to this book than the common perceptions about why people migrate. Immigration may ultimately be the result of personal decisions, but strip away the obvious, and what's revealed are underlying dynamics of business strategies and trade practices as well as politics and policies — global and domestic — that are pushing, pulling, and moving millions around the globe.

Humans are a migratory species. From the epic Exodus tale in the Bible to the story of Odysseus, our myths and legends attest to mobility as a central theme in the human saga. To escape problems and to seek out fresh prospects, we've been in the process of "globalization" for as many as a hundred thousand years, ever since our ancestral wanderers ventured out of East Africa in search of more hospitable living arrangements — better hunting, gathering, and fishing grounds. As we developed agriculture about fifteen thousand years ago, trade, commerce, and the eventual creation of cities spawned even more migration, a trend that continued as populations grew and as transportation and communications technologies advanced.

The world is experiencing an exodus on a scale never before seen, spurred by the same ancient motivations — the pursuit of opportunity and resources. Some have claimed that the unprecedented extent of globalization is "flattening the playing field." But if that is the case, why are so many switching teams?

While a large proportion of migrants move from poor countries to other developing nations that are less poor, most migrants live in the nations of the developed world. Today, one out of every thirty-five people in the world resides in a country other than the one he or she was born in. If the world's two hundred million people now living outside the nations of their birth were in one place, they would comprise the world's fifth most populous country.

I've reported on immigration issues on four continents and heard similar emotional and heated debates about "the immigration problem," discussions often tinged with racial overtones and xenophobia. The gut level reactions are often superficial and devoid of context.

Around the world, I've seen migrants pursued, rounded up, and deported as governments—and certainly the news media—treat the issue as a local phenomenon, arguing in a multitude of languages about fences, amnesty programs, border guards, guest worker proposals, linguistic purity, population growth, social services, crime, and the end of civilization as we know it.

Despite the fact that in raw numbers the United States is home to more migrants than any other nation, more than sixty other countries have even higher percentages of foreigners living inside their borders. Three quarters of the world's migrants are clustered in twenty-eight industrialized countries, nations that increasingly are becoming gated communities—as governments fortify boundaries, expand border police forces, and erect new iron curtains. Migrants go where the grass is greener, so just as the United States tries to keep out Mexicans, Mexico has beefed up security along its southern border to keep out Guatemalans. Malaysia deports Filipinos. Kosovo expels Bangladeshis. Along Europe's flanks, Spain, Italy, and Greece are expelling sub-Saharan Africans, while Poland is jailing Russians. In Russia, nationalist thugs are taking matters into their own hands by terrorizing dark-skinned migrant laborers from Tajikistan and Chechnya. In South America, Argentina deports Bolivians. Haiti throws out Dominicans. And in the United Kingdom, black-uniformed border police raid fast-food and curry restaurants looking for Pakistanis, Indians, and Bangladeshis lacking the requisite immigration papers.

On the world's political stages, the often fierce rhetoric over migration tends to overlook the issues that propel people to move, forces such as global supply chains, money flows, nomadic businesses, inequality, and trade policies. Instead, we fall into questions of control and management: How best to keep out unwanted foreigners and let in more desirable ones? What to do about the millions of illegal migrants who sneak across borders or overstay visas?

While people obviously migrate for many reasons, a chief focus of this book is the movement of labor. I began writing this book before the global recession hit. The economic downturn led to somewhat of a decline in labor migration, but nonetheless the same basic issues and trends persist. If anything, the increased competition for jobs has only sharpened the debates over immigration. The United Nations has estimated that nearly ninety million people worldwide are migrant workers. As many as forty million of them are believed to be illegal migrants. Millions more move as a result of conflicts, natural disasters, environmental degradation, or a combination of factors.

Even though migration can be complex, much of the political debate, at least in the United States, is one-dimensional, viewing migration through one prism, the legal status of migrants. The legal arguments mask a convenient historical amnesia and obscure more fundamental issues.

I once asked Joseph M. Arpaio, the tough-talking sheriff of Maricopa County, Arizona, which includes Phoenix, about his own family history. Arpaio has made a crackdown on illegal migrants a hallmark of his policing. I wanted to know whether the people he targets, mostly Mexicans, were much different from his own parents, who crossed the Atlantic from Italy in the early 1900s.

"I have a deep compassion for the Mexican people," he said. "However, if you come into this country illegally, you're going to jail in this county. My mother and father came from Italy legally. *Legally*," he repeated for emphasis.

Such indignation on the basis of supposedly unblemished family trees is widespread. But the claims to moral superiority reflect an "idealized history," as journalist Lawrence Downes has observed. The notion that U.S. immigration policy has a long and consistent legal record is a common misconception.

Until 1929, it was not a federal crime to enter the United States without authorization. The invention of "illegal alien" as a category is a relatively recent creation of twentieth-century restrictionists.

Besides which, the industrialized world's preoccupation with the legal status of migrants is only one facet of the larger picture.

Moving Millions attempts to fill a void by following the money and replacing a narrow spotlight with a broader floodlight. My goal is to illuminate some of the underreported economic aspects of the story—examining relationships between migration and globalization, as well as the constellations of enterprises that facilitate, encourage, and benefit from migration, both legal and illegal.

Policymakers trying to address immigration issues often seem to be flailing. If they really want to affect patterns of migration, they need to come to terms with the globally interconnected business engines that promote and support it. They should question whether the economic policies they enact and the trade policies they pursue encourage migration. They also need to make fundamental choices about priorities—about economic needs and human rights, matters that transcend national boundaries.

In other words, immigration should be seen more as a symptom or a reaction to policies and conditions than as a problem. Immigration is a fact of life. Given the right set of circumstances, people (not to mention our prehuman ancestors) have always moved and always will. Labor migration persists for at least two main reasons. First, global and local businesses rely on human mobility and on ready, vulnerable pools of labor, often available at bargain basement prices. Second, successful migrants—who number among the most assertive, determined, and entrepreneurial people in the world—are able to overcome the forces and obstacles arrayed against them. It's the law of supply and demand. Just as the drug trade feeds apparently insatiable appetites, overwhelming borders and policing, the world's migrants as well as the businesses and economies that love them make sure the human flow continues.

It is a global system that may be called "*coyote* capitalism."*Coyotes* are human smugglers, or as professors Gilbert G. Gonzalez and Raul A. Fernandez described them, "unauthorized Mexican labor recruiters." This neutral-sounding phrase filters out the legal baggage to arrive at a basic job description. It allows us to think of coyotes in economic terms rather than as fanged creatures of the underworld. Similarly, coyote capitalism straddles the realms of the legitimate and the unlawful, evoking a netherworld in which many migrants find themselves. This is not to suggest that most migrants are smuggled, although many are. Coyote capitalism describes a system of interlocking, dependent relationships, some "authorized," some not.

It is also a system of avoidance and transference. The coyotes' job is to ensure that human cargo gets from one place to another.

They are shippers who take no responsibility for the consequences of moving freight, either at the place of departure or the destination. Coyote capitalism allows businesses and governments (in both developed and developing nations) to pass workers around and pass the buck. If your policy is to export labor, there are fewer expectations to create jobs. If you import workers, you can excuse yourself for developing an economy dependent on migrant labor. And if you develop business or trade policies that encourage people to move around in search of opportunities, you are only the middleman, just the coyote.

Across the globe, migrants commonly perform the so-called 3-D jobs—labor that is dirty, dangerous, or demeaning. The migrant-dependent industries are the same everywhere. Many of the world's farms, fields, hospitals, nursing homes, and construction sites would be losing enterprises if not for the work of foreign laborers. Ditto for hotels and restaurants, labor-intensive manufacturing, and low-skilled services. Armies of migrant domestic workers clean, nanny, and nurse. Some are victims of ruthless traffickers, serving masters who keep them in conditions of indentured servitude.

Although migrants are overrepresented in low-wage, lower-skilled work, at the opposite end of the skills spectrum, global industries often compete for well-trained professionals.

Taken together, the promise of jobs, the willingness of employers to hire migrants, and the calculation by migrants that leaving is better than staying are all powerful incentives for crossing borders—legally or not. Migrant incomes are lubricants for the often extensive networks of recruiters, traffickers, and smugglers who get them to their destinations. Industries rely on the billions of dollars migrants send back to their homelands. The interconnected machinery comprising today's labor market forms a complex, global migration industry.

In the face of such forces, efforts to fashion rational, consistent, and humane migration policies have been elusive. Benjamin E. Johnson, director of the migrant advocacy group the Immigration Policy Center, eloquently summed up the conundrum: "We send two messages at our border: 'Help Wanted' and 'Keep Out,'" he told a congressional committee. Johnson nailed it, describing the default official approach as "schizophrenia."

Formulating sensible policy requires rulemakers to weigh competing interests. But a key issue is basic: Is it possible to formulate migration policies that balance the labor requirements of businesses and economies with the needs and rights of migrant workers? Or are migrant workers interchangeable parts, expendable widgets whose export and import should be calibrated and adjusted according to our needs?

Other questions flow from those.

Clearly, importing nations have come to rely on migrants as integral to their labor force. But what should be done in exchange? Do migrant-dependent businesses or economies have obligations to the families, communities, and countries left behind?

Developed nations and companies often adopt policies—both domestic and global—that have the effect of promoting migration. Should there be checks on such strategies?

At the same time, less wealthy nations actually encourage their citizens to leave, for both political and economic purposes. Should more be done to encourage sustainable economies that don't rely on the sacrifices that migration often entails?

Increasingly, businesses are forming tentative and unusual coalitions with immigrant advocacy groups. Who wins when partners in the "strange bedfellows" alliances have competing priorities?

Most Western countries argue over how many immigrants are too many. We focus on the size of the fences or the number of visas. But should we also pay more attention to the behavior of people importers? We go after human smugglers, but what about the other middlemen, the legal recruiters? Just as we try to monitor the importers of foreign food or toys, do we need to keep a closer eye on those in the people import business and hold them more accountable for the treatment of their human cargo?

Migration is a global phenomenon. Given that fact, how reasonable is it for politicians to adopt national immigration policies as if they were the equivalent of local zoning ordinances passed with a nod toward placating homeowners' associations with a NIMBY (not in my backyard) mentality?

Policymakers need to not only make sure economic interests do not trump human rights; they also should recognize that migration does not take place in a vacuum. Besides considering the international context, they need to reject the disease model of immigration that tries to treat it in isolation from its causes. Taking account of the reasons people migrate will allow them to shape humane and rational migration policies.

Careful readers will note a linguistic sensitivity about certain terms—in particular the use of the word "alien," which in this sentence appears between quotation marks. In this regard, I need to offer a note about the terminology you'll find in this book.

I've grappled for years over the best way to describe people whose residency in a country is unlawful, either because they crossed a border without permission or because the legal status they once enjoyed—in possessing a work or student visa, for example—is no longer valid. Are they "illegal"? "Irregular"? "Unauthorized"? Different countries, bureaucracies, and advocacy groups use various terms, often laden with baggage and meaning.

What about resident noncitizens (an awkward term)? Are they "aliens"? "Immigrants"? "Migrants"? "Foreigners"? (When Ted Turner owned CNN, he banned the use of the latter word. "We are trying to eliminate the word 'foreign' at CNN," he told an interviewer. "We have done away with the 'foreign' desk . . . we call them 'international.'")

The nouns "immigrants" and "migrants" suggest different standards of legitimacy. "Immigrant" usually refers to people who have gone through a legal process, while "migrant" describes someone who has merely crossed a border.

The various adjectives are fraught with political connotations, often conveying where the user stands on a continuum of attitudes ranging from sympathy to hostility. Many advocates of hard-line approaches prefer the term "illegal alien." Rights groups—justifiably, in my opinion—complain that "alien," while legally correct, conjures images of extraterrestrial space beings, while "illegal" should more properly refer to an act, not a person. The historian Mae Ngai raises the existential problem in using a term that denotes "'an impossible subject,' a person who cannot be and a problem that cannot be solved."

In my mind, "unauthorized" is too vague, while "irregular" is more suited to a product than a person. There's also the popular term "undocumented," one I've never been comfortable using, since most migrants do have some kinds of papers—even if they are forged, borrowed, or the wrong ones to satisfy the scrutiny needed for legal residency.

Then there's the squishiness factor. The labels we try to apply often don't stick. They can be as transitory as some of the people we're describing. "Irregular" or "illegal" immigrants one day may become "legal" the next if amnesty programs come into play (as has happened in recent years in the United States, Spain, Ecuador, Mexico, the Netherlands Antilles, and Argentina). On the flip side, today's legal "guest worker" might easily become tomorrow's deportee. (Similarly, while outside the focus of this book, the term "refugees" can be a temporary designation or a description passed from one generation to the next.) Rejiggering national boundaries also affects legal status. The breakup of the Soviet Union and Czechoslovakia, for example, transformed millions of people from internal to international migrants—accurately reflecting an old slogan of migrants' rights activists along the U.S. southern frontier: "We didn't cross the border; the border crossed us."

Contributing to the linguistic imprecision is the fact that many migrants move with the intention of returning. Not that they always do, but migration can be more of a fluid than a permanent arrangement. In 1993 I met Jesús Hernández-Rocha in the small town of San Diego de Alejandría in the state of Jalisco, about six hundred miles south of the U.S./Mexico border. On his first trip to the United States, Hernández was picked up by the Border Patrol and deported. He tried again and made it to Los Angeles, where he spent nineteen years working in a meatpacking plant. He saved his money and returned to his hometown, where, later, he became the elected mayor. When I met him, he was marching at the head of the parade during *el día de los ausentes* (the day of the absent ones), honoring migrants, and he showed me around his house, the biggest one in town. He pulled out pictures of his family. One son, born in the United States, was dressed in uniform—that of a U.S. soldier. In his binational family, the border was virtually a state of mind.

The legal categories of migrants are situational and fungible. So since this book deals mainly with economic and business issues relating to migration, I will not dwell on the legal status of people who cross borders. As for my preferred terms, I choose to use "legal" or "illegal" and "migrants." They are not perfect, but they convey the meaning and I intend no disrespect.

In my own family, migrants played footsie with the law. Although they undoubtedly left Russian-occupied Poland at least in part because of deteriorating economic conditions, my male ancestors might have been drafted into the Russian Army had they not left illegally to avoid conscription. When my mother visited relatives in the Polish town of Zduńska Wola before World War II, her father didn't accompany her, afraid the military would grab him.

For all families, migration is a delicate calculation. Are the likely rewards worth the risks? Will those who leave and those left behind be able to cope with the pains of separation? At the time we left England, my father's mother was frail, and he feared he might never see her again.

"I very reluctantly told my ailing mother," he wrote many years later. "She replied with a saying in Yiddish—*Gey mitn rekhtn fus*—which means 'Start with the right foot.' That meant a lot to me."

I have no idea how many other cultures and languages have similar send-offs for departing relatives. I'm sure that Sarah Kaye's benediction for her progeny has echoed through the millennia of human existence, although for many the tone is more of desperation than of hope.

In England not long ago, I met Alfonso Camiwet, then a fifty-six-year-old Episcopal priest from the Philippines who was working in a private house in London caring for an elderly man suffering the dual symptoms of a stroke and Parkinson's disease. Camiwet, a slight and intense man, was sending money home to his three college-age children and worrying that his youngest, a son whom he hadn't seen for more than six years, was getting into trouble. We talked about why so many Filipinos feel compelled to leave their country. His response was chilling.

"We have a term in the Philippines: *Kapit sa patalim*. There is no other way," he said seriously.

I asked him to elaborate. He raised his right hand, made a fist, and clutching an imaginary object, slowly pulled down as if doing a pull-up. "You hang on to a blade," he explained. "There's a knife, but you've got to hold it in order to hang on, to exist."

Migration experts talk about push and pull factors. Migrants are aware of rags-to-riches success stories as well as hardships. The tales abound of the upwardly mobile immigrant—the asylum-seeker from Nigeria who became Ireland's first black mayor, the foreign-born immigrants who helped start one of every four U.S. technology start-ups over the past decade, the impoverished Chinese ballet dancer who became a star in Australia, and the jeweler from England who accomplished his modest dream of sending his children to college.

Moving Millions assumes that human migration will persist no matter what we do to try to restrain or restrict it, particularly as the income gap between the haves and the have-nots continues to expand. Build walls, and people will go over, around, and under them. Hire border guards, and people will bribe them. Step up patrols, and migrants will find alternate routes.

As an English schoolboy, I was taught about King Canute, the Danish migrant who ruled England after he and fellow Viking warriors seized it in the eleventh century. According to legend, Canute was taken to the beach, where he commanded the tide not to rise. But it did. The common interpretation of the tale is that it shows the arrogance of a foolhardy monarch. Another, more flattering version is that the king, perfectly aware of his own capabilities, intended to demonstrate the limits of power to others.

I don't know which version of the story New York City mayor Michael Bloomberg had in mind when he testified before a U.S. Senate Committee that had solicited ideas about how to restrict immigration: "You might as well sit in your beach chair and tell the tide not to come in," said Bloomberg.

CHAPTER 1

Lures and Blinders

Hazleton's weathered downtown has seen better days. Some brick-facade office buildings sit empty, and even occupied stores at first glance appear abandoned. A much-needed face-lift along the main drag, Broad Street, has been delayed. Wood frame houses show their age. But there are signs of vitality in this small Pennsylvania coal country town in the foothills of the Pocono Mountains. Shopping centers and malls have sprouted up on the town's outskirts. Industrial parks have attracted brand-name tenants such as Amazon, Network Solutions, General Mills, ADM, Hilton, Cargill Meats, OfficeMax, and Pillsbury.

And up and down the side streets, there is other evidence of a city in transition.

"This is an Hispanic business," pointed out Ana Arias as we drove along Diamond Avenue. "This is an Hispanic business," she repeated moments later.

Arias, a local activist who works at Catholic Social Services, agreed to be my tour guide when I told her I was researching the politics and history of Hazleton. I had gone there to learn more about a place that in 2006 had made international headlines by passing one of the nation's strictest anti-illegal immigration laws. Like many of the town's arrivals over the past couple of decades, Arias is a native of the Dominican Republic who moved to Hazleton from New York City.

We passed La Bella Napoli on Locust Street. The pizza joint with the Italian name is owned by Dominicans, she told me. We turned into an upscale development with plush two-story homes on the outskirts of town. "This house is owned by a Dominican family. They own their own business," she explained.

The influx of Latinos has been striking. According to the Pew Hispanic Center, the number of Latinos in Hazleton's county, Luzerne, more than tripled between 2000 and 2007. Among counties with more than a thousand Hispanics, Luzerne has the eighth fastest-growing Hispanic population in the United States.

The growth began slowly in the late 1980s and picked up after the terrorist attacks of September 2001, when the area witnessed an economic resurgence and a population shift. Urban Easterners, many of them Latinos from New York and New Jersey, found country living, affordable housing, and jobs.

Newcomers obtained work on farms and in factories such as Pocono Knits, Chromatex, and the meatpacking plant Cargill. Jobs were coming on line thanks in large part to the economic development initiatives of Hazleton's cheerily named CAN DO (Community Area New Development Organization), which lured businesses with tax breaks and low costs. The influx of people and businesses reversed a trend. The city had been in decline, a demise that began in the 1940s after nearby coal mines began closing. Latino migrants not only came for jobs, they also opened up scores of businesses. Housing costs were cheap compared to places they had left, such as Queens in New York City; Victorian homes could be had for $30,000 to $40,000.

"The economy was good," Arias remembers. Her brother moved from New York in 1987. She and her mother followed in 1988. It was a boom town. People were buying and selling homes quickly. "You could put a house up for sale and two weeks later, it would be sold."

In addition to the cheap housing and available work, Arias said, Hazleton reminded her and other native Dominicans of their homeland. "This area was quiet and pristine. It was in the mountains like where these people came from originally."

Amilcar Arroyo arrived in Hazleton in 1989, when only about twenty-five Hispanic families lived in town. The urbane Peruvian native had been living in Miami when he spotted a newspaper ad offering free transportation to Hazleton for a farm job. He came north, took work packing tomatoes, and then went on to take a job in a textile company, followed by one in a printing firm. He's now the editor of *El Mensajero* (The Messenger), a monthly Spanish-language tabloid newspaper, which he founded in 2003 to cater to the area's changing population.

As a journalist, he not only chronicled the influx, he also benefited from it. His office, in a Broad Street shopping mall, is comfortable. In 2007, after building up to a readership of about twenty-five thousand, he sold the paper to the Wilkes-Barre Publishing Co. and a group of Texas investors who evidently saw merit in buying a Spanish-language paper in a growing Spanish-language market. The Wilkes-Barre Publishing Co. puts out nine other publications, including the *Dallas Post*.

Arroyo explained how migrants from New York had sold their homes there for twice as much as it cost them to buy comparable places in the Hazleton area. New arrivals, he said, paid for homes in cash, "and with the rest of the money, they opened a business. And what did they do? They work; they find a job, and they work for a factory, so we're talking about people who have three incomes. Renting house, a small business—grocery, barbershop, multiservices—and work in a factory."

Manuel Espinal used to deliver Budweiser beer in Brooklyn. The Dominican native moved to Hazleton, took a factory job at Chromatex (a now-defunct upholstery company), and, while working there, in 1996, opened the Jazmin Grocery Store on downtown Wyoming Street. His modest shop became his life. "It was the first Spanish store in town," he told me proudly. He was even prouder of the fact that two of his three children were U.S. Marines; one was in Iraq at the time I visited his store. "Every time the phone rings . . ." His voice trailed off without completing the sentence. "But it's not in your hands."

Espinal said town leaders have a bias against Latinos. "How can you say these people are bad for the town when they come to work for twelve or fourteen hours a day?" he asked. "We're doing good here."

For old-timers, the demographic shift and rapid population increase had changed a way of life. School enrollment had escalated. Housing conditions had become more crowded.

"You've got to get in the frame of mind of what we were deal-
ing with in a small town and how this was affecting our services,"
Hazleton's outspoken mayor, Louis J. Barletta, told me over breakfast.
Gregarious, immaculate, and distinguished in a starched white shirt,
Barletta resembled an Italian Mitt Romney.

We met in the Cyber Calf restaurant on the ground floor of
Hazleton's tallest structure, the hundred-year-old Markle Building,
described by its owners as a "wonderfully preserved 11-story skyscraper."
The landmark bears the name of a family once known for its prominence in coal mining and banking.

Over coffee and omelets, Barletta and two of his closest associates, Joseph Yannuzzi and John Keegan, described their frustration with the town's transformation. At the time of our meeting, the
Republican mayor was running for Congress. Daily, he had breakfast
meetings with Yannuzzi, who was the City Council president as well
as the owner of a computer company, and Keegan, a pharmacist.

"We're the mayor's brain trust—although he doesn't know that,"
joked Keegan.

To Yannuzzi, Keegan, and Barletta, it was as if the town were
under assault by invaders.

"People were moving in; people were moving out," said Barletta,
explaining that longtime residents were constantly complaining to
him. "So you had a nice home, modest home that you've taken care
of your entire life, and all of a sudden next door all of a sudden someone new buys it, now there's fifteen people in the house. You call
City Hall to complain; we're sending people down for violations time
and time again."

The character of residential neighborhoods began to change.

"It was obvious, you'd ride down the street and see a home with
ten [satellite] dishes, five on each side, which meant that in every
room in that house was somebody living there, as a family. That's
code violations right there," added Yannuzzi.

As complaints mounted, Barletta said he felt compelled to act.
"Believe me, I didn't just wake up one day and say, 'I'm going to start
picking on illegal aliens.' This has happened over *years* of seeing what
was happening in our neighborhoods."

What really spurred him, he said, was the crime. "We had more
and more cases of incidents involving illegal aliens; our violent crime

was beginning to rise. We started noticing more gang activity and more need for a greater police presence and for more money [for law enforcement]."

In 2001, a fatal shooting, involving drug dealers with ties to the Dominican Republic, made headlines.

Barletta complained about immigrants getting drunk in the park and creating domestic disturbances. They were responsible for neighborhood blight and overcrowded apartments, he said.

"The final straw for me was May 10, 2006. We arrested a fourteen-year-old for shooting a gun into a crowded playground. He was here illegally. That night, twenty-nine-year-old Derek Kichline was working on his pickup truck and was shot between the eyes by two individuals." Two illegal immigrants were arrested in connection with the shooting, but the charges were later dropped for lack of evidence.

Barletta decided he needed to send a message.

"Our police worked thirty-six straight hours in apprehending those who took Kichline's life. Our police department spent over half of our yearly budget for overtime on that one homicide. Our overtime in the police department was 150 percent over budget and we still don't have enough police on the streets to handle it now."

So on July 13, 2006, at a boisterous meeting, the Hazleton City Council, frustrated at what they saw as Washington's inaction, and led by Mayor Barletta wearing a bulletproof vest that he said was necessary for his safety, made international headlines by adopting in effect its own immigration policy. Hazleton's Illegal Immigration Relief Act Ordinance made English the official city language, imposed fines on landlords for renting to illegal immigrants, and revoked business permits of employers who hired them.

The new law put Hazleton in the forefront of a movement. For more than a century, the power to regulate immigration was assumed to be a federal prerogative. But in 2006, states, counties, and cities took matters into their own hands, passing hundreds of immigration laws.

"Illegal aliens are a drain on our resources, and they are not welcome here," Barletta warned at the time.

In discussing immigration, Barletta carefully sticks to issues involving crime and the demands put on a cash-strapped city. But he has had some trouble with actual proof and hard facts. He's been unable to document how many illegal immigrants live in Hazleton or their impact on city services. And while crime definitely increased as more people moved into town from big cities, in the six-year period between 2001 and 2006, Hazleton police identified no more than thirty crimes involving illegal migrants.

"I never say that illegal aliens commit all the crimes," Barletta explained. "I never attribute all these problems to illegal aliens. What I do say is that the drain on this city's budget, this very fragile city budget, affects the quality of life and our ability to protect the people of this community."

By the time of our conversation, Barletta had become used to the national limelight and sensitive to intimations of racism. He had been the subject of a profile by CBS's *60 Minutes*. He had been interviewed by the *New York Times* and was a frequent CNN guest. But while Barletta was circumspect, choosing to focus on high-minded public policy issues of budgets, tax bases, city resources, and competition for jobs, the other members of his breakfast "brain trust" did not feel similarly constrained about crossing the line that the mayor had carefully drawn. For Yannuzzi and Keegan, cultural stereotypes and broad-brush descriptions were very much a part of the conversation.

Keegan suggested that many Latino migrants were prone to violence. "How they dealt with conflicts in their country is what they brought in dealing with conflicts here, and it's not the way we deal with conflicts," he said. "I don't know if 'terror' is the right word, but [it's] the concern of the community because you didn't bring out a knife and gun to settle a conflict."

The men agreed that the new migrants had not made an effort to become part of community life. "They tried to establish their own Hispanic Little League, when our Little League was more than willing and continues to be open to every child," complained Keegan.

Yannuzzi chimed in with his own example. "The first thing they did, was they started their own Chamber of Commerce," he observed. "The Latino Chamber of Commerce. I think that's wrong."

In the minds of all three men, from high crime rates, to the disproportionate use of public resources, to the failure to assimilate, this wave of migration is unprecedented. And they should know.

Barletta's grandparents came from Italy, as did Yannuzzi's. Keegan's father's family was Irish. His mother's was Italian.

"They came here to become American," said Yannuzzi. "They came here to assimilate! The grandparents spoke Italian only when they didn't want you to know what was going on. 'We're in America! You speak English!' That's what was told to us by my grandmother and all, and that was the difference. Today, they're immigrating here for the benefits and I can't blame them, but they're looking for more than just the benefits."

"What do you think they're looking for?" I asked.

"They're looking for the programs, free medical, that kind of stuff," he answered.

Such generalizations about the Hazleton area's new arrivals sound as if they could have been uttered a century ago; in fact, they were.

- "Perhaps the most obvious result of the racial mixture is to be seen in the incapacity of the local government, and the wasteful administration of public funds."
- "Among the Italians, violence is more the result of quick temper than intoxication. . . . The Italians resort most often to the use of knives in their acts of violence."
- "The fact is there are some respected citizens in all the races except possibly the Italians. The average English-speaking person regards all of the immigrants as purchasable, ignorant, and vicious in a high degree."
- "The large number of Germans in Hazleton in 1880 made it almost a bilingual town. Attorneys and doctors advertised their ability to hold consultations in either English or German."

The first three quotations come from a 1911 U.S. government report on immigration to a town near Hazleton. The fourth is from a book by the historian Harold Aurand documenting life in Hazleton in the late nineteenth century.

The fact is that Hazleton is in a sense reliving its past. Present-day patterns of economic opportunity, ensuing migration, and the reactions to the influx of newcomers are recycled versions of old stories.

As they did then and as they do now, migrants move to where they can find jobs and opportunities. News of successes (sometimes exaggerated) travels through networks of families and friends, encouraging new settlers to take the leap and make homes in communities where the languages and cultures are familiar. While the consequences of migration (various degrees of hostility or acceptance) may vary, the magnet is usually the same: businesses need the labor and rely on warm bodies being in place at the right times and for the right costs. The effects on the destinations, the residents, or the migrants themselves are afterthoughts—if they are thoughts at all.

European migration to northeastern Pennsylvania propelled America's Industrial Revolution. It followed the development in the early nineteenth century of new technology that turned anthracite, a hot-burning coal, into the country's premier source of fuel for factory steam engines and for the home stoves of growing urban populations.

Northeastern Pennsylvania had the world's largest deposits of anthracite, but getting the mineral out of the ground and moving it to market were labor-intensive businesses requiring armies of men and boys who worked in construction crews and in the mines, extracting, hauling, crushing, and cleaning the coal. Those were jobs for migrants. They poured in, many of them experienced miners from coal regions in England, Scotland, Wales, and the German states. Later, they were joined by Irish immigrants—men who had earlier built the canal system that connected landlocked anthracite fields to inland rivers and eastern cities.

By the mid-nineteenth century, the anthracite industry grew in importance as coal barons became railroad magnates and as anthracite-fueled furnaces were put to use producing rails and locomotives, transportation that was far more efficient than the canals.

Industrialization, the demands of the Civil War, and the growth of the national railroad industry boosted the demand for hard coal. Anthracite production doubled to thirty million tons during the decade of the 1870s, and doubled again by the turn of the century. Increased production required more migrant workers. Between 1890 and 1908, the anthracite industry added nearly fifty thousand men.

But around 1875, the composition of the workforce started to change. Fewer miners were coming from English-speaking and northern European countries. Instead they moved from southern and eastern Europe. They were hungrier, willing to work more cheaply, do more dangerous jobs, and put up with the increasingly decrepit conditions in the overcrowded, company-owned "patch towns" around the collieries. Coal mine owners sent recruiters to New York to bring in workers in boxcars. Some company agents went across the Atlantic to try to lure cheap, compliant laborers who could replace more defiant union members. Poles, Lithuanians, Slavs, and Slovaks came first. They were followed by Russians, Hungarians, Croatians, Slovenians, Italians, and eastern European Jews.

The newest arrivals were typically at the lowest rungs on the job ladder, relegated to the most difficult and hazardous work. A derisive U.S. government report, sympathetic to the coal operators, defended the practice, suggesting that the workers' inferiority made them well suited for unsafe conditions. "The element of danger," it said, "does not act deterrently upon the immigrants, as their limited imagination shields them from the fears which would harass a more sensitive class of persons in such hazardous employment."

With jobs as the magnet, over a span of two decades, the anthracite-producing area of Pennsylvania saw a dramatic demographic shift with the influx of nearly ninety thousand immigrants from Italy as well as from eastern and central Europe. In 1880, settlers from those areas had accounted for fewer than 2 percent of the total foreign-born population, but by the turn of the century, they made up 46 percent of all immigrants.

Social and ethnic conflicts flared. Old-timers derided the "filthy habits and queer languages" of the "foreigners." Coal operators exacerbated the tensions by offering newcomers lower wages and providing worse housing than the first arrivals, who were rising socially and economically. As the earlier settlers were supplanted, the patch towns went through a "startling social change," as a contemporary writer put it. The newcomers could be "exploited—through company stores, company shanties, and other methods well understood by coal mine owners—in a manner that the old miners who were self-respecting English-speaking citizens would not have endured for a moment. . . . Their houses are now occupied by the newcomers from the polyglot proletariat of southeastern Europe; and under the roof where one miner's family formerly dwelt in humble decency there will now be found four or five families huddled together after the manner of the slums of Polish and Hungarian towns."

It turns out that the present-day depiction of old-time Hazleton ("They came here to assimilate!") with *kumbaya*, well-integrated migrant communities, is pure fantasy. In Hazleton, the Germans clustered in the southeastern and northwestern sections of town, the Irish in the south, the English in the central and northern parts, the Poles and Slavs mostly on South Vine Street, the Polish Jews on North Church, and the Italians and Slovaks north of Diamond Avenue.

"They all had their own churches, their own neighborhoods, their own social clubs," explained history buff Jane Waitkus.

Waitkus is an English instructor at Penn State who is fascinated by her grandparents' roots—Slovakian on her father's side, Lithuanian on her mother's. I met her at her house in Mountaintop near Hazleton and talked about the area's ethnic history as she and her eighty-six-year-old mother, Ann Michaels, placed silverware into napkins that they folded in preparation for the wedding of Jane's daughter. It was to be a Slovakian wedding, Ann explained, offering me a plate of homemade Slovakian jellied pastries called *kolachy* filled with *lekvár*, a prune jam imported from Slovakia.

"Until this day, I call Sacred Heart in Plains the Irish church, because that's the way we were brought up," said Jane. "That was Irish. The Polish church was St. Peter and Paul in Plains; the Lithuanian church was St. Francis in Miners Mills."

Instruction in the public schools was in English, of course, but preschoolers generally learned their parents' language first.

"I never spoke English when I was a child, it was Lithuanian," Ann explained. "And I learned the other languages, too, because in the neighborhood, if I had friends who were Slovak or Polish and their mothers were baking something, I wasn't gonna get any unless I asked in their language. Nobody spoke English. I'll tell you, when I became a nurse, I was an interpreter in the emergency room more than once, because nobody could speak the languages. I could understand the Slovak, Russian, and Polish, and I spoke Lithuanian very well."

In the latter part of the nineteenth century, ethnic divisions led to undisguised conflicts and hostilities. Hazleton newspapers called Slavs and Hungarians "peculiar," described Hungarians as "an ignorant, immoral and filthy race who create disgust wherever they locate," and labeled Italians as "the most disreputable."

Divisions and resentments among migrant communities were aggravated by working conditions and pay. Mine owners, motivated by the desire to maximize profit and production, showed little regard for the safety of their employees, whom they could easily replace, since there were more workers than jobs. Tunnel explosions and cave-ins were common. For every one million tons of coal extracted, close to fifteen workers perished on the job.

While cultural changes, ethnic differences, and outright racism often bubble to the top in immigration arguments, time and again, at the core of the real divide are underlying issues beyond the control of people they affect. When one group loses good jobs, and another finds itself in precarious straits, finger-pointing and power struggles inevitably thrust immigration issues and migrants into the spotlight.

In Hazleton, class and professional differences intensified ethnic rivalries. Ann Michaels remembers stories told to her by family members who worked in the mines: "My brothers came in contact with the Irish because they were the bosses in the mines, and they hated them. Our people hated the Irish because they really made them work very hard. From what I hear, they used to come home and they were actually abused, and they used to call them 'dirty Irish.'"

Tensions rose when times were tough and had particularly tragic consequences in 1897, a bad year for the anthracite industry and for newly arrived southeastern European immigrants.

The nation was at the end of the "Long Depression," and long-time residents blamed newcomers for depressing coal miners' wages. Pennsylvania legislators came up with two laws to protect the existing workforce—both with startling parallels to Hazelton's Illegal Immigration Relief Act Ordinance, which came 109 years later. One statute was a language test that required job applicants to "answer intelligently and correctly at least twelve questions in the English language pertaining to the requirements of a practical miner." Another became known as the "alien tax." It was supposed to penalize employers for hiring immigrants by requiring them to pay a tax of "three cents for each day of such foreign-born un-naturalized male person as may be employed." In fact, the levy on employers became a worker tax, since bosses typically paid the money by garnishing the miners' wages.

For miners, the problems were piling up. Coal prices were low, so to save money, operators cut workers' wages and hours and stopped paying them on time. In the late summer of 1897, miners began staging protests. At the Audenreid Colliery, miners went on strike. Communities were in turmoil as miners marched from one colliery to another to gather support and to shut down coal mines. By Labor Day weekend, some ten thousand northeastern Pennsylvania coal miners, largely Polish, Slovak, Italian, and Lithuanian, were involved in protests.

On September 10, 1897, miners began a march with the intention of shutting down the mine in Lattimer, about two and a half miles northeast of Hazleton. When they got to West Hazleton, the local sheriff, James Martin, ordered them to disperse. Instead the miners agreed to take a different route, and set off, led by Steve Jurich, a Slovak carrying an American flag.

As three hundred to four hundred marchers approached Lattimer, they were met by the sheriff and his posse. Martin had deputized more than eighty volunteers, a force consisting mainly of professional men with English, Irish, or German backgrounds, many with connections to the coal operators. The posse was armed with new Winchester rifles. The sheriff again ordered the marchers to disperse, but they refused. Shots rang out. The first man killed was the flag bearer, Steve Jurich. In all, the sheriff's deputies shot and killed fourteen Poles, four Slovaks, and one Lithuanian. As the wounded cried out for help, one deputy reportedly responded, "We'll give you hell, not water, hunkies!"

The following year, Sheriff Martin and eighty-three deputies were tried for murder. All the men were acquitted.

The site of the shooting is now an intersection in a quiet suburban neighborhood. A blue and gold marker put up by the Pennsylvania

Historical and Museum Commission describes the Lattimer Massacre as "one of the most serious acts of violence in American labor history."

During the century that followed the massacre, ethnic divisions among Europeans dissipated and were forgotten. Mayor Louis Barletta's wife is of Irish descent, an intermarriage that would have been unthinkable fewer than a hundred years ago.

But the twenty-first-century wave of migrants ushered in modern conflicts. Once again, old-timers resent the newcomers. Descendants of those Slavic, English, Scottish, Welsh, Irish, Italian, and Lithuanian mineworkers, who once engaged one another in a maelstrom of ethnic tumult, united in common cause in speaking out against their new Latino neighbors. Like a long-abandoned coal mine, Hazleton's old vein of resentment and hostility found a new life.

Cycles of short memories and disassociation are stitched into the fabric of the immigration debate. The eighteenth-century remarks of one noted son of a migrant and grandson of an indentured servant imported from England serve as a poignant reminder of historical myopia. German migrants were "the most ignorant Stupid Sort of their own Nation," Benjamin Franklin famously declared.

Despairing about the preponderance of Germans and of German speakers, he wrote, "They begin of late to make all their Bonds and other legal Writings in their own Language, which (though I think it ought not to be) are allowed good in our Courts, where the German Business so encreases that there is continual need of Interpreters; and I suppose in a few years they will be also necessary in the Assembly, to tell one half of our Legislators what the other half say." Survival, said Franklin, required immigration restrictions: "[U]nless the stream of their importation could be turned from this to other colonies . . . they will soon so out number us, that all the advantages we have will not in My Opinion be able to preserve our language, and even our Government will become precarious."

As I finished the kolachys that Ann Michaels had so hospitably served, our conversation turned to the latest wave of migrants. We had talked about intolerance toward Lithuanians and Slovaks. I wanted to know what she thought about Latinos.

"I'm not saying all of them, but they're certainly not morally fit, believe me," she said. "They're committing crimes, and you never saw that, you never saw that before, and drugs and anything to make money. I don't see them working. I'm not saying all of them, but they don't have a job promised to them here when they come here illegally. They should go back to the old days, I'm telling you—make sure they had a sponsor if they were coming here, make sure they have a job."

Hazleton's Latino leaders view the familiar denunciations with consternation. "It's been happening throughout history and we haven't learned anything," said Ana Arias.

Amilcar Arroyo, the newspaper editor from Peru, is worried about the pattern continuing.

"You know what will be the funny part to this one?" he asked rhetorically. "I hope I'm wrong. I say, 'God tell me that I'm wrong.' You know what's going to happen? I hope not. This Hispanic people of the second or third generation, they will forget, so the next wave of immigrants to this area probably, they will have the same problems as I have . . . and they will be doing the same as [they] did, the same generation of Irish, Italians, Polish people to this Hispanic people who came now. Because it's like that. It's a cycle. Believe me, it's a cycle, but I hope that doesn't happen. I hope so."

Modern-day restrictionists take umbrage at any suggestion that race or national origin shapes their view. "People think we're after Hispanics," Hazleton City Council president Yannuzzi explained. "We're not. We're after illegals."

"People ask, 'Don't you have compassion for those who came here?' Of course," added the mayor. "I would sneak into this country, too, if my family depended on it. . . . We're seeing small-town America, the life being taken out of it, because we don't have the money to deal with the problem."

But legal avenues to attack the "problem" have themselves proved problematic. In 1898, the U.S. Supreme Court overturned Pennsylvania's "alien tax," affirming a lower-court judge's ruling that declared it a "hostile" and "arbitrary" law that discriminated against noncitizens in violation of the Constitution's equal protection guarantees.

As for Hazleton's 2006 Illegal Immigration Relief Act Ordinance, it was struck down as unconstitutional by a district court judge. "Whatever frustrations officials of the City of Hazleton may feel about the current state of the federal immigration enforcement, the nature of the political system in the United States prohibits the City from enacting ordinances that disrupt a carefully drawn federal statutory scheme," wrote federal judge James Munley, criticizing officials for enacting their own municipal immigration policy. As of this writing in December 2009, the case, *Lozano v. Hazleton*, was on appeal and seemed destined to make its way to the U.S. Supreme Court.

Still standing in Hazleton law is the preeminence of English. The declaration did not come under legal challenge. As a result, "the English language is the official language of the City of Hazleton," so no other languages shall be required in City documents, and Hazleton officials are obligated to "take all steps necessary to insure that the role of English as the common language of the City of Hazleton is preserved and enhanced."

Score one for Barletta, although his 2008 bid to unseat the twelve-term Democratic congressman Paul E. Kanjorski was less successful. Barletta lost by 3 percentage points, a narrow defeat he attributed, with a dexterous spin, to his popularity. "Many people tell me they didn't want me to leave," he told a reporter.

The Hazleton saga has an interesting coda, one in which anti-immigrant resolve gave way to economic pragmatism. Just eighty-five miles to the southeast, another small town whose character also had been altered by an influx of migrants took note of the Hazleton example and decided to follow suit.

On July 26, 2006, two weeks after Hazleton enacted its immigration policy, a crowd of some three hundred people came to a meeting of the Riverside Township Council, whose members had prepared a copycat ordinance. The small New Jersey community had witnessed an influx of newcomers, mostly illegal migrants from Brazil, many of whom had moved into Riverside and surrounding areas to work in housing construction. Estimates of their numbers ranged between 2,000 and 5,000, a massive and jarring adjustment in a community whose population the 2000 census pegged at just 7,911.

"They're everywhere. There's more of them than there are of us," lifelong resident Carolyn Chamberlain told newspaper reporter Jennifer Moroz, who wrote a three-part series on Riverside in 2005. "Brazilians are taking over this whole town."

The immigration issue aroused such passion and interest that to accommodate the crowds, the hearing on the Hazleton-like ordinance had to be moved from Town Hall to the Riverside High School auditorium. The vote was preceded by screaming and shouting matches. Eight police officers—half the force—came to keep order. By a 5 to 0 vote, the council adopted the Riverside Township Illegal Immigration Relief Act, seeking to yank the licenses of businesses that hire illegal immigrants and to impose fines starting at $1,000 on landlords who rent or lease to them.

The immediate consequences were, in part, predictable. Within three weeks, church groups sued the township in federal court in an attempt to get the law overturned. Business groups that formed the Riverside Coalition of Business Persons and Landlords soon followed their lead and filed suit in New Jersey Superior Court.

But as the lawsuits proceeded, the new statute remained in place, resulting in repercussions beyond the courthouse. News reports indicated that Brazilian migrants, the ordinance's intended targets, were leaving town by the hundreds. Business owners boarded up stores and residents abandoned their homes.

"The exodus is insane," said the owner of a rental property vacated by immigrants. "People just left their lives in the trash."

With legal bills mounting, fourteen months after its passage, Riverside officials rescinded the law, which had never been enforced. Attorney fees had reached $82,000, costs which forced the delay of road-improvement projects and repairs to Town Hall.

The new mayor, George Conard, who had voted for the original ordinance, conceded that the law's supporters had not fully considered its consequences. "I don't think people knew there would be such an economic burden," he said. "A lot of people did not look three years out."

It's easy to see the moral to these stories as "See how much immigrants are needed?" Or, "See how quickly people forget their own immigrant heritage?" Or even, "Locals have every right to defend and preserve their way of life, even at the risk of jeopardizing economic stability." But the key lesson is about how closely immigration and economics are linked. Often, the public responds to immigration and cultural change as it does to a power plant, a prison, or a big new mall—NIMBY! (not in my backyard). In those cases, ensuing debates involve spreadsheets and calculators and determinations about whether gains outweigh losses. But for all the attention and time devoted to the immigration debate, the simple truth is that global migration is just a part of global trade. Developing resources, manufacturing, and trading commodities is sometimes a good idea, and sometimes it isn't, but in the end, when government or corporate decisions help create opportunities, often people are moved to cross borders to take advantage of them—regardless of local consequences.

For employers throughout the developed world, migrants make perfect economic sense. Often they perform work that many long-time residents will not do—at least not for the wages offered. Just as in the United States, where a common refrain is "Mexicans will do the jobs Americans won't," in the United Kingdom it is said that eastern Europeans will perform labor that the English won't. In Poland, Ukrainians and Belarusians will work for wages and in conditions not tolerated by Poles. In Argentina, Bolivians fill low-paid jobs that Argentinians shun.

Global and local businesses rely on human mobility and on ready, vulnerable pools of labor often available at bargain basement prices.

In turn, migrant incomes are lubricants for the often extensive networks of recruiters, traffickers, and smugglers who get them to their destinations. Industries rely on the billions of dollars migrants send back to their homelands.

The complex and interconnected machinery and interrelated businesses that comprise today's global market for labor has been called the "migration industry." It's an apt description with an implicit message for those concerned about "immigration reform." That is, addressing migration on a piecemeal, local, or even national basis flies in the face of the obvious. The NIMBY approach favored in the industrialized world has no more chance of success than efforts to resolve global warming by exporting coal-fueled industrial production from the United States to China. Destination countries are just one piece of the larger picture. To grapple seriously with global migration requires at the very least an understanding of why migrants leave home to begin with.

CHAPTER 2

Growing People
for Export

Along the crowded streets of the Tondo district in northwestern
Manila, homes, small factories, and storefronts are jammed together in an urban mishmash that blends industry and squalid housing.
For residents of the Philippine capital, Tondo is synonymous with
slums and poverty, disease and crime. It's a place where shantytown
residents sell their kidneys and where squatters comb through garbage
piles looking for salvageable scraps.

The Tondo Medical Center is a reflection of the community's
woes. Viewers of Manila's evening news often see the public hospital
as a destination for injured gang members stabbed or shot by feuding drug dealers. Driving through the gates of the shabby, two-story
Tondo Medical Center, I thought at first I'd come to the wrong place
and was arriving at a run-down industrial building instead of a hospital.

The government facility was built in 1971, but it seems much
older. With a two-hundred-bed capacity, it serves Manila's most densely
packed and poorest population. Hallways are dim. Equipment is aging.
Furniture is sparse. The walls can use a paint job.

I had come to Tondo to learn more about the Philippine
health care system and the people working in it. Seeing Filipinos
in a health care setting is a normal experience for most people in
developed countries, since the Philippines produces a third of the

world's nurses. In Los Angeles, it's surprising *not* to hear snippets of Tagalog, the main Philippine language, spoken by at least some staff members in hospitals.

The Philippines has come to rely on an absent workforce whose jobs abroad and at sea provide the wherewithal for an otherwise unsustainable economy. Their remittances, the hundreds of billions of dollars that foreign workers send home from around the world, are part of an international, migration-fueled economy. Think of a global maze of pipelines through which migration's economic life-blood flows, connecting wage earners at one end with families and communities at the other. National economies that have come to rely on the work of migrants, combined with the lucrative and growing business of remittances, a key component of the "migration industry," demonstrate the dynamic forces that not only propel global migration, but also benefit from it.

In 2008, the top-ranking destination countries for remittances were India ($45 billion), China ($34.5 billion), Mexico ($26.2 billion), and the Philippines ($18.3 billion).

Migrant labor accounts for the Philippines' second-largest source of export revenue, after electronics. Remittances accounted for nearly 11 percent of the GDP in 2008 and helped offset the nation's growing trade deficit.

With about 10 percent of its population working abroad, the nation of ninety-two million people has developed a culture of migration.

The government has developed a vast and profitable bureaucracy, the Philippine Overseas Employment Administration (POEA), to manage and promote migration. A business infrastructure trains, recruits, and markets Filipino workers the way that banana republics used to cultivate crops. Government officials and publications boast about the number of OFWs (Overseas Filipino Workers) that have been deployed. And no, "deployed" is not a typo for "employed." The word "deploy," meaning "to spread out strategically," is very much a part of the official game plan.

Each year, the Philippine president hands out Bagong Bayani (modern-day heroes) awards to the country's "outstanding and exemplary" migrant workers.

"Our OFWs have contributed in no small measure to our financial stability and economic growth," said President Gloria Macapagal-Arroyo on Migrant Workers Day in 2005. "Their remittances have shored up our foreign exchange reserves, driven investments in the cities and countryside, and kept alive the hopes of millions of Filipino families."

Until recently, Philippine government officials pointedly countered the unseemly suggestion that they had actively encouraged their own people to leave the country. As proof, they trotted out the country's 1995 Migrant Workers Act, pointing to Section 2, paragraph (c) of the law: "The State does not promote overseas employment as a means to sustain economic growth and achieve national development."

But the glaringly obvious could not be ignored, and in December 2008, as global financial clouds darkened, President Macapagal-Arroyo issued a fiat that essentially swept aside the statute. She declared that "challenging times require out-of-the-box, not-business-as-usual solutions."

Despite her claim, "Administrative Order No. 247" was most definitely not "out of the box." The new policy merely accelerated a long-term practice. But the language was striking, an edict from the president to send her fellow countrymen and women packing. She directed the POEA to move "full blast" to "aggressively deploy Filipino expatriates . . . with urgency and unbothered by institutional hurdles . . . to update and expand its Rolodex on its country-contracts, global companies recruiting expatriate workers, international head-hunters and manpower placement agencies with a global reach."

She declared, "The target shall be to increase the countries currently hosting Filipino workers and break through the 200-country barrier," referring to the fact that at the time of her order, Filipino workers were deployed to 198 nations.

The tradition of Filipino labor migration began in 1906, when workers left what was then a colonial outpost of the United States for the sugarcane and pineapple plantations in the U.S. territory of Hawaii. Others went to work in agriculture on America's West Coast. The Philippine government's encouragement of emigration dates back to the dictatorship of former president Ferdinand Marcos. In 1974, faced with rising unemployment, political instability, and a stagnant economy, Marcos saw a way to export young men as contract laborers in response to the rising demand for workers created by the oil boom in the Middle East.

By 2007, more than a million people a year—on average, three thousand Filipinos a day—were leaving the country to work abroad. Labor migration is such a common and expected occurrence that at the Ninoy Aquino International Airport, outside of Manila, one of the last sights departing passengers see before going through the metal detectors is a large, brightly lit sign bidding farewell to migrants: "Maligayang Paglalakbay!! OVERSEAS FILIPINO WORKERS." Translation: Bon voyage!!

Arriving at the airport, preparing to learn more about migration, I felt a little like someone going in the wrong direction down a one-way street. Most traveling American reporters know the mantra from editors is to find a U.S. angle on a foreign story: "What does it mean for Americans?" And that's the way the immigration issue is generally reported: How do immigrants affect *us* and *our* economy? But I had hoped to turn the telescope around, to try to get some understanding of what it means for the country and for the people left behind. I wanted to find out more about why migrants were making the journeys and get a better understanding of the effects of their absence.

The subject was not completely uncharted territory for me. I had spoken to Filipino migrants in the United States, and had been particularly struck by an essay written by a community college student who had migrated from the Philippines as a teenager. He had grown up without his parents.

"When I was born, my parents left me to my aunt in the Philippines because they went abroad to work," he wrote. "As I grew, it was hard for me to accept that they left me, so whenever I remembered them I cried. When I was twelve years old, I came up with the idea of forgetting them, and pretended to myself that I had no parents. As time passed, I realized that I had just forgotten them mentally, but not emotionally, because whenever I saw parents around me, I felt like crying again."

In America, the Philippines has long been the main foreign source for nurses. In 2004, more than fifty thousand Filipino-trained RNs were working in the United States. The importation of Filipino health care workers is a colonial legacy. Americans began training Filipino nursing students in the early twentieth century. During the post–World War II nursing shortage, U.S. hospitals were eager to attract nurses who had been trained there under the auspices of a U.S.-sponsored training program intended to promote goodwill during the Cold War. After 1965, when changed U.S. immigration laws overturned long-standing policies excluding Asian migrants, entrepreneurs set up nursing schools in the Philippines to meet the growing demand in the United States.

Between 2000 and 2007, nearly seventy-eight thousand qualified nurses left the Philippines to work abroad, according to the government. The majority went to Saudi Arabia—a popular destination, not so much because of any deep desire to go there, migrants told me, but because the salaries were relatively good and immigration restrictions were fewer than for the United States. Some researchers have said that the official migration statistics understate the full picture because many nurses move without telling the government. I had seen disturbing reports suggesting that while the Philippines was producing nurses for export, training them to meet foreign requirements and pass foreign tests, it was unable to satisfy its own domestic needs. Nurse-patient ratios were skyrocketing, and patients were dying from neglect. Researchers had found that hospitals were closing as a result of a shortage of health care workers. But it was one thing to read statistics in reports and another to see them for myself.

On the day I visited the Tondo hospital, members of an employees association wearing hospital uniforms rallied in the outside courtyard, demanding pay raises. By American standards, the staff is grossly underpaid. The nurses at the hospital were making about $261 a month. No wonder they wanted to leave. In the United States, nurses on average earn more than fifteen times that rate of pay.

Emma S. Manuel, the supervisor of the hospital's radiology department, organized the demonstration. Smartly dressed in a black pantsuit, she said patients were suffering as a result of too few nurses on staff. She said that each nurse had to care for forty to sixty patients. (By comparison, California law requires a nurse-patient ratio of no more than one to five).

"They're suffering from overfatigue, and they can't give bedside care," Manuel said.

As a result, taking care of sick patients at Tondo becomes a family affair, she explained.

"Patients must have relatives take care of them," she said. "Relatives stay and buy medicines for them outside the hospital. They have to pay for lab tests and assist in bedside care. They have to give patients baths and sponge baths, clean the rooms, and change the linens. The nurses cannot do that, so the relatives do it."

Conscientious nurses, she said, often work extra days and long hours that run to twenty-four-hour shifts. They don't get any more pay for their work, she explained, but feel obligated to their patients.

The problem, she and others said, is not that there's an actual shortage of qualified nurses in the Philippines, since nursing schools pump out a hundred thousand graduates annually. The trouble is that they are trained mainly for export. Domestic hospitals typically do not hire sufficient numbers of nurses because of budget constraints, and those they do hire are low-paid. As a result, qualified nurses either go abroad or work in other fields. Many take jobs as nursing instructors, for example, where starting wages are about $4.00 an hour, ridiculously low by American standards but still much higher than salaries for entry-level nurses in the Philippines.

Other staff members at the Tondo Medical Center told me they also were trying to make do with a shortage of doctors. Even when positions became available for physicians, sometimes no one applied for the jobs. The reason is that thousands of doctors have retrained to become nurses to join the medical exodus, go abroad, and earn more money. The average pay for doctors in the Philippines is about $4,000 a year. Thirty-seven schools offer two-year courses to retrain doctors to become nurses. Filipinos even have a term to describe professionals—doctors, pharmacists, and others—taking up nursing careers. They are known as "second-coursers." Between 2000 and 2008, more than six thousand doctors-turned-nurses left the country.

The shortage of doctors places an extra burden on those who stay. One of the four doctors at the Tondo hospital told me that in some cases physicians were too busy to attend to gravely ill patients.

"They perished," he said.

"Were the deaths preventable?" I asked.

"Yes, sir," he replied.

Another doctor explained that at busy times, hospital staff, knowing patients wouldn't be seen, set quotas.

"We took twenty in the morning and twenty in the afternoon. Any more than that," he said, "we sent them away and told them to come back."

To learn more about the nurse export business, I went to visit the Manila Doctors College, which does not, as its name implies, train doctors. Its actual mission is more in keeping with its advertising slogan: "We Nurse the World." The private college is operated by the Metrobank Foundation, the philanthropic arm of the Philippines' largest bank.

The school is set on a spacious, grandly appointed campus and is one of hundreds of nursing schools that have been established over the past twenty years to cater to the growing needs of the foreign market. In 2008 it had forty-two hundred students enrolled in its four-year nursing program.

Dr. Lino Reynoso, the college administrator, acknowledged that the reason why most students come to his institution is to get overseas jobs. The more prestigious Philippine nursing colleges are known for affiliations with overseas agencies, and the Manila Doctors College has a formal association with Health Care Corporation of America (HCCA) International, a Tennessee-based global recruiting company that, in turn, is an arm of America's largest operator of for-profit health facilities, Hospital Corporation of America (HCA).

"Basically we use that as our marketing strategy to encourage our parents," Reynoso said, explaining how the school tries to appeal to families to enroll their sons and daughters. He said that the message is that if the students "do good in college, after four years of training, we promise them opportunities in the United States."

The college is designed basically to be part of a colonial supply chain. While the curriculum is "Philippine-based," Reynoso explained, "we improved it to cater to our expected country of deployment. . . . Our textbooks are all foreign-authorized, and we have adopted our evaluation tools following the United States and it must be certified by the HCCA. They look into the curriculum and they align it with the U.S., otherwise they would not enter into an agreement with us."

U.S. placements have not gone as planned because of a backlog in the United States in granting nursing visas. But Reynoso hoped that would change. Sensitive to criticism that Philippine nursing schools are sometimes seen as breeding grounds for exportable commodities, the college has imposed a requirement that students work for two years at an affiliated Manila health center, the Doctors Hospital, before they sign on for an international job placement with HCCA International.

"Our problem in education is 'How do we instill nationalism?'" said Reynoso. "So we begin training them: 'It's okay to want to go abroad, but once you have enough money, then come back and serve the country.'"

It's a token gesture. As I was escorted around the college, watching fourth-year students training on modern equipment and using dummies to practice techniques such as tracheotomies and catheter insertions, the ultimate goal for trainees was reinforced by signs posted around the classrooms: "Let's speak English."

Watching a young man named Christopher work on his feeding tube skills, I asked where he was planning to go after he received his degree.

"I love the Philippines," he replied, saying he expected to stick around.

My escort, a nursing instructor, voiced skepticism as we thanked Christopher and walked on. "He'll change his mind in due time," she said.

Sure enough, when I interrupted a class of fifty students and asked them to raise their hands if they intended to remain in the Philippines, not one arm went up.

Besides the obvious wage disparities between the Philippines and industrialized countries, I wanted to get an idea about what drives the exodus of Filipinos. Another physician, Dr. Geneve "Beng" Rivera, agreed to show me a vivid illustration. Rivera is secretary-general of the Health Alliance for Democracy, an organization of health professionals. Our destination was a Manila neighborhood known as Isla Puting Bato (White Stone Island). The idyllic-sounding name is misleading. Isla Puting Bato is a shantytown perched on the edge of Manila Bay. It's a squatters' neighborhood that has been gradually growing since the 1960s. Shacks, crudely assembled from scrap materials, lean up against each other and provide rough housing on a breakwater of the harbor.

Many of the huts are perched with one side resting on the breakwater and the other propped on stilts that go down into the water. Narrow planks over the water run between homes. Sewage runs into the bay, where kids swim and fishermen try their luck.

The neighborhood is a densely packed area of some fifteen thousand people where violent crime and communicable diseases thrive. Rivera's group provides weekly clinics in the barrio. As we walked down narrow alleys between shacks on the breakwater, she ticked off a catalog of poverty-related ailments that health care workers treat: "upper respiratory conditions, diarrhea, coughs, pneumonia, and tuberculosis."

The barrio has its own economy. People sell produce, chickens, and fish from the polluted bay, containers of water, and pedicab rides to the nearest public transportation, nearly a mile away. Many of the residents are employed outside the neighborhood in menial jobs working as domestics or doing laundry.

Like many of her neighbors, Luzviminda Solayao and her family run a small business common to the community. It's a garlic-peeling enterprise, and Solayao's dry, swollen fingers are evidence of her labors in what is quite literally a cottage industry. Middlemen drop off sacks of garlic onions, which she and family members peel on a table in her shack. The garlic peeling business earns the family about $25 a day.

Government officials refer to the three thousand families of Isla Puting Bato as ISPs (informal settlers in the port). But a number of families are not so settled. They've split up as migrants have left to find work overseas. So far, no one from Solayao's family has gone away, though they've had the desire.

"We would, but we've got no money," she said, referring to the cost of recruiters and visas. "We can't afford the placement fee just to become a factory worker."

Not far away, in another shack, I met twenty-three-year-old Grace Ongutan. She and her two-year-old daughter Patricia lived with her sister's family of five. Ongutan's husband was away on a ship working as a mechanic, one of the 266,000 seafarers the Philippines has deployed aboard oceangoing fleets. She said she expected him to be gone, except for brief visits, for most of the next twenty-five years, until he becomes eligible for retirement.

"We have no choice," Ongutan explained. "He has to do it for the future."

Little Patricia had met her father only once, for a short time at the age of five months, when he returned for additional training. Ongutan's husband earns about a thousand dollars a month. He sends half to his parents and half to his wife.

In May 2009, Philippine congressman Roilo S. Golez authored legislation proposing to elevate the nation's migrant export policy beyond a presidential administrative order and enshrine it into law. Calling his bill "An Act Liberalizing and Accelerating the Processing and Deployment of Overseas Filipino Workers," Golez bluntly declared, "Our local economy cannot adequately sustain our population growth." As a consequence, he said, migrant workers "form the nation's economic edge."

Migrant rights groups were outraged. "Economic edge is really simply economic sacrificial lambs!" said Garry Martinez, chairperson of Migrante International, an advocacy group for migrants.

"Instead of getting down to business and looking for genuine solutions to the country's chronic and ever-worsening crisis, such as implementing a genuine land reform program and engineering a national industrialization program, the COWA [the House Committee on Overseas Filipino Workers Affairs, which gave initial approval to the legislation] is choosing the easier route preferred by the greedy and the corrupt by offering its citizens as slaves [so] that unscrupulous scallywags in government and the private sector, both here and abroad, can pocket more money from the billions of profit earned from government fees and remittances," Martinez said.

Bombast aside, it is hard to fault the notion that governments of migrant-sending countries should focus more on cultivating sustainable economies than on the "Processing and Deployment" of human beings. When I went to the building of the Philippines Overseas Employment Administration and met with Hans Leo J. Cacdac, the POEA's deputy administrator, I posed a question that seemed to surprise him.

"Is it a good thing to have so many people going abroad?" I asked.

He paused for a good ten seconds before venturing a reply.

"You know what? I'm not really sure," he said. "Er, I'm not really sure if it's a good thing, so I guess that means it's not necessarily a good thing. Let me put it that way."

Migrants' rights organizations have complained that institutionalizing and relying on labor migration as a prime source of foreign exchange is a misguided policy. Not only does it callously break up families, it also reduces the incentive to press forward with meaningful economic development programs that would reduce the need to migrate. Since the 1970s, the outflow of "modern-day heroes" has been not only a valuable economic crutch, but a political safety valve in a country of high unemployment and low job creation. Annually exporting a million of the nation's most capable and ambitious citizens means there are that many fewer residents who might involve themselves in the nation's civil affairs and politics.

Forty percent of the population lives on less than $1 a day. The poverty is deepest in rural areas, where the government has failed to invest evenly in education, infrastructure, and health care. The poorest regions are in the South, in areas such as Mindanao, where armed conflict has displaced thousands of families. Nationwide, while per capital income increased over the past fifteen years, the benefits went mostly to the wealthier sectors, and the income gap widened.

In the face of such deep-rooted and seemingly intractable problems, it is easier to send people abroad than it would be to correct structural issues and redress inequality.

While the dependence on the income of migrant workers may have masked issues and bought time, it also has made the government vulnerable. A high birth rate has meant increasing numbers of workers coming onto the job market at a time when the global economic meltdown was not only threatening jobs at home but also those of overseas Filipino workers. Thousands of OFWs were expected to return home, even as employment opportunities dried up in the Philippines. The government promised financial assistance for returnees, while migrants' rights activists saw them as likely catalysts for political action.

"We will call for the ouster of this government," said Martinez of Migrante International. "It's happened before, and it will happen again for sure."

The Philippines is not alone in adopting a labor export policy as an economic prop. Bangladesh, Indonesia, Sri Lanka, India, and Vietnam also have bureaucracies that promote worker migration.

Just as the global economic downturn led the Philippines to more aggressively market workers abroad, other countries also adjusted their strategies. In May 2009, Bangladesh's Expatriates' Welfare and Overseas Employment Ministry announced it was sending emissaries to East Europe and Africa, beyond the more conventional destinations for Bangladeshi workers, "in the pursuit of new labor market[s]."

As the global economy soured, the heavy reliance on foreign labor by developing countries was shown up as a sorry and precarious policy. Migrant workers, vulnerable during the best of times, found themselves to be among the first laid off or with reduced pay. For migrants, even worse conditions back home meant that returning was not an option.

"Going back to Bangladesh now would be a problem for me," Momen Bhuiyan, an out-of-work day laborer living in a shelter in Malaysia, told a reporter. "I already sold the land, I have a loan, I don't have money to pay them back, I don't have my passport." And, of course, there were no jobs.

But it is too simple to place all the blame for labor export policies on undeveloped nations. As we shall see, much of the responsibility for moving millions of migrants can be traced to corporate suites and government centers in the industrialized world.

CHAPTER 3

Migrants in the Global Marketplace

For years, news reports have graphically documented the aftermath of desperate voyages by African migrants, crammed into flimsy fishing boats trying to reach beaches in southern Europe. The tens of thousands who made it or who were intercepted by authorities were the lucky ones. Thousands of others have drowned at sea. Often their corpses wash up on shore. For many, a mass grave in a church cemetery in southern Spain became their final resting place.

Initially, the main points of departure were along the coast of Morocco on Africa's northwest corner. But as border policing made it more difficult for migrants to leave that country, increasingly they turned their attention southward, at first to Mauritania, then farther south to Senegal, Africa's westernmost nation. A goal of European-bound Africans leaving Senegal's beaches was to get to the Spanish-owned Canary Islands nine hundred miles to the northwest. Once there, they were technically in Spain. Without papers, it was difficult to deport them. Spain has brought thousands of African boat people from the Canaries to the European mainland.

On a beach in the coastal village of Kayar, an hour's drive north of Dakar, the capital of Senegal, I met Biram Sarry, a thirty-four-year-old struggling fisherman who had tried to adopt another vocation, smuggling. But things didn't work out. Cocky and athletic, he had tried twice unsuccessfully to take boatloads of migrants to the Canaries. In addition to being the ship's captain, he was a would-be migrant himself. Both times, he and his passengers were deported.

Sarry told me he was aware of the risks of undertaking a four- to five-day voyage out into the Atlantic. He said many of his passengers were terrified. "There were people with mental breakdowns," he explained in his native Wolof, speaking through an interpreter. "Sometimes I had to control them and tie them until they had their minds back. But sometimes the boat hit things at sea. I knew that it was hitting the bodies of people who had died. It made a noise. I knew what it was, but I didn't want to tell people because they would have been afraid."

Despite the dangers, Senegal's migrants are treated as folk heroes. Most families in Senegal have at least one family member living abroad. In 2008, remittances they sent home accounted for an estimated 8.5 percent of the nation's gross domestic product.

I spoke to Sarry's mother and to one of his three wives (Senegal is a Muslim nation). They were worried about his safety, but they expected and hoped that he would try to make the trip again.

"I would really prefer that he would go by plane instead of by boat," said Binta Gueye, Sarry's mother. "If he'd go by plane, I'd be much happier."

Sarry's youngest wife had a similar attitude.

"I just want him to go and get some work and bring back millions in his new work," she said, smiling as she held their baby. We stood outside a hut that served as a kitchen. Inside, a boy of four or five watched over a pot cooking on a small wood fire.

"Were you disappointed when he came back?" I asked.

"I was," she replied. "I want him to return, but this time I want him to take the plane. This is what we pray for."

Decisions made by the Biram Sarrys of the world to migrate, to leave relatives and communities, to take risky journeys, and to cross international borders (either lawfully or illegally) are bound up with individual values, shaped by cultural expectations, and guided by family needs. But personal calculations are not made in a vacuum. Often, migrants' decisions are influenced by policies that originate in the world's trade offices, executive mansions, government buildings, and financial centers.

Think of these powerful institutions as present-day incarnations of Janus, the Roman god of gates, doors, beginnings, and endings. In sculptures, he is depicted as having two heads or faces looking in opposite directions. Sometimes he is shown holding a key. As modern governments guard their own gates, attempting to deter migration with immigration police and border controls, their policies and trade deals often have the countervailing effect of promoting migration. Along the borders of the developed world, while one of the two-faced Janus heads presents a stern, law-and-order countenance, the more permissive counterpart looks the other way, dangling carrots and encouraging migrants to bypass sentries and seek out opportunities.

That's the context needed to understand global labor migration. In an international marketplace, human mobility is as much a part of the economic system as nomadic companies that hopscotch the world in search of low prices, strategic alliances and trade arrangements, exports and imports, industrialization and currency shifts. On the surface, none of these issues has much to do with migration. But scratch a little deeper and it becomes apparent that seemingly unconnected policies can have a direct bearing on the movement of people, albeit unintentionally. Nonetheless, institutions and nations—both destination as well as source countries—that would claim to be passive forces in global migration are, time and again through their actions, unwitting collaborators.

One way to appreciate Senegal's migration picture is to start with a cooking lesson. In one pot, fry onions and fish. Stir in tomato paste, add water and rice, and bring to a boil. Then add vegetables such as carrots, sweet potatoes, turnips, eggplant, and cabbage. Simmer until done. The result is Senegal's classic national dish, *thieboudienne* (pronounced "cheb-oo-JEN"). The fish most commonly used in the concoction is thiof or *Epinephelus aeneus*, similar to white grouper.

What does thieboudienne have to do with immigration? The answer lies in the ingredients.

At the outdoor market up from the beach in Kayar, vendors display octopus in metal containers and thiof laid out on the concrete sidewalk. Close by, fishermen haul in canoes used to scour the seas. As each colorfully painted pirogue nears the crowded shore, the men go to the water to push the fishing boat up on the sand, using wooden logs as rollers. Women along the beach and at the fish markets wait to process and sell what the men have caught. But the catch is getting increasingly meager, so the fishing industry and local economy are in crisis. In 1997, there were an estimated 10,707 pirogues in Senegal's fishing fleet. Eight years later, that number had been cut in half.

"We have nothing to live on," Astou Faye told me. Dressed in a brightly colored headscarf and matching dress, she had sat with other similarly attired women on the beach all day, but their husbands, the fishermen, had provided them with few fish, and there had been no customers.

Faye and her friends saw one way out of their predicament: migration.

"I had one of my sons who went and they sent him back," she said. "If we find some other way to put him on a boat again, we will do it. The men leave, because they don't have a choice, there is no way to get enough money."

Sitting next to her, her friend Sada Diouf echoed her words.

"There is nothing here at all," Diouf said. "Our husbands try to make money with their fishing boats, but it is difficult for them, because oil [for the engines] is becoming more and more expensive. This is another problem."

Fishing is not only a major source of employment for Senegal, it also is a chief source of protein for the country's fast-growing and poor population.

However, 60 percent of the labor force works on the land. The name of the town, Kayar, refers to the area's two food sources: the seas and the fields. But both fishing and agriculture have faced tremendous difficulties.

Kayar's one paved road runs along the shore. Transportation around the village area is by foot or by horse and cart. I rode one out of town, passing cinder-block houses where most of the cooking is done using pots placed on open fires. Goats wandered around picking at garbage, and children played with kites made of plastic bags. When I arrived at the fifteen-acre family farm owned by Ndiaga Fall, president of Kayar's eight-hundred-member association of vegetable farmers, he explained how it had become difficult to make a living.

He and his family grow eggplants, carrots, potatoes, onions, and tomatoes. But his techniques are crude. The crops are irrigated by means of a leaky pump that brings water from an underground aquifer to a pond and then to handheld hoses. Weeding also is done by hand.

Fall explained that farmers couldn't get adequate financing to become more efficient, and they couldn't compete with foreign imports.

"We work six months to get the products to sell, but the problem is the imports," he said. "They import at the same time we're growing, and we have problems selling our products because the imported products are much cheaper."

Fall said some family members and friends had left their farms in Senegal and crossed the seas in search of greener pastures in Europe. They couldn't make their land in Kayar profitable or productive.

Senegal is a country where life is hard, and anyone wanting a better life might try to leave. But the root causes of some of the nation's economic woes are profound.

At the port of Dakar I watched as dockworkers unloaded fifty-kilogram sacks of rice from a boat and loaded them onto waiting trucks. The scene was a snapshot of a globalized world. As Filipino sailors stood by, Senegalese stevedores removed Uruguayan rice from a Greek-owned ship operated by Seacor, a Miami-based transnational company.

At local outdoor markets, I saw sacks of rice imported from Thailand, and bags of onions from the Netherlands. Senegal also imports tomato paste from Italy. All of this brings me back to Senegal's classic dish, thieboudienne. Besides the fish, Senegal produces each of the essential ingredients in the recipe. But the population's ability to harvest and trade these commodities has been severely affected by many factors, most of which are outside their control.

Industrial-size trawlers from Europe, Japan, the United States, and elsewhere have seriously depleted the once-abundant fish population. Senegal's government sold fishing rights to the Europeans, and now its own fishermen are paying the price. Their small wooden boats can't compete with factory ships that hold up to two thousand tons of fish at a time. Foreign fleets get millions of dollars in government support for fuel and equipment.

Some of thieboudienne's other ingredients are exported from countries where growers receive state subsidies. Dutch onions and Italian tomato paste are underwritten by their respective governments, as is much of the rice from the United States. In addition, Senegalese farmers can't compete with cheap rice that is produced industrially in South America and Thailand.

"We are importing 80 percent of our national supply of rice, while we have here the conditions, all the expertise to produce even more than what we need," lamented Hamath Sall, Senegal's minister of agriculture.

The American-educated official calculated that self-sufficiency in rice would generate two hundred thousand Senegalese jobs. He said Senegal can't compete with industrialized foreign farms, backed by much wealthier governments.

Between 2006 and 2008, rice farmers in higher-income economies received 60 percent of their rice receipts in the form of government subsidies. In 2008, governments comprising the thirty member states of the Organisation for Economic Cooperation and Development (OECD) provided $265.5 billion worth of price supports to farmers, an amount equal to 21 percent of their total income. About a quarter of those subsidies went to farmers with no requirement that they produce any commodity.

"We can help lessen the price of fertilizer for our farmers and subsidize quality seeds, but in the European countries, they can subsidize everything," said Minister of Agriculture Sall. "Even sometimes they don't put an area into production and receive revenue."

Senegal's president, Abdoulaye Wade, also has strongly criticized Western-financed food assistance programs, suggesting that they "should be progressively abandoned in favor of a 'help to stand up policy,' of help for self-assistance."

A 2008 investigation by Laurie Garrett, a senior fellow at the Council on Foreign Relations, revealed that most food assistance programs support domestic farmers and shipping companies instead of the people most in need.

"The real beneficiaries of food aid, then, are the domestic food producers of Europe, Canada, the United States, and Australia and shipping giants like Maersk, Mitsui, and American President Lines," she wrote. "Genuine food aid would aim at improving the technology of agriculture, directly investing in small-scale farming operations in poor countries, provision of mechanized irrigation systems, and fair trade practices," Garrett suggested.

Senegal's agriculture minister agreed. "Instead of actually giving us or throwing commodities in our countries, I believe that it's more efficient to help our administrations to build up these agriculture systems, allowing our own people to produce," said Sall.

To be fair, doling out cash assistance to notoriously corrupt governments such as Senegal's is an iffy proposition. Sall conceded that corruption impedes efficiency, but he suggested it not stand in the way of providing his nation with the resources it desperately needs. "Of course, the help in the form of commodities might be useful when we are facing a situation of hunger or something like that. People have to eat, and then it's useful to have the commodity, but if you put this in long-term perspective, it's better to prevent the situation and invest in helping the government to set up the infrastructure necessary to improve the production of agriculture commodities."

The United States did provide some $35 million worth of aid to Senegal in 2008. Of that, $6.4 million was targeted for economic growth, which included working to "improve the agricultural investments sector." To put those amounts into perspective, during the same year, Senegalese migrants abroad sent home about $1 billion in remittances.

The stories from Wolof-speaking Senegalese farmers and fishermen echoed the accounts in Spanish that I had heard from Mexican migrant farm workers in California. Besides the languages, only the details about the produce differed. The messages were the same: financial and agricultural policies beyond their control had pushed them to migrate. Senegalese were leaving because fishing and farming didn't provide a living. The Mexicans told me they could no longer support themselves by selling the corn they grew. Unable to compete with cheaper produce flooding the market, they came north.

Many Mexican migrants followed in the footsteps of generations, but, beginning in the mid-nineties, three major factors helped stimulate the continuing exodus into the United States: an international trade treaty, a banking crisis, and a domestic political decision.

The North American Free Trade Agreement (NAFTA) signed by the United States, Mexico, and Canada, which took effect on January

1, 1994, abolished many existing agricultural tariffs. It also devastated many small-scale Mexican corn producers.

Corn cultivation originated in Mexico some five thousand years ago. In Mexico, corn is not just a food staple and a cultural icon, it also is a source of income for some two million farmers. The Mexican government promised that free trade would mean lower prices for consumers, and it pledged to provide more assistance to the farming industry. About 40 percent of the country's agricultural land is used for producing corn—most of it by subsistence farmers growing on twelve acres or less.

U.S. corn producers saw the deal as a long-sought opportunity to penetrate the Mexican market. American growers had achieved remarkable efficiency using heavy machinery, chemicals, high-yield corn varieties, and large-scale irrigation. By contrast, 90 percent of Mexican farmers rely on the rain to water their corn. Much of it is on steep slopes in poor soil, and only 35 percent of corn farms have tractors.

Not surprisingly, Mexican farmers were little match for American corn growers, who in addition to using industrial farming techniques, could take advantage of U.S. government subsidies that dwarfed Mexican assistance to its farmers. After NAFTA broke down the doors, American corn producers rushed in. Within six years, exports of corn to Mexico from the United States increased eighteenfold. A quarter of all the corn consumed in Mexico was now grown in the United States. Corn prices tumbled, and so did the number of farm jobs. Hundreds of thousands of Mexican peasants were unable to live off the land. And even though NAFTA proponents had argued that the agreement would lead to a decrease in illegal migration, after 1994 the rate increased.

NAFTA was not the only reason why Mexicans moved north.

Just after Christmas of 1994, Alan Greenspan, then chairman of the Federal Reserve Board, was in New York City for a few days of concerts and shopping with his wife, Andrea Mitchell, a correspondent for NBC News. Soon after they had checked in at the Stanhope, a posh Fifth Avenue hotel, the phone rang. On the line was Robert E. Rubin, a former partner in Goldman Sachs who at the time was serving as President Clinton's chief economic adviser.

The problem, as Rubin told Greenspan, was Mexico. The country had taken a gamble, borrowed billions of dollars, mostly from Wall Street investors, was in over its head, and was about to default on its debts. The year 1994 had not been a good one for Mexico. A candidate for president had been assassinated. The Mexican Army had been called out to put down an armed uprising of peasants in the southern state of Chiapas. Domestic and foreign investors, nervous about the political instability, had withdrawn money. As a result, the peso had been devalued by more than 40 percent, and Mexico, without nearly enough money to repay its loans, was in crisis. The need for urgent action derailed Greenspan's plans for a cozy dinner at Le Périgord with his wife, and it quickly became a consuming priority for Rubin, who was about to be sworn in as Treasury secretary.

Within two weeks, the Clinton administration, with the backing of congressional Republicans, put together a proposal for a $40 billion package of loan guarantees. But popular sentiment in the United States was against the scheme. Critics charged that it was in reality a bailout for Wall Street banks. In response, instead of going to Congress, Rubin, Greenspan, and his top lieutenant, Lawrence H. Summers, worked up a plan to tap into an emergency Treasury Department fund to provide Mexico with loan guarantees of $20 billion. Canada and the International Monetary Fund agreed to pony up more, bringing the total to $40 billion. Summers and Treasury official David Lipton flew to Mexico City to visit the new president, Ernesto Zedillo, at his official residence, Los Pinos, and explain the deal. There would be stiff conditions—a cap on wages, high interest rates, and a loosening of rules restricting foreign ownership of banks, they told him. Zedillo agreed, and on February 21, 1995, Rubin and his Mexican counterpart, Guillermo Ortiz, signed the agreement in the ornate Cash Room of the Treasury Building in Washington, D.C.

The effects of the deal were staggering for lenders and borrowers. Citigroup (which Rubin joined after leaving the Clinton administration) became a major Mexican creditor, then acquired Banamex, Mexico's second-largest bank. The U.S. Treasury earned $580 million because Mexico, eager to pay off the loan quickly, repaid it ahead of schedule. As Rubin, Greenspan and Summers knew, Mexico had swallowed a bitter pill.

"Larry could be shrewd," Greenspan wrote about Summers, who later became Clinton's Treasury secretary and more recently

President Obama's chief economic adviser. "It was his idea to put such a high interest rate on the Mexico loans that the Mexicans felt compelled to pay us back early."

The repayment plan coupled with the conditions extracted by the United States officials meant dire times for the people of Mexico. Following the loan agreement, Mexican interest rates on business, automobile, and farm loans, as well as on credit cards and home mortgages, exploded. A 2008 report by a special commission of the Mexican Senate summarized the painful consequences: "The excessively high real interest rates introduced at the beginning of 1995 led to the bankruptcy of hundreds of thousands of companies and the disappearance of several million jobs. The policy recommended in 1995 by Rubin and his colleagues and accepted by the president of Mexico against the counsel of his team of advisers resulted in most families going bankrupt and most companies falling behind in their loan payments. *The loss of employment and the economic collapse mean that beginning then, more than six million Mexicans would emigrate to the United States in search of employment."* (italics mine)

The commission's report was clearly hyperbolic. The majority of Mexican families did not go bankrupt, nor did most companies default on their loans. It also is impossible to accurately pin specific numbers of migrants to one fateful agreement, the loan package. (How many people would have left Mexico anyway?) But the pointed conclusion reached by the Mexican senators made a clear link, one that is rarely discussed in the United States—namely, decisions to migrate are based not only on individual and personal calculations. In this case, public policies hatched in Washington and endorsed by Mexico set off a chain of events that helped launch an exodus.

While both NAFTA and the lending deal involved international participation, one other purely domestic decision by Mexico also led to the remarkable rise in border crossings.

Beginning in 1991, the Mexican government gradually dissolved a subsidy program known as the Compañía Nacional de Subsistencias Populares (National Company for Mass Subsistence). CONASUPO, as it was known, was a state food distribution monopoly that operated food stores, offering milk, beans, corn, and other staples at affordable prices. It subsidized farmers and sold food at below-market prices. Responding to complaints about corruption and inefficiency, and faced with pressure by major corn producers to privatize, the government cut back on corn subsidies. On January 1, 1999, it eliminated them altogether.

With the end of the program, the migrant trail widened. "We used to sell all our crops to CONASUPO," said Antonio López, a farm worker in Lindsay, California, explaining why he and his family moved from their village in the southwest Mexican border state of Michoacán. "But when CONASUPO went out of business, there was nowhere to sell them. We couldn't compete."

Just as trade and financial policies affect migration, "globalization"—the movement of goods, capital, ideas, and services around the world—also has an impact on human mobility.

As transnational companies rely on migrants to overcome cultural, linguistic, and legal barriers, at the same time they stimulate migration. The phenomenal growth of the Indian high-technology sector provides a good example. During the run-up to the year 2000, companies worried that what became known as the "Y2K" programming glitch would doom computer systems worldwide. Many computers had not been programmed to recognize dates beyond December 31, 1999. Increasingly, they turned to low-cost but technically savvy Indian workers to fix the problems. In doing so, they helped created a boom in information technology services and launched the Indian outsourcing industry. But many Indians didn't remain in India. High-tech firms that became used to working with Indians brought them to work in places such as California's Silicon Valley and Massachusetts's Technology Highway. Instead of exporting work, it became convenient to import workers to the United States. The next logical step fueled even more migration.

As transnational computer companies expanded globally, they saw India as a natural place to establish operations. The high-tech firms turned to Indian migrants, transferring them back to their home country to help set up corporate outposts. As a report for Manpower, Inc., a leading global recruitment and placement firm, put it, "Companies like Hewlett Packard and General Electric opened operations in India largely because of the confidence infused by the presence of many Indians working in their U.S. operations."

With increasing numbers of firms operating globally, migration has become part of their competitive strategy, either by design or inadvertently. Expanding or contracting in response to perceived opportunities or downturns, transnational firms depend on human mobility, moving personnel for long- or short-term assignments, training managers and experts in foreign countries, and relying on staff who can demonstrate cultural fluidity and international experience.

Transnational companies move millions. Ever in search of efficient and low-cost supply chains, they play off one region against another, consolidating, moving, outsourcing, and offshoring, opening and closing offices and factories, chasing ever-cheaper sources of labor and tax rates. Service and information industries set up shop anywhere and everywhere. Assembly plants can be relocated to wherever costs are low and supply is reliable.

Europeans call the process "delocalizing," an antiseptic term that disguises its often broad consequences. Ever-shifting global supply chains can have the effect of creating disruption and vacuums in areas where work has come and gone. When the jobs evaporate, workers, too, will pick up and leave. By the same token, employees will move if they see fresh opportunities in newly industrializing areas.

Human migration reflects the larger picture of international trade and commerce. The rapidly expanding universe of transnational corporations—there are about seventy-nine thousand such companies employing eighty-two million people—make international borders increasingly irrelevant. Fast-paced and cheaper communications combined with speedy production lines, improved cargo transportation, and a globally interconnected banking system have all led to the expansion of world trade and foreign investments. In 2007, of the world's hundred largest economic entities, sixty-one were nations and thirty-nine were transnational companies. During the 2008 global financial meltdown, dominoes fell rapidly, with little regard to political boundaries.

A poster child for the nexus between globalization and migration is the textile and garment industry, whose products have traditionally been among the first produced by newly industrialized economies. That's been the pattern since the Industrial Revolution erupted in Britain in the eighteenth century and spread to Western Europe and the United States. Reliant on a low-wage, vulnerable workforce, garment sweatshops and textile factories have traditionally been a magnet for migrant workers.

The U.S. fabric and clothing industries have long shown a penchant for corporate mobility. In the 1950s textile production moved from the Northeast to the less industrial states of the South, where companies could find cheaper, non-union labor. At the same time, retailers increasingly turned to imports from the newly industrializing countries of Singapore, Hong Kong, the Republic of Korea, and Taiwan, nations that relied to a great extent on migrants. As labor costs increased in those countries, Asian companies subcontracted to factories in cheaper nations—China, Sri Lanka, Thailand, Indonesia, and Bangladesh. In turn, U.S. manufacturers, taking advantage of falling trade barriers, increasingly moved production to Mexico, Central America, and the Caribbean Basin.

But with even more liberal international trade policies, quotas fell, and manufacturers moved out and on. Soon China, followed by Vietnam, became the production sources of preference.

In both China and Vietnam, officials have been trying to manage huge migrations of workers from rural areas to cities as jobs in urban centers—in a variety of industries—become available. In the past thirty years, China's growing economy produced the largest migration in history, as an estimated 130 million people left the countryside to find work in the cities. By late 2008, however, the trend went into reverse, with yet another mass movement of Chinese. As the global economy cooled and demand for consumer goods eased, thousands of factories closed their doors and, according to official estimates, as many as 10 million laborers returned to China's countryside.

In the Socialist Republic of Vietnam, the rapid pace of industrialization has also meant a steep increase in migration, as people moved from rural areas to the cities in search of jobs created by the *doi moi* (renovation) policy of economic development. Vietnam's industrialization is part of a broad strategy to become an industrial nation by the year 2020. Since 1987, the Communist country has been shifting from central planning to a mixed market system that encourages private and foreign investment. Between 2006 and 2008, overseas businesses of all kinds pumped in about $40 billion worth of investments. Textiles and apparel ranked among the nation's biggest earners of foreign currency, accounting for 15 percent of total exports. By 2008 there were more than 2,500 textile and garment businesses in operation, employing about two million workers. Among them were migrants who had poured out of the countryside into the urban centers of Ho Chi Minh City (formerly Saigon) and Hanoi, the capital. The influx was swelling the populations there considerably. According to one estimate, by 2008 the flow of migrants into Ho Chi Minh City was 430,000 per year. At that rate, the population of the city was expected to increase from 5.7 million people in 2004 to 7.9 million in 2009.

Government officials were trying to carefully steer Vietnam's industrial revolution in the right direction.

"We start law for [encouraging] foreign investment in 1987," Bui Quoc Trung, the number two man at Vietnam's Foreign Investment Agency, explained to me when I visited his Hanoi office in 2008.

"That was more than twenty years ago. We have reached very great achievement concerning this issue. Up until now, we have 10,000 foreign enterprises in Vietnam," he said.

Bui took pride in telling me that a growing number of companies had selected Vietnam instead of China, or had expanded to Vietnam from China. "They think that if they have investment from Vietnam, they get more profit than they have investment in China."

The main reason, he acknowledged, was the wage scale. "Because we have competitive advantage, especially for our labor force. It's more cheaper. Lower cost than in comparison with China."

Vietnamese workers, on average, earn about half as much as their Chinese counterparts.

The growth pangs of rapid urbanization are evident. Migrants have moved into dilapidated housing on a bank of the Red River in Hanoi. And hastily constructed though relatively new apartment blocks, intended to house growing populations, have become casualties of neglect and disrepair. They resemble American public housing projects gone bad, with peeling paint, cracked sidewalks, and vacant lots with weeds where parks had been promised.

The economic surge has created an explosion in the number of motorcycles, the preferred mode of transportation. One in four Vietnamese has one. But the motorbikes are a major contributor to Vietnam's worsening air pollution, and an epidemic of motorbike crashes and head injuries led Vietnam to pass a mandatory helmet law.

Đăng Nguyên Anh, a professor of sociology at the Vietnam Academy of Social Sciences, who has studied Vietnam's migration, took me to the once-tranquil residential neighborhood of Sai Dong, a suburb of Hanoi.

"Four to five years ago, it was very quiet," he said. "And then some businesses started, and people kept coming to live and stay for years in this area to work for the factory nearby here." In a short period of time, the community had changed from a sleepy suburban area of two-story apartment buildings to a crowded mix of housing and commerce. Vendors attached makeshift storefronts to the buildings and set up shopping stalls in the streets. The water pressure was inadequate for the growing population, and the apartments were crowded with tenants from the countryside working in the adjacent industrial area.

"The housing is problematic," Đăng said as we walked around the neighborhood. "Because to get cheap rent you have to share the house with other workers, so maybe three to four persons in one room."

In Vietnam's cities, migrants can be commonly spotted doing odd jobs to supplement their incomes to make ends meet. They polish shoes outside cafés, peddle newspapers, or work as street vendors selling goods from twin bamboo baskets suspended from poles slung over shoulders.

Meager wages amid an inflation rate of nearly 23 percent, the highest in two decades, have drawn protests, particularly from workers in the lowest-paid textile and garment sectors. There were 650 wildcat strikes throughout the country in 2008, according to the government, up from 540 the previous year. Most of them occurred in Japanese-, Taiwanese-, and Korean-owned factories.

The Hanesbrands factory in the center of Vietnam is outside the city of Hue, in the Phú Bai Industrial Park. The spacious facility is adjacent to an open field that is part of what used to be a military airbase that was the site of heavy fighting during the Vietnam War. Concrete bunkers are still scattered around. In late 2008, Hanesbrands was paying the nine hundred garment workers at the plant an average of $80 per month for a six-day, forty-eight-hour workweek, which, managers pointed out at the time of my visit, exceeded the monthly minimum wage of about $50. Employees get free lunches during thirty-minute breaks in the company canteen. Many of the workers stand all day at sewing machines, but those who sit, it was pointed out, do so in ergonomic chairs.

The North Carolina–based maker of such underwear brands as Hanes, Playtex, and Wonderbra is a globetrotting company that has opened up and closed factories around the world. From North Carolina to the Dominican Republic, from Mexico and Puerto Rico to Vietnam, the Hue plant was one of two Hanesbrands facilities in Vietnam. The company had another one, outside Hanoi, as well as one in Thailand and a textile factory in China.

Hanesbrands has put in place what the company describes as "a carefully managed facility migration process." As the nomadic firm evolved its global strategy, its facilities were not the only resources to have migrated. Its business decisions have resulted in the movement of thousands of workers.

As it expanded in Southeast Asia, Hanesbrands closed eight plants in Latin America and the United States and fired sixty-four hundred people. Worldwide, the company's globalization strategy has resulted in the closing of some twenty-nine factories worldwide and the loss of more than three thousand North Carolina jobs since 2006 (when it was spun off from Sara Lee).

The Vietnamese employees in the Hue factory, most of them women in their twenties, were working in a modern, well-lit, air-conditioned factory, sewing men's briefs, stuffing them into plastic bags, and boxing them to be shipped to the United States for sale. Working in teams, each wore a colored smock with his or her work title in bold capital English-language type sewn onto the back of the uniform: SEWING OPERATOR, SUPERVISOR, SUPERVISOR HELPER, INSTRUCTOR. For 50 percent of the employees, these were their first factory jobs. Previously they had worked on farms, making subsistence wages.

Plant officials introduced me to sewing operator Tran Thi My Nang, a shy eighteen-year-old who told me that her life had been changed because of the factory job. She took me to her family home, where she lives with her parents and brother. The modest house is on the outskirts of Hue in a rural area. They have running water for drinking and use well water for washing. The family grows rice on a small plot of land, but unable to provide for themselves, had sent Tran at age sixteen down south to Ho Chi Minh City to live with an uncle. She worked long and hard hours in his tailor shop as a seamstress, sending all the money she earned back home. But when Hanesbrands opened its Hue factory, she was able to return home and was glad to do so.

"It was difficult in the South working such long hours—from six or seven in the morning until six or eight at night," she said. "Now I feel more comfortable, working only eight hours a day."

The jobs created by Hanesbrands have prompted migration. Just as Tran Thi My Nang returned home from south Vietnam, other employees moved away from farms to find work at the company's plants. But I wondered about Hanesbrands's long-term plans. Its record of commitment was spotty. Might its workers have to move again? Hanesbrands has shuttered factories throughout the Western Hemisphere.

I put the question to Javier Chacon, Hanesbrands's Bangkok-based vice president for Asian apparel operations. Chacon himself is from the Dominican Republic, where the company closed three factories in 2007.

"At what point does Vietnam become unaffordable for you?" I asked.

"Not for a long time," he said. "We have been doing this in other countries as well, and so far we see that we stay a very long time in communities that we set up operations."

I pressed the point. "But at some point, might you be reassessing and moving on to another country where the labor costs are cheaper?"

"Twenty, thirty years from now, probably," he acknowledged. "We cannot say 'never.' But we usually stay for a relatively long time in the communities where we establish operations."

In the meantime, he said, Vietnam was providing the company with what it needed. "Vietnam has a good labor force, a good labor cost, a good infrastructure, and good energy costs, and it is convenient for our fabric location in China in terms of flow and logistics," Chacon explained.

Taxes were another draw. A Hue provincial official told me that Hanesbrands, which had become the area's largest employer, would pay no taxes for the first four years, followed by 50 percent of the normal corporate tax for nine subsequent years.

"Our supply chain strategy is very simple," explained Richard A. Noll, Hanesbrands's chief executive officer and board chairman. "It's to balance it equally across hemispheres between the Western Hemisphere and Asia." Even though the vast majority of the company's workers are overseas, 90 percent of its sales are in the United States—mostly through big box stores Wal-Mart and Target. According to Noll, the wage rates in Asia are a half to a third of the pay in Central America.

The company's approach "has been consistent for many decades," he said. "It's to always operate in the lowest-cost places that we can that allows us to use the cost advantage to invest in our brand, invest in innovation, and keep prices low for our consumers."

The veteran CEO has been well rewarded for the strategy, with a 2008 compensation package of $9,280,711, including stock options. Based on their respective 2008 pay rates, it would take the average worker in his Hue factory 806 years to earn what Noll made in a single month.

Noll believes that both Hanesbrands and the Vietnamese benefit from the relationship.

"As you look at the places we go and we operate, as industrialization is taking hold and we're able to bring jobs to those localities so that they can get their economic engines going, actually I think on a worldwide basis, when you take a view across all boundaries, you're helping a lot of people raise their standard of living, which is good for all of us," Noll said.

Unsurprisingly, that view is not shared by former Hanesbrands workers in the United States or in Mexico.

"I don't even buy their products anymore," Willie Hill, a former factory worker, told me in Winston-Salem, Hanesbrands's headquarters town.

"I don't either," added her friend Barbara Plater. Both were veteran Hanesbrands employees whom I met in a state unemployment center. Ironically the office was housed in a building that had been used and abandoned by Hanesbrands.

"I don't let my family buy Hanes. Nobody. I'm like—we don't do Hanes anymore. Anything but Hanes," said Plater, visibly upset at the layoffs.

"There was a lot of anger at first, then we've moved through depression," explained job counselor Anne Cannon. "Fear is out there, too. . . . It's an evolving economy; it's a changing economy; and there are people who are having the ground fall out from under them."

Farther to the south, I visited workers who had been laid off from Hanesbrands factories in Mexico. There I discovered to my surprise that the firm's global strategy had resulted in even more migration, but this time across an international border.

My meeting took place in the industrial town of Monclova, 125 miles south of the Texas border. Hanes had operated three factories in the area but closed them in 2004 and 2006 as it shifted production to Haiti and Central America. Because of the closures, some five thousand workers lost their jobs.

I went to a small house that serves as an office for Servicio Desarrollo y Paz (Service, Development, and Peace), or SEDEPAC. The organization was founded in 1983 to organize the predominantly female workforce in foreign-owned manufacturing and assembly plants along the border—factories known as *maquiladoras*. SEDEPAC's founder, Betty Robles, who worked at one of the factories, said that at first the main issues were low wages and objectionable working conditions. Workers complained that production lines were speeded up unreasonably and that women had to take monthly pregnancy tests. If they were found to be pregnant, they were fired. When Hanesbrands announced plans to close the factories, organizers switched their focus. With the support of sympathetic organizations in the United States, they tried to keep the Hanesbrands facilities open but lost the campaign.

Half a dozen other women in the room told me their stories, asking me not to use their names.

"When the factory closed, my husband got $3,000 in severance pay," one explained. She said there were no jobs in town, so he decided to put the money to good use. "He needed $2,000 to pay a *coyote* [human smuggler] to get across the border. I couldn't go because I needed to stay with my children, so he went by himself."

"My husband went to San Antonio when the plant closed down," another woman said. "When he calls me, I ask him where he works. He stands on a street corner and asks people if they need workers and he goes with them. He sends me $50 a week. He lives with other men, also from Monclova."

Each woman sitting around the room told a similar tale. Hanesbrands had unwittingly underwritten an exodus.

"I believe that about 40 percent of the people who worked in the factories migrated to the United States," said Robles.

Their stories of separation were heartbreaking. Neither the jobs nor the men, apparently, were returning.

"My husband is in Alabama working for a construction company that installs roofs," said a woman in the corner, the mother of two girls—one seven, the other eleven. "He sends money every two weeks. But he married another woman. That's one of the problems. The men go, and find Americans, and we're alone."

"He says he has no money. He has to pay rent," said another woman about her absent husband. "I don't know if that's the truth or if he's lying. But the problem is with our children. They can't forget that their father isn't with us. My older daughter—she talks on the phone with her father, and he tells her that he's coming back."

"Does she believe him?" I asked.

"Yes," she answered. "Because he says he'll return."

"Do you believe him?"

"No, I don't," she said. And she laughed.

CHAPTER 4

Switching Course: Reversals of Fortune

Leaving Ireland in the mid-nineteenth century was not only a quest for a better life; it also was a bid for survival.

"The quays are crowded every day with the peasantry from all quarters of the country, who are emigrating to America," reported the *Cork Examiner* in 1847. "When a ship is put on the berth here, she is filled in a day or two, and the agents say if they had 100 ships, they would not be sufficient to meet the demand."

In the decade spanning 1845 and 1855, more than two million Irish people went abroad, a number equal to a quarter of the population before the migration.

"Each day brings with it its own horrors," wrote one correspondent. "The mind recoils from the contemplation of the scenes we are compelled to witness every hour. . . . Each day—each hour produces its own victims—Holocausts offered at the shrine of political economy."

The immediate cause of the horror was *Phytophthora infestans*, more commonly known as potato blight. Potatoes were susceptible to disease, so when the fungus struck, it ravaged crops, blackening them, turning the vegetables into rotting, stinking plants. Since potatoes were practically the only food for much of the population, the result of the blight was widespread famine. As many as 1.5 million people died from starvation and disease.

Although it played a central role in the Irish exodus, *Phytophthora infestans* is just one part of the story. Irish migration in the nineteenth century was profoundly affected by political and economic decisions—just as it has been for more contemporary migration into and, more recently, out of the Emerald Isle.

During the famine, Ireland was a colonial outpost of England. Much of the land was owned by absentee landlords and was cultivated by Irish peasants who produced grain and meat for export to a rapidly industrializing England. Catholics were not allowed to buy land, so as their population grew, they divided the acreage they owned or leased into smaller and smaller plots. Since potatoes were easy to grow in small areas and could feed large families, Irish peasants came to depend on the vegetables as a subsistence crop.

"The potato blight was unavoidable, but the Great Famine was largely the result of Ireland's colonial status and grossly inequitable social system," according to the historian Kerby A. Miller. "The continued exportation of Ireland's grain, cattle, and other foodstuff to feed British markets while the Irish perished from hunger was an especially poignant example of Ireland's political and economic subservience to British interests."

The escape, mostly to America, was often perilous. Tens of thousands died of communicable diseases such as typhus, cholera, and dysentery at sea aboard what came to be known as "coffin ships."

In Ireland today, more than a dozen memorials commemorate the famine and its consequences. In Murrisk in County Mayo, a bronze sculpture of a three-masted ship contains representations of human skeletons. On the Dublin Docklands, a group of statues, one of a scraggly dog, the others of seven painfully gaunt people—one being carried over the shoulders of another—represents Irish famine victims walking toward a ship. The display haunts a walkway in the financial district along the Liffey River. There is probably no better symbol of the old and the new Ireland than the emaciated figures of poverty and powerlessness juxtaposed with the imposing building across the street from where they stand—the glimmering, eleven-story, International Financial Services Centre.

As Ireland's fortunes changed, its migration picture also ebbed and flowed. Even after the nineteenth-century famine subsided, Irish emigration continued, and the population continued its decline.

Up until 1961, more people were leaving Ireland than were entering or being born. For most of the 1980s, unemployment hovered around 16 percent. Limited economic opportunities offered few incentives for Irish people to remain in the country, and emigration continued.

However, the tide was turning. After Ireland joined the European Economic Community in 1973, the stage was set for migration patterns to change. E.U. membership made Ireland eligible for subsidies and provided it the opportunity to step out of the shadow of England. Foreign companies saw possibilities and began investing in the country.

During the 1990s, Ireland unleashed the "Celtic Tiger." Generous tax benefits, relatively low wages, and an educated, English-speaking workforce lured computer, medical technology, and pharmaceutical companies eager to expand. Companies such as IBM, Lotus, Microsoft, and Bausch & Lomb set up shop. As Ireland put more money into its infrastructure and educational system, multinationals seeking to expand to Europe in an era of prosperity saw Ireland as a useful platform. Foreign investments multiplied twenty-five fold, leaping from $1.1 billion in 1993 to $25.5 billion by 2000. American companies, in particular Intel Corporation, Microsoft, Dell, Hewlett-Packard, Motorola, and IBM, established Irish operations, as did nine of the world's top ten pharmaceutical companies. Between 1995 and 2000, the Irish economy grew by more than 9 percent a year, twice the annual growth rate during the previous five years.

The foreign investments helped alter long-standing migration patterns. Along with the influx of money came an inflow of people. By 1996, Ireland had turned a corner: more people came into the country than left it. A large number were natives of Ireland returning as the luck of the Irish reversed course.

A country known for exporting its people became a country workers wanted to move to.

Pat Phelan had studied engineering in Ireland, but in the early 1980s, with no job prospects, he got a job as a butcher instead. "I hated it," he said.

Phelan went to London, where he found work managing a pub. Eventually he became a cook. As the economy improved in Ireland, he returned to his native Cork, where, in 1994, he was hired as the chef at the Taste of Thailand restaurant on Bridge Street. But unable to attract workers for low-wage restaurant jobs, he found himself working almost around the clock. With more attractive alternatives, Irish people who had not "taken the big plunge for the gold-paved streets of New York or Boston," as he put it, just weren't interested in taking low-paying work in the restaurant.

To brush up on Thai cuisine, Phelan had attended a cooking class in Bangkok. On the way back from Thailand in transit at the Kuala Lumpur airport, Phelan fortuitously met an Irishman who owned a Malaysian recruitment agency. The two came up with a plan to address Phelan's needs.

Back in Cork, he convinced his boss, the restaurateur Jim Ryan, to go into the recruitment business with him. The two started a company, PR Recruitment, and began importing workers from South Asia in partnership with Phelan's newfound colleague in Malaysia. Other eateries also were interested in what Phelan and Ryan had to offer.

"We went to an employer and we said, 'How many people do you need?'" he remembered. "And it was not one, but ten. 'I need kitchen workers, chefs, waiters.' We showed as many CVs as we could find. 'Would you like this guy? Read the CV.' Apply for a work permit, and we have the guy in ten weeks."

A business was launched. Phelan and his partners brought in Bangladeshis, Pakistanis, Indians, and Malaysians to work in the Irish hospitality industry. They were among the first waves of migrants brought in to ride the Celtic Tiger.

"What happened to them?" I wondered.

"They're all still here," Phelan said. "They all stayed and became Irish citizens. Their sons and daughters are in school. It was like the Irish who went to America. They went too far to come home."

Over the next few years, Irish prosperity created a massive ripple effect—a spectacular real estate boom, particularly in housing.

"The Celtic Tiger is back, or if not the tiger, perhaps the Celtic Panther," the *Irish Times* reported enthusiastically in 2004.

"It is a bit of a downer to see the roads dug up," the Bank of Ireland's chief economist, Dan McLaughlin, told the paper. "But I think sometimes we lose sight of the fact that it is a golden age of construction."

In ten years, building industry revenues multiplied threefold. The number of construction industry jobs doubled to two hundred thousand. The pace of home building was frenetic. Ireland's growth in housing construction surpassed all other Western European countries.

As Conn Ó Muíneacháin, a broadcaster and former computer programmer in Ennis, County Clare, told me, the Irish people are obsessed with homeownership.

"This is probably a legacy from the days when we didn't own our property or own land, but paid money to absentee landlords for the pleasure of living on their patch of ground," said Ó Muíneacháin, who has an English-language morning radio program and a regular Irish-language podcast. "And I think as a result of that, Irish people have always had this fascination or this special love for property and so we had a housing and construction boom."

As Irish expatriates returned home, immigration to Ireland also climbed. By 2006, nearly 15 percent of all Irish residents were foreigners. The largest numbers of expats were Brits who had migrated west. The second-largest category was Polish nationals. Since Poland and Ireland both belong to the European Economic Area, passports are basically irrelevant, and people who are citizens of any of its thirty member countries can work in one another's nations freely, so official census figures are unreliable. The 2006 census counted 63,100 Poles in the country, but there were likely two or three times as many living there. Migrants hailed from 188 countries. Behind the United Kingdom and Poland as chief home countries for Irish foreigners were immigrants from Lithuania, Nigeria, Latvia, the United States, China, Germany, the Philippines, and France.

Immigration changed the face of Ireland dramatically and rapidly. From dim sum in Dublin to curry in Cork, restaurants and grocery stores allow migrants to savor familiar items from home and provide Irish natives the opportunity to expand their horizons. The hip, tourist-packed Temple Bar district south of the Liffey River in Dublin offers a wide array of international cuisine and cosmopolitan nightspots along its cobbled streets. Not far away, off Parnell Street, migrant workers take packages to a shipping company to send goods home to Nigeria, the Philippines, Malaysia, and elsewhere.

Poles can buy Okocim beer in Polish bars, find kielbasa sausages in specialty grocery stores, listen to Polish-language radio stations, or read magazines in their native language.

In Cashel in County Tipperary, I met three Polish migrants in their mid-twenties who had left Bydgoszcz in northern Poland to take jobs in the Irish service and hospitality sectors. They were college graduates who decided they could earn more in Ireland than they might have in Poland.

Kryzysztof Matuszevski was working as a chef at the Rock House Restaurant, which prides itself on "traditional Irish food." Posters for Guinness beer, hurling (similar to field hockey), and Gaelic football decorated the dining area. Matuszevski, who came without any previous cooking experience and who told me that his favorite Irish dish is chicken curry (€9.95 on the menu—with basmati rice), said he could make the equivalent of $600 to $750 in a good week. In Poland, it would have taken him a month to earn the same amount.

His friends Dominika Rydwelska and Malgorzata Tuzylak came together from Poland and lived in a flat above a shoe store. Both women were college graduates who worked in Cashel as shop assistants. Their goal was to stay for a couple of years, save money, return to Poland, and buy homes.

Our conversation was interrupted by a brief Internet chat on Skype that Rydwelska had with her mother back home. It was an almost daily ritual that she said made living so far from friends and relatives less difficult.

"It's hard to live in a different country, even if you know English. Even if you have good money here, and everything is fine, it's still not your country," she said. "The food and everything is different, and people, mentality and everything. In your country, you're like at home, you know. You feel relaxed and everything."

By the autumn of 2008 when I met the three young Poles, the economy was changing quickly. If the tiger had morphed into a panther in 2004, as the *Irish Times* put it, four years later it had mutated into a purring pussycat.

"The money was cheap. Interest rates were low; banks were shoveling money out to people," explained Neil Prendeville, a Cork radio personality and developer. "Developers were building housing estate after housing estate after housing estate. Labor was cheap. They built too many houses."

The collapse of the housing market and the onset of Ireland's recession preceded the U.S. economic crisis by several months. "We had our time in the sun. And we spent like drunken sailors," Prendeville said, offering a pithy analysis, not only of Ireland's economic misfortunes, but also of the developed world's. "We thought that every day was going to be a glory day."

Instead, Ireland's glory was fading. By 2008, unemployment was rising, foreign businesses were packing up and leaving, and construction was sagging. The lousy economic picture was reflected in the migration numbers.

Immigration into Ireland had peaked.

Fewer and fewer migrants were moving in, and more and more people were going abroad. As many as a hundred thousand left Ireland in 2008, and a survey by a recruitment firm indicated that a third of the Polish population in Ireland was planning on returning to Poland within the next year. Once again, investment decisions and economic policies had profoundly affected migration patterns.

In late 2008, as construction workers in Cashel put the finishing touches on a new Tesco supermarket, site supervisor Kevin Carroll, wearing a yellow hard hat, walked around the entrance to the parking lot measuring the dimensions of a newly installed and still drying cement curb. The project was one bright spot in a declining economy. The supermarket would create about eighty retail jobs. But Carroll's own employment was in jeopardy. His employer, Sisk Contractors, Ireland's largest construction firm, had announced a 7.3 percent drop in profits and had laid off 10 percent of its workforce. Carroll worked out of the Sisk office in Limerick, which had taken a disproportionate share of the cuts.

"This time last year, we had 102 staff in Limerick, workers on the ground, company engineers, surveyors, foremen, site agents, and a contracts manager. Now we've only got 62 at the moment," he said.

With only a few weeks left to go on the job, Carroll was fully expecting to be laid off, a prediction that came true by Christmas. His solution, he said before losing the job, was a ticket out of Ireland. "I'd probably go to Dubai or the UAE or somewhere like that," he conjectured, not anticipating that only one year later, the real estate bubble in the United Arab Emirates would also burst.

In Cork, plumber's apprentice Ruairí O'Callaghan also was finishing up a job and expecting to follow some of his construction worker friends out of the country.

"I know a lot of people who have gone to Australia, which seems to be the big destination now at the moment," he said. "A lot of people are heading for London, trying to get a job." Things had slowed down in the British economy, but many construction workers were trying to get work at sites where building was taking place in preparation for the 2012 Olympics.

To commentator Conn Ó Muíneacháin, Irish history was being repeated.

"It's the revival of a traditional cycle," he said. "Irish people have been immigrating into the United States since the mid-nineteenth century. And that came to almost a complete halt, and indeed many of my friends and relatives who would have lived and worked in the United States, many of those came home in the mid- to late nineties, and now we're looking at a situation in which Irish people are once again talking about going to work abroad."

Ó Muíneacháin had worked for eight years as a software engineer at Dell Computer in Limerick. The American manufacturer had established its Irish presence in 1990 to take advantage of the cheap labor pool and low corporate tax rates.

"Products were being built in Limerick, Ireland, and then being shipped to the United States. So I guess you could say they were American jobs that had been exported to Ireland," Ó Muíneacháin observed. Dell eventually became the country's second-largest employer.

As a Dell employee, Ó Muíneacháin had a front-row seat to unfolding preparations for even more job migration as the firm moved farther afield. One of the biggest projects for many of his colleagues was to set up a lower-cost operation. The company was reducing the workforce at its three Irish facilities and preparing to open up a new one abroad. His coworkers were being asked to plan their own demise.

"Where was the fourth one going to be?" was the question he said needed to be resolved. "Somewhere in Eastern Europe. And there were a lot of people who were in Limerick at the time to select and build and set up and start that manufacturing facility in Europe built outside of Ireland, which was built in Łódź, in Poland."

In a January 2009 press statement, Dell announced its much-anticipated decision to "release" nineteen hundred Limerick employees over a twelve-month period and shift operations to its new plant in Poland.

"This is a difficult decision, but the right one for Dell to become even more competitive, and deliver greater value to customers in the region," said Sean Corkery, vice president of operations for EMEA—a common corporate acronym for a marketing area comprising Europe, the Middle East, and Africa.

The exodus was picking up steam. "A lot of my friends went back to Poland because all the constructions over here are nearly finished," explained Paulina Mieroslawska, manager of the Gospoda Polska restaurant in Dublin. "Plenty of people in this kind of business went back."

As the lateral journeys of Irish and Poles illustrate, far from all the world's migrants move from desperately poor countries to wealthy ones. While it is true that most migrant workers on the globe are low-skilled, it is also a fact that just about the same number of migrants move from one developing country to another ("south-to-south," in the vernacular of development experts) as migrate between developed nations ("north-to-north"). As the recent histories of Ireland and Poland indicate, the old distinctions between "countries of origin" and "countries of departure" have become more and more vague. Most labor migration takes place within regions, and countries such as Ireland, Poland, Italy, Spain, Malaysia, South Korea, and Thailand, which once saw legions of citizens going abroad in search of work, have themselves turned into employment destinations for migrants. The flows turn this way and that, depending on changes in laws, incentives, as well as global financial conditions—circumstances that affect the flow of money and the building or closing of factories.

In the case of Ireland, as fortunes there declined, the luck of the Poles was ascending. Dell Computer was just one example. In January 2008, Dell opened a sprawling nine-acre manufacturing facility in Łódź, Poland's third-largest city, in the center of the country. The firm's namesake, CEO Michael Dell, flew out for an opening ceremony.

"As we saw our Central and Eastern European businesses grow, we knew we needed a manufacturing base here to maintain our ambition for the region," he told employees and Polish dignitaries assembled for the ribbon-cutting. "Our operations in Łódź mean we can maintain this momentum and offer a superior service to customers." The factory, built at a cost of almost $300 million, was expected to eventually employ three thousand people.

Since the end of World War II, Poland's history has been characterized by waves of mass migrations—in the main, Poles moving out. After the war, the rejiggering of Poland's borders resulted in the resettlement of millions of people. During the 1950s, thousands of ethnic Germans living in Poland moved to the Federal Republic of Germany. In 1968, as many as twenty-five thousand Jews left the country in reaction to anti-Semitism. During the rise and suppression of the Solidarnośći (Solidarity) anti-Communist movement at the beginning of the 1980s, another quarter of a million Poles left the country.

Since the collapse of the Soviet empire in 1989 and the emergence of a market economy, Poland's migration picture has been in a state of flux. After the fall of communism, Poland, like former Soviet republics, liberalized its travel policies. Many workers headed out of the country to find low-wage jobs in Western Europe. High unemployment during the late 1990s and early 2000s pushed out more emigrants. When Poland joined the European Union in 2004, Poles were able to legally move west to find work. At least two million of them emigrated, mostly to the Republic of Ireland and England.

Exact numbers are impossible to come by since so much of the migration was under the radar and because many migrants often traveled back and forth. By 2006, British officials had counted 229,000 Poles living in the United Kingdom, although unofficial estimates put the number at closer to 600,000. The *Times* of London reported that "the word Pole has become shorthand for cheap, reliable worker." As a result largely of Polish migration, according to a 2007 study, Catholics were found to outnumber Anglicans in Great Britain—a first since the Protestant Reformation of the sixteenth century. The Church of England protested that the numbers were inflated.

But another church, the English-speaking Roman Catholic parish in Warsaw, had been experiencing the flip side of Poland's migration story. The collapse of Polish communism, followed by the country's membership in the European Union (what the Europeans grandly and quasi-religiously refer to as "ascension"), meant good news for its membership figures.

The Sunday I visited, the two-story church was packed for Mass—a reflection of the increase of English speakers living and working in the Polish capital.

"If you go on the streets of Warsaw today, you can see a more cosmopolitan city," explained Wieslaw Dawidowski, a priest. "If you see our parish, for example, you see we have people from all over the world, right? So Poland is now facing a new face of the European Union. . . . Usually, we are used to the fact that many Poles left Poland looking for a job in England or Ireland, right? And here, we have people who left their countries to work in Poland. For various reasons, perhaps for bigger money, but they left their country."

At a secular venue, Jimmy Bradley's Irish Bar in the heart of Warsaw, patrons were watching rugby matches on big-screen televisions. I met Cathel Moynihan, who had arrived the day before from Dublin.

"I'm a qualified bricklayer," he told me. "I was working for a company there for five or six years and there was no more work left over there." A friend pointed him to a job in a stone quarry outside Warsaw, and he was ready to start. He'd earn less money, but Poland was a cheaper place to live.

"It's a small drop. Not that big of a drop. In Euros you're talking losing maybe €200 in a week, but it's much cheaper to live here. I'll probably be gaining more here than I would be at home."

Poland's entry into the European Union opened a door for foreign businesses, which sped through. A *Who's Who* of transnational firms set up operations. Manufacturers, including Bridgestone, Sharp, and Toyota, opened factories. General Electric, Samsung, IBM, Motorola, and Siemens started research and development centers. Other companies, such as Accenture and Shell, established outsourcing and business service locations.

Encouraging the growth were generous corporate tax breaks from the Polish government, which established fourteen special economic zones. To sweeten the pot, officials baited companies with subsidies from the European Union. Dell received nearly $74 million, just about a quarter of the cost of its plant in Łódź.

Poland's boosters tout the combination of an educated workforce and low wages. Despite many outward signs of prosperity, Poland is still very much a developing nation. The average salary is about $17,000 a year.

"Poland's employment costs are among the lowest in all of Europe," crowed the Polish Information and Foreign Investment Agency. "The country's wage costs are not only less than those of Western Europe, but also lower than those of Slovenia, Estonia, Slovakia, the Czech Republic, Hungary, and Latvia."

One area that had attracted businesses and was seeing returning and new migrants was Łódź. This once-depressed city has witnessed a noticeable transformation. Old brick factories that prior to 1990 marked the area's prominence as a center for the apparel industry are being converted to other uses. Textile and clothing companies have moved to Asia. In their place are such transnational firms as Gillette, DHL, Dell, and Sonoco. They moved in, hired locals, lured back Polish ex-pats, and brought in foreigners.

In Łódź I met business executives who explained the importance of Poland to their international operations. "Our overall strategy is about moving the tactical jobs from people being located all around the places in Europe, in North America," said Arkadiusz Rochowczyk, who runs a purchasing division of the Dutch electronics giant Philips. The company has been moving operations from Western to Eastern Europe since 1991. On one floor of an office building, some fifty buyers sat at computer terminals, scouring the globe for deals on equipment and services the company needed. Their purchases total about $300 million a year.

"I think the wage difference is of importance here," said Rochowczyk, explaining why Philips had moved to Poland from the West. "We are talking probably the difference between annually €40,000 to €50,000 in West Europe to €15,000 to €20,000 annually here in

Poland, which is a significant delta," he said. (In U.S. terms, the buyers were earning $21,000 to $28,000 a year.)

In addition to the attraction of lower wages, Philips's move to Łódź was motivated by a $4 million package of benefits in the form of subsidies and tax reductions from the Polish government.

Between 2005 and 2008, foreign investors sank more than $67 billion into Poland. During the same time period, the country's economy grew by about 5.3 percent a year—outpacing the European Union's average annual growth rate. Poland's unemployment was cut in half. And even though wages were low by U.S. standards, between 2007 and 2008, salaries increased by 6 percent. Growth slowed by the end of 2008 and into 2009, but still was better than European countries whose economies were contracting.

Paul Jack moved his wife and teenage daughter from outside Dublin to Łódź in 2007, as opportunities faded in Ireland and increased in Poland. He'd grown up in the printing industry, but, as he tells it, the business virtually died out in Ireland. Even the vaunted Guinness brewery, which used to print its own beer bottle labels in Dublin, moved its printing operations overseas. Jack, a quiet-spoken forty-five-year-old, said the move had been difficult. "It's been quite traumatic," he said. "But really it was essential for me if I wished to stay within this industry."

Jack worked as a technical manager for Amcor, an Australian-owned packaging company that has shifted production from Western to Eastern Europe. It opened up three separate plants in Łódź, printing plastic bags for snack foods.

Amcor executives told me the wages there were about a third of what they were paying for comparable work in Western Europe. In addition, the tax rate was unbeatable.

"Here, in the special economic zone, we have no taxes," said Cezary Wojciechowski, who ran Amcor's Polish operations. Wojciechowski explained that in return, the company had to commit to stay in the area until at least 2017.

Łódź mayor Jerzy Kropiwnicki took much of the credit for the city's resurgence and for the unemployment rate, which plunged between 2002, the year he came into office, and 2008.

"In six years, from 21 to 6.5 percent. It's enormous, I think," he told me as we sat in his office in the city hall on Piotrkowska Street, a three-mile revitalized thoroughfare. "And today, our unemployment rate is less than the national average and is lower, much lower than the regional one, so we transformed from the black hole of Poland and of the region to the machinery of development for the region and very soon, also for Poland."

The Polish resurgence made the country an attractive destination for returnees. In 2008, Poland Street, a British organization of Polish ex-pats, started organizing conferences in the United Kingdom with representatives of twelve Polish cities to prepare returning Poles for "re-immigration."

Recognizing a trend, and eager to attract a needed and talented labor pool of Polish exiles, in 2008 the Polish prime minister's office hired Paweł Kaczmarczyk of the University of Warsaw's Centre of Migration Research as a consultant to help design a plan to reach out to the Polish diaspora.

"We are going to provide migrants, people who are staying abroad, with reliable information covering all the information important to them, issues related to [Polish] social security, to the taxes system, labor market, family issues, all kind of issues you can imagine," Kaczmarczyk told me. "There will be kind of a guidebook, a booklet distributed in Ireland, in the United Kingdom, and other important destination countries. And also there will be a Web site for migrants containing all this information, but additionally it will be interactive. We assume that all migrants will have a chance to ask questions, to chat with Polish politicians and experts."

The Internet site, titled in Polish *"Masz PLan na powrót?"* (You have a PLan to return? ["PL" is the common abbreviation for Poland]) was cofinanced by the Polish government and the European Union. Its logo is a depiction of a large white stork, ubiquitous in Poland, landing in a large nest built of twigs.

Attempts by Polish authorities to lure back migrants reflect a broader trend among governments to better manage migration according to perceived economic needs. However, managed or selective migration is far from an exact science. Needs change. Walls, fences, and doors are imperfect.

The politics of migration control are inevitable land mines, particularly since the requirements of policymakers are likely to trump the rights and aspirations of migrants. At the same time, recent history has proven just how fickle the economics of migration also can be.

On a trip to Sweden in 2007, I met Sten Andersson, an earthy former merchant marine who had won election to the town council of Malmö, a port city in the South. Andersson had earned a reputation as a racist for his attacks on Sweden's generous and welcoming approach to migrants.

"I don't know why there are more immigrant criminals," he told me, trucking out a timeworn antimigrant shibboleth. "Many people say it's because that's what they did before they come here, but that's not something we can prove. A lot of the drug trade in Sweden is handled by foreigners."

I asked him what he would do about the growing number of migrants being admitted to the nation. Sweden being Sweden, where, by U.S. standards, many conservatives would be considered raving leftists, Andersson's proposed "solution" seemed tame and ever so Scandinavian.

"We should pay them to leave," he suggested.

Sweden has not adopted that policy, but as the global financial crisis sent unemployment rates soaring, other developed nations did get out their own financial brooms. In late 2008 and early 2009, the Czech Republic, Spain, and Japan all launched programs to pay immigrant workers to go home.

The Czech Republic offered €500 per worker ($700) plus the cost of tickets home. Japan said it would pay temporary workers from Latin America whose ancestors were of Japanese origin ¥300,000 ($3,200) to return, while Spain was the most generous, tendering €14,000 ($19,600) to every migrant laborer who pledged not to come back for three years.

Only a year earlier, Spain, a nation that had been making deals with African nations to send migrant workers, was paying for them to return, an emblem of the delicate dynamics of migration—situational and subject to quick reversal.

The *Wall Street Journal* mused about the wisdom of a fickle migration policy. "Critics also wonder what will happen when the financial crisis abates, re-opening the labor market gaps that led the Czech Republic and its aging workforce to recruit foreigners in the first place." The critics were unnamed.

One answer came from Demetrios Papademetriou, a veteran immigration expert who heads the Migration Policy Institute in Washington. "In many of these countries, you see a form of buyer's remorse," he said. "But they're going to need some of these workers again."

CHAPTER 5

Recruitment Agencies
and Body Shops

R ene Urbano arrived before dawn at the U.S. consulate in
Monterrey, a gritty industrial city in northeastern Mexico. Clad
in a black polo shirt and jeans to match, topped by a baseball cap
with a brown camouflage design, and carrying a canvas bag slung
over his right shoulder, the stocky entrepreneur strode briskly through
the plaza outside the concrete building. A group of about thirty men
gathered around him as he took roll, handed out instruction sheets,
and explained the plans for the day. Zulma Medellin, his business
partner, stood nearby holding on to the stack of passports she had collected from the men earlier. Working with agents throughout Mexico
and with a U.S. placement firm, Urbano and Medellin run a company, Asesores Consulares Integrales (Complete Consular Advisers),
that recruits temporary laborers, mainly farm workers, and sends them
off to jobs across the border.

The men listened attentively to Urbano, who took on the role of
team coach, describing consular procedures and encouraging them
to work hard for their American employers. By nightfall, his recruits
would be boarding buses that would take them to farms in the southern
United States.

The laborers had left their homes to spend the night in housing
that Urbano and Medellin had arranged for them near the consulate.

The recruiters' task now was to hand their clients' documents to consular officials, then wait for most of the day as the men went inside to be photographed, fingerprinted, questioned, and, if everything checked out, eventually issued temporary work visas. By early evening the two would make sure the men were on their way to the border checkpoint at Laredo, heading to job destinations in North Carolina.

Before he started his own recruitment company, Urbano worked as a migrant farm laborer himself, picking cucumbers. These men, he said, had worked mostly in orange groves in the northeastern state of Tamaulipas. He and his colleagues had recruited them by going into the fields and promising them legal jobs in the United States. Many had worked illegally previously, but Urbano offered an alternative.

"They were having too many problems," he said. Instead, they can "go there for six or seven months, bring back $6,000, $7,000, and the next year go back. They're going to be preferred workers because the employers are going to ask for them." Business, he said, was picking up. "Last year we send in like two thousand workers, and this year we're going to send like four thousand workers," he exclaimed enthusiastically as his recruits lined up outside the consulate, waiting to go through security and, from there, to the various stations manned by consular officials.

Similar scenes play out throughout the world's human export centers and help form the machinery of migration. On the spectrum of respectability and legality, recruitment and transportation networks range from publicly traded global companies on the one end (the focus of this chapter), to clandestine smuggling operations (the subject of chapter 6) on the other. But whether they are licensed "headhunters," recruiters, staffing agencies, placement services, or illegal "snakeheads" and *coyotes* (human smugglers), the business is essentially the same: to procure and deliver migrants.

With as many as fifteen thousand firms, global recruitment enterprises comprise a multibillion-dollar-a-year industry. They include publicly traded companies that dominate the market—among them Manpower, Inc., Adecco of Switzerland, and the Dutch giant Randstad. Private recruiters are widespread in Asia, where sending nations have put in place government regulations designed to oversee the industry and protect departing migrants. Companies have to be licensed, registered, and bonded, and are supposed to follow rules concerning salaries and fees. In 2007, Sri Lanka had 691 licensed agencies, a fourfold increase in two decades. The numbers were similar in Bangladesh. In India, the Office of the Protector General of Emigrants had registered 1,887 recruiting agents by the end of 2008. And in Pakistan, the government's Bureau of Emigration and Overseas Employment had published its list of 2,532 Licensed Overseas Employment Promoters, or OEPs, as they are known.

In the Philippines, competition among 1,363 registered recruitment agencies is intense. Much of it plays out in southern Manila along Mabini Street, a crowded thoroughfare that has become a job bazaar for overseas recruitment agencies. On a recent visit, it seemed as if the world was hiring. Along the road, three-wheeled pedicabs and small, colorful jeepney buses made up much of the street traffic. On the sidewalks, peddlers selling wristwatches, packages of Viagra, SIM cards for cell phones, and "dates" with "boom-boom" women hustled Western tourists. But the real action was inside the office buildings, which were crowded with job applicants. Companies with such names as Job Lane, Ample Laborpool, Al-Masiya Overseas Placement Agency, GreenGate Manpower Services, and Creative Artists Placement Services, advertised "Jobs Worldwide" and plastered their windows with signs in large block letters offering a wide variety of positions: MACHINIST, AUTO PAINTER, FARM LABORER, FLOWER ARRANGER, TAILOR, DIESEL MECHANIC, STEEL FABRICATOR, DENTAL TECHNICIAN, CARPENTER, TANKER DRIVER, GRAPHIC DESIGNER, and on and on. One company's six-foot-long sign touted a government award for "deploying the highest number of professional overseas Filipino workers." Many of the posted jobs spelled out "KSA"—the Kingdom of Saudi Arabia. Fewer were in Australia and New Zealand but hardly any in the United States, where legal entry is much more of a challenge.

Along Mabini Street, even the recruiters have recruiters. As he left one of the agencies, a man told me that the company paid him a finder's fee of $200 for each worker he brought in who could be placed.

The recruitment industry is notorious for kickbacks, extravagant fees, and lax enforcement. In May 2009, the Philippine government admitted that twenty-nine thousand arrest warrants were outstanding against illegal recruiters, suspected of charging high fees and promising jobs that didn't exist. Stories of abuse and corruption are familiar ones in a business with a long and checkered history.

John Lawson Burnett of Alabama may have been short in stature, but he carried a huge grudge. After his death in 1919, a fellow U.S. congressman eulogized him as a champion of the doctrine "America for Americans," a man who "awakened [the] consciousness of millions of Americans to the menace of the unassimilated mob." Burnett, a staunch advocate of a literacy test for immigrants, had been chairman of the House Committee on Immigration and Naturalization. During a 1912 committee hearing on immigration restrictions, Burnett recounted a conversation with a coal operator in northeastern Alabama, the area Burnett represented.

"I said to him, 'What is the best laborer in the coal mines?' And he said, 'Welsh is about the best, and next the Scotch, the Irish, the English, and the Germans.'"

This line of conversation was common for the times. The period of mass migration from Europe had kindled a virtual obsession among restrictionist politicians and their enablers in the pseudoscientific eugenics movement who were fanatical about cataloging the relative and what they considered innate abilities of ethnic and racial groups.

"What is the poorest?" the chairman remembered asking the mine owner.

"The dagos," was the reply.

The Alabama congressman expressed surprise.

"Worse than the Negro?" he pressed. "Yes," replied the coal operator, explaining that even so, he would prefer to hire Italians than Negroes.

Burnett was confused. "Then why do you want the Italian?" he asked.

The preference was a matter of pure economics. "For the purpose of regulating the price, not the quantity," the businessman explained.

A fellow committee member understood immediately why Italian immigrants were a better value. "The padrone system," clarified Congressman William G. Brown of West Virginia.

The padrone system was a corrupt practice in which international networks of recruiters, placement agents, bankers, contractors, and subcontractors trafficked in Italian immigrants, turning most of them into indentured laborers. The system flourished after the Civil War, when American industries needed a supply of workers to sustain production. In 1864, Congress had obligingly passed the Act to Encourage Immigration, allowing employers to require migrant workers to "pledge the wages of their labor" for up to a year to "repay the expenses of emigration." Even though the law was repealed four years later, abusive practices of private recruitment and placement agencies continued for decades.

In 1890, congressional investigator Victor L. Ricketts described the padrone system as "probably the worst evil connected with our modern immigration."

"Twenty-seven thousand Italian immigrants were landed at New York last year, and probably two-thirds of them are subject to a bondage almost as pernicious as the African slave system that prevailed in the Southern states thirty years ago," Ricketts told a newspaper reporter.

As the padrone (master, landlord) received requests from railroad firms, construction companies, or other employers of unskilled labor for men, he put in orders with recruiters in southern Italy. Paid by the head, their job was to round up peasants for whom the promised wage of $1.00 a day seemed a fortune compared to their accustomed daily pay of $0.20. The padroni made money in various and insidious ways. They received commissions on the steamship tickets they sold to immigrants. They boarded the newcomers at exorbitant prices, overcharged them for food, got a percentage of their wages, and forced them to deposit their earnings with unlicensed "banks." These "padrone banks," often operating out of grocery stores, beer saloons, and lodging houses, nonetheless had impressive names such as Banca Roma or Banca Italiana. Record-keeping was sloppy; deposits were often "lost," and fees for routine services, remittances to Italy, and occasional bail also were excessive.

The padrone system was not confined to Italians. It also was used by Armenians, Turks, and Greeks. Over time, the system died out. As immigrants adapted to U.S. customs and language, they no longer had to rely on the cruelty of strangers.

While the padrone arrangement was a particularly odious practice, U.S. immigration history is bound up with the active recruitment of migrants, a practice dating back to the colonial era when businesses advertised in Europe their growing need for workmen and artisans. In the early nineteenth century, construction firms sent agents to Europe hoping to attract canal builders.

At the end of the century, U.S. railway companies and farmers seeking cheap labor looked south, to Mexico. They developed a system known as *el enganche* (the hooking), in which labor contractors along the U.S. side of the border paid commissions to agents in Mexico (*enganchadores*) to procure hundreds of thousands of Mexican workers. Like the padroni, the contractors often made their money by renting housing in labor camps to migrants and charging them inflated prices for food and supplies.

Recruitment of migrant workers during the nineteenth century provided the English language with colorful expressions. In the garment business, the widespread use of contracted labor was referred to as the sweating system. The middlemen were known as sweaters because they made their profits by sweating the difference between what they earned from contractors and what they paid their workers. Sweatshops were the places where the work was done. In China, flesh peddlers abducted people from the streets to be used as laborers in colonies in Southeast Asia, South Africa, Cuba, Australia, and Canada. Those tricked into working were said to have been Shanghaied.

Over the past century, various U.S. government programs authorized the use of temporary foreign employees, often referred to as "guest workers." (It's a term that strikes me as an oxymoron.) Early programs were adopted to address wartime complaints by the agricultural industry about worker shortages. Between 1917 and 1921, tens of thousands of Mexican workers came to work in sugar beet and cotton fields. Some twenty years later, under the bracero program begun during World War II and lasting until 1964, some 4.6 million Mexican laborers worked on U.S. farms. Controversy over the program persists. Some forty-five years after it ended, former braceros and their survivors were still trying to collect money deducted from workers' paychecks as incentives for them to return to Mexico. The funds were deposited in savings accounts in Mexican banks but never returned to the workers.

In 1952, the Immigration and Nationality Act established categories for "nonimmigrant" workers coming to the country temporarily to perform both agricultural and nonfarm work. By 2008, the government was issuing fifteen categories of temporary work visas, including "specialty workers," farm laborers, nurses, internationally recognized athletes, entertainment groups, and people with religious occupations.

Between 2004 and 2008, American employers imported 1.4 million workers from abroad on "nonimmigrant visas." Just about every legal occupational category was represented—from bank vice presidents and accountants to teachers, shrimpers, nannies, and fashion models. About half of the temporary workers were in the H-1B category of "specialty" occupations such as computer programming and engineering; the others held H-2A visas for farm work and H-2B visas for other blue-collar labor in forestry, seafood processing, landscaping, construction, and other nonagricultural industries.

All of the programs have come in for criticism. U.S. high-tech workers in particular have charged that H-1B visa holders take jobs from Americans and undercut U.S. wages. For employers of H-1B workers, the bar is low, since there is no independent certification, audit, or requirement for companies to prove they are meeting responsibilities to pay prevailing wages. Companies need only *attest* that "the importation of the foreign worker will not adversely affect the wages and working conditions of U.S. workers." In addition, according to the U.S. Department of Labor, "H-1B workers may be hired even when a qualified U.S. worker wants the job, and a U.S. worker can be displaced from the job in favor of the foreign worker."

When the U.S. Government Accountability Office (GAO), the investigative arm of Congress, examined the H-1B program in 2006, it found that the Department of Labor was falling down on the job by failing to provide adequate oversight. It determined that the vast majority (99.5 percent) of applications were automatically approved by government computers. Investigators found that more than three thousand applications had been certified "even though the wage rate on the application was lower than the prevailing wage for that occupation in the specific location."

Among computer programmers and high-tech workers from India, recruitment agencies are derisively referred to as "body shops."

The industry got its start in the 1990s after Congress, responding to the urging of U.S. employers, passed the Immigration Act of 1990, creating the H-1B visa program to give fast-growing high-tech companies access to foreign professionals. The influx of tech workers from overseas mushroomed as the computer industry saw spectacular growth. But American software engineers and programmers were incensed that they were being displaced by cheaper Indian workers. A 1993 *60 Minutes* episode on CBS television took up their cause.

"When any American company needs programmers, the body shops can often deliver employees all the way from Bombay for rates that are so cheap, Americans just across town can't compete," reported Lesley Stahl. "This is an employment agreement between one foreign programmer and an India-based body shop called Blue Star. It tells her she'll be assigned to Hewlett-Packard in California, that her salary of $250 a month will still be paid back in India, and that she'll receive $1,300 a month for living expenses in the United States."

Work and workers were going in opposite directions simultaneously. U.S. companies were saving money, not only by bringing Indian-trained technicians to America, but also by outsourcing—shipping work overseas to have it done by Indians in their own country. In doing so, they gave a boost to the staffing and recruitment operations of homegrown computer companies in India. Because of time zone differences and the need to better service and communicate with their American customers, Indian "consulting firms" expanded beyond the subcontinent and set up operations in the United States. They staffed them by using the H-1B program to import thousands of Indian high-tech workers.

The numbers grew exponentially. By 2007, Indian computer firms had not only established a major presence in the United States, they also were among the main users of the H-1B temporary visa program. Tata Consulting Services had about eight thousand H-1B workers. Infosys had at least seventy-one hundred H-1B workers, while Wipro Ltd. and Satyam Computer Services—all of them Indian-based firms—reported that H-1B workers made up the bulk of their U.S. staffs.

At the same time, recruitment firms sprang up to act essentially the same way the old-time sweaters operated, as middlemen. So-called body shops import high-tech workers to the United States through the H-1B program, then basically hire them out to domestic U.S. companies paying rates that, according to a number of studies, are below the wages paid to American-trained workers. Computer programmers critical of the H-1B program described the imported professionals as "techno-braceros," comparing them to migrant farm workers.

Eager for the work and the money, many Indian high-tech workers have put up with abuses, often unwilling to speak out for fear of jeopardizing an opportunity to work in the United States.

In Edison, New Jersey, I met Subbu (he asked me not to use his full name), an Indian national, in the United States on a work visa. He had just returned from taking his wife, an Indian-trained scientist, for her New Jersey driver's test. As we left their sparsely furnished apartment and drove down Oak Tree Road, one of America's most densely populated areas for Indian ex-pats, Subbu said the concentration of Indian-owned businesses and restaurants and the sari-clad women made him feel as if he were back in India.

Subbu moved to New Jersey from Bangalore in 2007. He had expected to work full-time, but after a year he lost his job as a systems analyst for JP Morgan Chase, even before the financial tailspin. When I met him, he was biding his time, hoping for another placement.

At any given time, as many as five hundred thousand people—there are no accurate figures—are working in the United States on nonimmigrant "specialty occupation" H-1B temporary work visas. Each year, the government issues eighty-five thousand such visas (sixty-five thousand for holders of bachelor's degrees or higher, and, since 2005, an additional twenty thousand for foreigners with masters' or Ph.D. degrees from an American university), good for a maximum of six years. During the go-go economic boom years of 2007 and 2008, so many companies were applying for foreign workers that the quota was reached soon after the April application period started, and federal immigration officials cut off petitions after the first week. But the recession of 2008–2009 seemed to dampen enthusiasm for importing workers. The number of applications dropped, and the application window reverted to preboom levels of months instead of a week.

Subbu had been sending money home to his mother in his hometown of Mysore near Bangalore, and had planned to return there himself with his wife and children. He wanted to care for his mother and see that his kids become fluent in Kannada, his native tongue and one of India's official languages. So, like many migrants, Subbu was not planning a permanent stay in the United States.

He paid a body shop a $3,500 fee and arrived in New Jersey from India in 2007. He expected to be hired out as a systems analyst earning about $70,000 a year. Once settled, he would send for his family. As a condition of employment, the recruiter had him sign a seven-page agreement pledging to work for the agency for eighteen months or face a lawsuit if he didn't. Subbu didn't know it, but that requirement is illegal according to an immigration attorney I asked to review the agreement. The recruiter was attempting to treat Subbu as a bonded laborer.

But as it turned out, the contract was the least of Subbu's difficulties. There was no job. The recruiter, who has offices in India and New Jersey, put him up in a four-bedroom house in New Jersey with eleven other recruits. (The recruiter was later cited for operating an illegal boardinghouse.) Subbu stayed there for five months, and in that time was paid $500. Unemployment is common in the recruitment industry, despite assurances to the contrary. H-1B workers describe the downtime as being "on the bench." Another Indian H-1B worker who was at the house at the same time confirmed Subbu's story, and said he had similar problems—no work for three months.

The recruiter eventually placed Subbu after transferring the visa to another body shop. As he put it, one recruiter "rented me out to another one, and then rented me out to JP Morgan Chase." He said the bank, his ultimate employer, was unaware of the convoluted arrangements. Each of the body shops took a cut from his pay, even though he wound up with a still respectable $100,000 for the year he worked there.

Subbu reckoned that he was owed about $6,000 by the recruiter who brought him to the United States, and he was bitter.

"I have been exploited to the maximum," he said. He was angry at fellow Indians, those who run recruitment agencies and tell their workers that if they complain, they'll be sent back to India. "They are trying to swindle us by not giving us proper salary and creating fear. People who are coming with this type of visa are not coming as illegal immigrants. They are coming in with a valid visa. They have valid degrees and a valid education, so they are afraid [that if they speak out] they will not only spoil their image, they will spoil their family's reputation also."

Subbu's experience is not isolated. I spoke to half a dozen H-1B employees with similar stories, who asked to remain anonymous. In 2000, the *Baltimore Sun*, after reviewing hundreds of court records and government documents, found numerous cases in which unscrupulous body shops billed U.S. companies at rates three to four times the salaries they actually paid the workers. They also interviewed H-1B workers who were not paid what they had been promised and were threatened with deportation if they challenged their employers.

In 2007, Patni Computer Systems, a global technology company headquartered in India, agreed to pay more than $2.4 million to 607 H-1B workers following a U.S. Department of Labor investigation that determined the workers had been underpaid. Patni supplied IT workers to such companies as State Farm Insurance, MetLife, and General Electric.

High-tech worker advocacy organizations such as the Programmers Guild and the Institute of Electrical and Electronics Engineers–USA have complained that many employers and recruiters abuse the H-1B visa program by phonying qualifications and applications of foreign workers and bringing them in under false pretenses. A number of high-profile cases have buttressed their contentions. In 2008, the Los Angeles attorney Daniel E. Korenberg was sentenced to two years in federal prison for his role in a visa fraud scheme that included bringing in paralegals for his law firm. Korenberg, another lawyer, and two employment agencies were convicted of falsifying job titles and salaries on visa applications, citing jobs that didn't exist, and lying about the foreigners' work experience.

In July 2008, authorities arrested Nilesh Dasondi, an elected zoning commissioner in Edison, New Jersey, owner of a recruiting firm called Cygate Software & Consulting. The feds accused him of bringing eight workers from India, claiming he was going to place them in high-tech jobs. But, prosecutors said, instead he put them to work doing nontechnical work such as running a greeting card store. Six of the eight admitted they paid Dasondi thousands of dollars in fees. Dasondi pleaded not guilty.

Even more damning than the criminal cases was a September 2008 audit conducted by the Department of Homeland Security suggesting that visa fraud was pervasive in the H-1B program. The Office of Fraud Detection and National Security, which is part of the U.S. Bureau of Citizenship and Immigration Services (USCIS), concluded that based on an assessment of 246 cases, one in five H-1B visas are either fraudulent (13.4 percent) or contain technical violations (7.3 percent). The auditors said it was reasonable to extrapolate those numbers for the entire H-1B program. They concluded that fraud and error rates were higher in smaller companies (those with fewer than twenty-five employees and with annual gross incomes of less than $10 million) than in larger businesses.

The economic downturn made the extensive use of H-1B visas by American firms particularly controversial. Major companies, notably Microsoft, Deloitte & Touche, IBM, Oracle USA., Inc., Cisco Systems, Intel, and Motorola, Inc., have imported thousands of H-1B workers themselves, without relying on outside consulting agencies. In 2008, as the economy was tanking, each of those companies was seeking approval to import more foreign workers—even as they were laying off employees or preparing for staff reductions.

JP Morgan Chase, where Subbu had worked, received permission from the U.S. Department of Labor to directly hire 684 foreign workers with H-1B visas. Job titles ranged from $200,000-a-year vice presidents to $50,000-a-year tax analysts. During the same period, the company cut hundreds of jobs, then acquired Washington Mutual, and slashed thousands more employees from the payroll.

The ironic juxtaposition of foreign worker recruitment and domestic employee layoffs was not lost on Obama administration officials, legislators, and even federal prosecutors.

- The February 2009 economic stimulus package signed by President Obama contained a provision called the Employ American Workers Act, designed to prevent companies receiving federal bailout money from displacing U.S. employees when hiring H-1B workers.
- In April 2009, senators Dick Durbin (D-IL) and Charles Grassley (R-IA) proposed legislation aimed at making it more difficult for U.S. companies to hire H-1B workers and easier for the government to investigate fraud allegations in the program.

- At about the same time, federal prosecutors in Iowa pressed a novel argument against a company charged with H-1B visa fraud. Expanding beyond the confines of the fraud allegations, assistant U.S. attorneys said the firm, Vision Group, Inc., had "substantially deprived U.S. citizens of employment." The prosecutors' argument contained a frontal assault on the H-1B program itself, declaring that "[I]n January of 2009, the total number of workers employed in the information technology occupation under the H-1B program substantially exceeded the 241,000 unemployed U.S. citizen workers within the same occupation." Company lawyers, astounded by the thrust of the case, pointed out that the "theory is supported with evidence that does not distinguish between violating the law and obeying it." The defense attorneys argued that the "courtroom is an improper venue for a policy debate about immigration."

The high-tech industry is not alone in a global competition for professionals and a worldwide market for recruiters and suppliers. Of all the migrant employees who have become essential to U.S. enterprises and critical to the well-being of their patrons, perhaps none are as vital as workers in the health care industry. Walk into just about any hospital, nursing home, or retirement facility, and the chances are good that among the staff—ranging from cleaners of bedpans to inserters of intravenous drips—migrants play key roles. That's particularly true in California, where nearly 30 percent of registered nurses were trained abroad. In Florida and New York, about 11 percent of RNs received their training overseas.

The United States is not alone in looking abroad for qualified medical personnel. Health care businesses in the United Kingdom, Australia, and Saudi Arabia also import nurses from Africa, the Philippines, India, and Canada.

The demand in the developed world for healthcare professionals, particularly since 2000, has spawned a dramatic growth in the number of international nurse recruiting businesses. A landmark 2007 study by AcademyHealth, an influential organization of health services researchers, policy analysts, and practitioners, found a largely unregulated industry that included 267 U.S.-based international nurse recruiting firms, a tenfold increase since the late 1990s.

The report found that the companies were recruiting in seventy-four countries. Most charged health care organizations fees of $15,000 to $25,000 per nurse and required nurses to make two- to three-year commitments. If nurses resigned before the end of their contracts, they were obliged to pay "buy out" fees of $10,000 to $50,000.

Most of the larger recruiters are staffing agencies, meaning they employ the nurses rather than placing them with health care organizations. The largest U.S.-based international recruitment firms are Cross Country Healthcare, AMN Healthcare, Maxim Healthcare, ATC Healthcare Services, On Assignment, and HCCA International. Cumulatively, in 2007 those firms had revenues of $2.8 billion.

AcademyHealth researchers also interviewed nurses and found numerous abuses—all of them in nursing homes rather than hospitals. Although their report did not identify employers or judge the extent of the problem, researchers found that many nurses had not been given contracts or had discovered that the ones they signed were later altered. Employers, they said, had withheld or delayed wages for foreign recruits, or were paying less than they had promised. They were requiring imported nurses to work excessive hours, threatening them with deportation if they refused. Some nurses were provided substandard housing and required to pay higher-than-expected "buy out" fees.

Filipino nurses with grievances against employers or recruiters are often reluctant to speak out—publicly or privately. But one case involving some two dozen health care workers became an international cause célèbre, an episode that eventually involved government officials in the United States and the Philippines, and included the filing of criminal charges.

In January 2006, the then thirty-one-year-old Noralyn Ortega arrived in the United States after a six-year-long odyssey that began when she enrolled in medical school close to where she lived in Parañaque City, a suburb of Manila. It ended after she received permission to immigrate to the United States, qualified as a nurse, took international nursing exams, and signed on with a recruitment agency that brought her to work in Nassau County, New York. Hoping her husband and children would eventually follow her, Ortega followed in the footsteps of family members who had migrated to Texas, California, and Canada, joining the far-flung diaspora of Filipino migrants who turn a medical education into a ticket out of their homeland.

Things did not turn out exactly as planned. Ortega had thought she was going to be employed by the Garden Care Center, a short-term rehabilitation facility. Instead, she wound up working for a New York agency at the Bayview Nursing and Rehabi-litation Center, a twenty-four-hour nursing home. The agency, the two health facilities, and the recruiting company were all part of affiliated businesses—the Sentosa Recruitment Agency in the Philippines, Sentosa Services (a New York employment agency), and SentosaCare LLC, which owns a chain of nursing facilities in the New York area.

But it wasn't just that her employer and place of work had been switched on her. In a way, those were the least of her problems.

"The benefits and promises told in Philippines, it was not mate-rialized when I'm in the United States," she said. Instead of paying me for thirty seven and a half hours, they just paid thirty-five hours, but I'm working more than forty hours and they don't pay me overtime. They said they gonna to give us medical insurance, I don't receive any of that. They said they would reimburse the expenses that I spent on exams, but they didn't.

"The work was overwhelming," she explained. "I was doing three jobs. I was doing medication, treatment, and I was a charge nurse for forty to sixty patients. The last night, before I quit, they gave me two units—a total of seventy-four patients. It's not possible to give very good care for the patients by myself alone."

Ortega was miserable. She was placed with other Sentosa nurses in a house that she said didn't have adequate heating. She thought about returning to the Philippines, so she went to the Philippine con-sulate and asked for assistance. Consular officials provided her with a lawyer, Felix Vinluan, who advised her that because her employ-ers had breached the contract, she could resign without a problem. So after just three months, she left, as did twenty-three other Filipino nurses in SentosaCare facilities. Soon afterward, she found one new nursing job in San Diego at a hospital where a cousin-in-law works, and she took a second position at a nearby medical center. Her hus-band and two children flew out from the Philippines to join her.

But the story didn't end there. Lawyers for the nurses and for SentosaCare battled in legal cases filed in New York State and the Philippines. In New York, authorities rejected a complaint by SentosaCare that the nurses had abandoned their patients. And in the Philippines, where the matter received press coverage and attention from politicians, authorities denied the nurses' petition to have Sentosa's license suspended but ordered that some of the nurses be paid damages.

More seriously, in March 2007, the Suffolk County district attorney indicted ten of the Sentosa nurses who left one of the SentosaCare homes, alleging that by quitting without sufficient notice, they endangered the welfare of patients. He also charged their lawyer, Felix Vinluan, with conspiracy for advising them to quit. Ortega was not charged.

Facing the possibility of year-long jail sentences, the nurses and Vinluan tried to stave off the prosecution. In January 2009, the Supreme Court of the State of New York cleared the nurses and their lawyer. The court said Vinluan's advice to his clients was protected under the First Amendment right of free speech. And the nurses, said the court, should not be prosecuted because the Thirteenth Amendment, prohibiting slavery and involuntary servitude, gave them the right to resign.

The ruling suggested that no patients were in danger because there was time to find replacements for the nurses who quit. "Under the facts as presented herein, the greatest risk created by the resignation of these nurses was to the financial health of Sentosa."

Although the court ruled in favor of the ten nurses in the criminal case, in late 2009, Ortega and the others were still defendants in a Nassau County, New York civil case brought by Sentosa. Nonetheless, Ortega was glad to have made a new life in San Diego, even though she eventually found that working six twelve-hour shifts a week was too much. She had no time for her two young children nor for her husband, Vincent, a former nurse in the Philippines, who was studying to pass examinations in order to work in nursing in California. So she quit one of the jobs.

"I can't say how I made it," she said, thinking back on her exhausting schedule. "It's less money, but it's okay. We survive."

Complaints about the treatment of professional migrant recruits have parallels to allegations of abuse in the H-2 programs for less-skilled foreign laborers. Human rights groups, unions, and prosecutors have documented case after case in which recruiters failed to provide promised wages or accommodations. There have also been numerous instances of temporary workers being charged excessive fees, sometimes totaling thousands of dollars.

"These workers . . . are not treated like 'guests,'" complained the Southern Poverty Law Center in a forty-seven-page report, *Close to Slavery: Guestworker Programs in the United States*, issued in 2007. "Rather, they are systematically exploited and abused. Unlike U.S. citizens, guestworkers do not enjoy the most fundamental protection of a competitive labor market—the ability to change jobs if they are mistreated. Instead, they are bound to the employers who 'import' them." The center said workers had been "routinely cheated out of wages, forced to mortgage their futures to obtain low-wage, temporary jobs, held virtually captive by employers or labor brokers who seize their documents, forced to live in squalid conditions, and denied medical benefits for on-the-job injuries."

In 2002, an employment agency with offices in Los Angeles and Thailand brought forty-eight Thai welders into California under the H-2B visa program promising jobs on the San Francisco–Oakland Bay Bridge. Instead, a labor contractor put most of them to work in his Los Angeles–area restaurants, held them against their will, confiscated their passports, restricted their movements, and paid them little or nothing.

In 2007, I met Mexican welders recruited to work at Signal International, an oil rig construction and repair company in a Mississippi shipyard. The workers were living in a compound adjacent to the shipyard inside wooden sheds, sleeping in bunk beds, six to a cabin without windows, plumbing, or insulation. Not far away, inside the shipyard, were about five hundred workers imported from India. Using borrowed money and life savings, the Indians had paid as much as $20,000 each to travel to America, lured by false promises made by Global Resources, Inc., a placement firm run by a Mississippi sheriff's deputy. They had been told that they would be able to live in the United States permanently. Instead, said the workers, they ended up living in crowded labor camps and were given food they claimed made them sick. In March 2008, about a hundred walked off the job and filed a class action lawsuit. A dozen went to Washington, D.C., and staged a four-week hunger strike. Signal International blamed the problems on the recruiter, who denied the allegations.

Back in Monterrey, Mexico, Rene Urbano told me that the migrants he recruited generally invested about $600 each. Of that, nearly half went to fees charged by the consulate, and the rest were for his services as well as food and transportation costs. Urbano was just one link in a worker supply chain stretching from the interior of Mexico to the fields of the southeastern United States. By 2009, as a labor supplier for businesses, Urbano had developed a new advertising catchphrase: "Your worker is my client."

Urbano's firm was one of ten companies that provided hundreds of farm workers to a Virginia company named másLabor (*más* is Spanish for "more"). The firm supplied workers to eastern and southern U.S. firms under both the H-2A and H-2B programs. Company co-owner Dave Fulton explained the partnership with Urbano. "We're the employer agent," he said. "He's the worker agent and we meet in the middle."

Employers pay másLabor a flat fee of $3,000 to $5,000 per worker. For that, they get delivery of a ready-to-work Mexican or Central American laborer with all the necessary and completed legal paperwork.

As Fulton sees it, everybody wins. The employer gets a worker, and the migrant gets to provide for his family, earning $9 to $10 an hour.

"There are unlimited numbers of millions in Mexico who would love to be making five dollars an hour, much less ten dollars an hour," he said. "These are the same people dying in the desert to take minimum-wage jobs. If we give them an air-conditioned ride to the United States, isn't it for the benefit of both the worker and the employer?" he asked.

He discounted the complaints of migrant rights advocates. "People whose jobs depend on there being an oppressed brown-skinned minority, their whole worldview depends on there being oppressors," he said. "Some folks always look at employers as the oppressors, but . . . the worker is not just a victim. These people are serious, smart heads of households and shouldn't be viewed as victims. I believe there's going to be a huge number of Spanish-speaking Mexicans in heaven."

Of course, the conviction that there are eternal rewards in store for migrants misses the point. The mere fact that workers can improve their lot by saying *adios* to their families, crossing a border, and taking jobs with salaries that beat those back home is no excuse for what, by U.S. standards, are low wages and subpar working conditions.

Toughened border controls and stepped-up immigration enforcement have led many U.S. employers and farm workers alike to conclude that using the official temporary worker program is more reliable and safer than the alternative of crossing the border and working illegally.

"The price is worth it," explained farm worker Daniel Ramírez as he stood outside the Monterrey consulate waiting to be called in and processed. "A *coyote* costs a lot, and you risk a lot when you go with them."

Mike Nobles, president of a Tennessee-based recruiting and contracting firm, H2AUSA.COM, expressed the same sentiment. I ran into Nobles at a convention of citrus growers in central California, where he was manning a booth and handing out leaflets describing his services: "If you can't get enough American workers to complete your project, we can get you as many non-American workers as you need."

In previous years, California farm workers had shown little interest in the official temporary worker program, since there was a ready supply of illegal immigrants available to do the jobs. But, he said, interest by farmers was picking up.

"I believe any farmer that wants workers, legal workers, can get them right now through the H-2A program. So I believe it is salvation," he said, sounding like a recruitment evangelist. To hear Nobles tell it, he also was something of a patriot, greasing the economic wheels and filling gaps left by unwilling Americans.

"My son doesn't want to pick oranges. Do your children want to pick oranges?" Nobles asked. "Every American I know wants their children to go to college, get a degree, and become a professional. I don't know too many parents that say, 'Oh, I want my child to be an orange picker.' I don't know any eighteen- and nineteen-year olds that are going to college, that want to go pick oranges, or build pallets, or carry mud, or dig ditches. We no longer have a labor class."

That's a common, but flawed argument. The contention that importing migrants is a salvation for a nation lacking "a labor class" is self-fulfilling. If certain jobs pay more than others, people in need of work will gravitate to them. The desirability of the actual tasks becomes a secondary consideration. As the labor activist and author Beth Shulman has written, "There is nothing inherent in welding bumpers onto cars or manufacturing steel girders that makes those better jobs than caring for children or guarding office buildings. Workers organizing through unions, and the passage of social legislation, raised wages and created paid leave and health and retirement benefits in these initially 'bad' manufacturing jobs, changing them into good middle-class positions."

"Fortunately," she wrote, "we can make choices as a society to make today's 'bad' jobs 'good' ones." And that might include the work performed in the groves by some of the people Nobles recruits from Mexico.

Nobles, too, fit the classic definition of an old-fashioned sweater. He recruited Mexican farm workers, paid them $8.56 cents an hour, then supplied the workers to U.S. companies, which paid him $14.50 for each hour the migrants worked. The difference—41 percent of the hourly rate—was his.

Determined to right wrongs, the Obama administration pledged to cut down on abuses and fraud in temporary worker programs and proposed to hire more investigators. But the extra degree of oversight was relatively modest, posing little threat to companies that import workers to save money and are intent on skirting the rules, particularly in a weak economy.

The allegations of corruption in licensed, government-authorized temporary worker programs invite a logical and inevitable comparison. In the global recruitment and people-running business, legitimate and authorized procurers of foreign labor are not too distantly related to the more outlaw strain of body shops, namely human smugglers.

If you make a living by providing overseas workers with visas, jobs, and transportation, you are considered a bona fide staffing or recruitment agent. But "bringing in illegal aliens for financial gain" makes you a felon, in violation of Title 8, U.S. Code, Section 1324(a)(2)(B)(ii), subject to fifteen years in federal prison and a $250,000 fine. Clearly, violating the law is not the same as following it, but the occupations are certainly kissing cousins.

CHAPTER 6

Smugglers as Migration Service Providers

For more than twenty years on reporting trips to the U.S./Mexico border I've seen the barrier between the two countries become increasingly formidable, with more and more resources devoted to troops, guards, fences, and high-tech detection equipment. As a reporter, I have driven many times along the U.S./Mexico border between Tijuana and San Diego, generally escorted by a U.S. Border Patrol agent eager to make the case for ever more federal funding devoted to stopping people from crossing what many border residents refer to simply as *la línea* (the line).

But not long ago, a visit to Tijuana offered a different perspective—a smuggler's-eye view from *el otro lado* (the other side). My guide was "Amelia" (she asked me not to use her real name), a forty-four-year-old woman who had spent most of the past two decades as a professional smuggler, much of that time as the chief executive of a Tijuana-based smuggling network.

To Amelia, the border represented an opportunity rather than a barrier. The Mexican entrepreneur considered her niche business a specialty travel agency catering to clientele with very narrow objectives— to cross the border safely and undetected.

My conversation with Amelia provided a rare peek into the organization of smuggling networks—businesses with sales and marketing branches, transportation departments, delivery operations, and collections systems, a system comprising a multibillion-dollar-a-year global industry.

The fortunes of the smuggling business are tied to the actions of governments. The basic economics are simple, as a Federal Reserve Bank of Dallas report drily explained: "Migrants are more likely to hire *coyotes* [smugglers] when they perceive a higher chance of apprehension were they to attempt a crossing on their own. If coyotes are more in demand or if risks increase, as is the case when criminal penalties on smuggling are increased, then we expect coyote use and prices to rise."

In other words, as border controls tighten, people smugglers raise their fees (even if they may not always deliver what they promise). On the U.S.–Mexico border, coyote prices doubled and tripled between 1995 and 2007. As the border became more militarized, border crossers came to rely more on smugglers. To try to reduce their risks, by 2007 some 90 percent of illegal migrants were resorting to the use of coyotes, compared to 69 percent before 1995.

The pan-European police agency Europol refers to human smugglers as "illegal immigration facilitators." Operators of Chinese people-smuggling networks are known as "snakeheads," after a predatory fish. In Ecuador, they're called *tramitadores* (facilitators). In Morocco, Khalid Zerouali, the head of Morocco's Department of Migration and Border Control, told me how he had been cracking down on human smuggling rings he called "mafias." In Mexico, the people smuggling business is known generally as *coyotaje*, based on the term most often used to describe the occupation of the person who guides migrants across the border, a coyote.

("Coyote" is an old term. Besides referring to the small wolf *Canis latrans* common to North America, it originally meant an "illegitimate intermediary for cutting red tape.")

Amelia prefers to be called a *coyota*, a feminized version of the word. As we raced through the Tijuana area in her beat-up Honda, I received a tour not found in the guidebooks. Amelia pointed out a smuggler walking with his *pollo* along the concrete banks of the Tijuana River, which runs adjacent to the border. (The coyotes' clients are often known as *pollos*—Spanish for chickens.)

When we passed a downtown church, Amelia described it as a prime location for guides to troll for would-be customers. On the way out to the beach area, Amelia took note of a parked police car, a base of operations, she said, for cops who are notorious for stopping coyotes and shaking them down, extracting a fee of $150 per pollo. Closer to the Pacific Ocean, where the U.S. fence runs out into the water, we looked down at the aptly named Smugglers Gulch, a steep ravine that, until recently, when American earth-moving equipment performed a massive makeover, was a longtime favorite crossing place for migrants and a major headache for U.S. agents on the other side of the border.

Amelia said that stricter border enforcement—combined with the weak U.S. economy—had affected her industry.

"Business has been bad for two years," Amelia told me. She was getting fewer calls from pollos. But, as the Federal Reserve Bank of Dallas accurately predicted, she was able to charge more for those who did use her services. Her going rate at the time of our meeting in the summer of 2008 was $1,400 per customer, nearly five times as much as when she started twenty years earlier.

As U.S. border enforcement tightened in the urban areas, routes for border crossers and smugglers gradually shifted to more treacherous terrain, such as the Sonoran desert, which spans southern Arizona and northern Mexico. American officials had hoped they could slow or stop migration by forcing migrants to trek through the wilderness.

Though many were deterred, others calculated that the eventual rewards would outweigh the risks. Their decisions and fates often highlighted the desperation of their gambits. The *Arizona Daily Star* compiled a gruesome tally of deaths of migrants who perished crossing through the Arizona stretch of the U.S.–Mexico border. On average, between 2004 and 2008, records from county medical examiners amounted to 219 deaths a year.

Horror stories about dangerous crossings abound and are spread by word of mouth among would-be migrants. Since they are often easy prey for bandits and rapists, getting picked up by the U.S. Border Patrol can come as a relief to migrants making the often treacherous journey. One gruesome rumor circulated among migrants in Lindsay, California. They had heard about a woman who died coming through the desert. As she lay on the ground, the baby she had been carrying continued to suckle at the dead mother's breast. Both supposedly had been abandoned by the guide and the other migrants.

As the United States stepped up border enforcement, Amelia tried to adapt her operations. Talking shop as she sat in the comfortable living room of her house in a noisy Tijuana neighborhood, she explained that televised news reports of border crossers' deaths had put a serious dent in the people-smuggling trade.

By all appearances, Amelia seemed a typical middle-class Mexican housewife, slightly overweight, her dark hair pulled back to reveal an attractive face with a ready smile. As we spoke, her infant daughter played on the floor, and her nineteen-year-old son walked back and forth to the refrigerator. Above the television console, set off by salmon-colored walls, was a display of sports trophies he had won in high school. Amelia said her son's birth had provided the impetus for her and her late husband to launch their coyote enterprise.

She had trained as a legal secretary in her native Nayarit, a Mexican state in the country's central-western area, and moved to Tijuana in 1985 with her husband, "José," a horticulturalist. She got a job in a mall, and he worked as a buyer for a store. Four years later, José got a taste for human smuggling when he helped Amelia's sister cross the border. With an extra mouth to feed and their budget stretched, the couple had found a way to make some extra money.

Mexico was mired in an economic depression, so the services of smugglers were in demand, and not just from working-class Mexicans. The economic crisis had slashed wages of the middle class, and teachers along with professors, engineers, bankers, and other professionals were seeking to find better-paying though often menial jobs across the border. One Mexican engineer referred to himself and other migrating professionals as "braceros técnicos," a reference to the temporary farm worker program begun during World War II.

As her husband's business and ambitions grew, Amelia and José worked out a division of labor. José acted as a guide, escorting migrants across the border, and Amelia became a sort of den mother, putting up customers in Tijuana, providing them with food, letting them use the bathroom.

"I would feed them and take care of them. He would cross them," she explained.

José generated a customer base by arranging partnerships with taxi drivers outside the Tijuana airport. When passengers arrived looking for coyotes to take them into the United States, cabdrivers referred them to José, who returned the favor with referral fees of $50 a head. In turn, José charged his customers $300 each, then the going rate for smugglers' fees.

As the couple's reputation spread and as the demand increased, their business improved. The mom-and-pop enterprise expanded, and they brought in nephews and brothers to help out. By 1993, Amelia and José employed twelve people. As illegal border crossing became more difficult, they raised their fees. In four years, they more than doubled their prices, to about $700 per person.

Although she was busy raising their three children, Amelia wanted to play a larger role in the business, but José wouldn't let her. She got her wish in 1997. Living on the edge of the law, José had been having an affair with a woman whose boyfriend was a drug smuggler. The man shot and killed José.

The murder left Amelia in a quandary. Should she abandon the business or continue it? At José's funeral, associates of her husband promised to help her carry on. Two corrupt Mexican officials offered her protection. Amelia felt she had no choice.

"I had three children. I had to take care of them," she explained.

The business grew. Amelia rented a separate apartment in Tijuana as a way station for migrants passing through. She installed a refrigerator and a television. Repeat customers found out about her by calling José's old phone number, and new clients came to her by word of mouth. The company relied on a loose network of associates spread throughout Mexico. As a coyota, Amelia's job was to set the prices and coordinate the activities of the other members of the organization. It is a common business model used by human smugglers, an enterprise described by the San Diego–based researchers Jezmín Fuentes and Olivia García as "an extensive hierarchy of workers who collaborate to provide smuggling services." Their investigation revealed a sophisticated business model. "Through an elaborate division of labor," they reported, "the coyotaje network has developed into a quasi corporation."

Human smugglers along the U.S./Mexico border first got into the business in the early 1900s. But the coyotes' customers were not Mexicans. They were Chinese, crossing over in violation of an 1882 federal law, the Chinese Exclusion Act. It was the first law in American history to bar immigrants solely on the basis of race and class.

In the 1890s, Chinese migrants entered the United States from Canada, using networks that had smuggled opium and other contraband substances. Smuggling fees ranged from $23 to $60 a person (about $600 to $1,500 in 2009 currency), but by the following decade, the price had multiplied tenfold. By 1906, effective crackdowns along the Canadian border forced human smugglers to shift their business to the south. Since Mexico had continued to import Chinese laborers, considering them useful to the country's development, many U.S.-bound migrants were able to use Mexico as a back door. Chinese laborers paid smuggling organizations in China $500 each (the rough equivalent of $12,000 in today's money) to bring them to ports along the Pacific coast of Mexico.

U.S. newspapers carried story after story about Chinese sneaking across the border aided by "wily" smugglers. Mexican and American coyotes stashed their contraband cargo in with shipments of furniture, truckloads of hay, smuggled diamonds, and opium. Some were hidden in the iceboxes and closets of railroad dining cars. The following decade, with the advent of Prohibition, rum runners forced them to "pack bootleggers' hootch along with them."

"For some time, immigration officers have known that extensive smuggling of Chinese was going on," reported the *Los Angeles Times* in 1907. "It has been found impossible to control the entire length of the Mexican border, and hundreds of Chinese and Japanese coolies are making their way into this country in spite of stringent regulations."

Between 1907 and 1909, U.S. officials arrested 2,492 Chinese for crossing into the country illegally from Mexico. In 1909, Chicago authorities broke up a ring that they believed had smuggled more than a thousand Chinese migrants in Pullman railroad cars across the border at El Paso, Texas. The multinational outlaws—Americans,

Chinese, and Mexicans—paid cooks on the trains $50 a head to deliver the stowaways.

Smugglers provided Chinese immigrants on their way to the United States via Mexico with American money and railroad maps, Chinese-American newspapers, and dictionaries. "Two schools in Juarez [Mexico] did nothing but coach Chinese in answering questions inquisitive government agents might ask," reported a newspaper wire service.

One enterprising immigration business ran an underground railroad using stagecoaches, boxcars, and burros to transport and escort Chinese across the border. Working with Chinese recruiters in Mexico, the smugglers disguised the migrants as Mexicans and taught them a few Spanish phrases. In an office in the back of the Palace saloon in Cananea, across the Mexican border south of Bisbee, Arizona, one member of the ring, C. A. Springstein, used rubber stamps, a sealmaker, and a metal plate for printing to produce hundreds of bogus U.S. residency certificates, which he sold to his customers for $100 apiece (about $2,400 in 2008 currency).

Because Mexican migration was virtually unrestricted, Chinese migrants remained smuggling networks' chief customers. But their business model changed when Congress enacted the Immigration Act of 1917. For the first time in American history, the United States applied immigration restrictions to Mexicans, and in the process created a new and lucrative revenue source for the smuggling industry.

With the advent of World War I, the Bureau of Immigration diverted its attention from Chinese migrants not only to Mexicans, but also to suspected enemy aliens, anarchists, and draft dodgers.

The responsibility for enforcing immigration laws along most of the southwest border fell to Frank W. Berkshire, the Bureau of Immigration's supervising inspector in the newly created Mexican Border District. Berkshire had been transferred to the region in 1907 after impressing superiors at the bureau with his competence in overseeing enforcement of Chinese exclusion laws, first in Chicago, later along the New York–Canadian border and in New York City. At the U.S.-Mexico boundary, he became alarmed by the ease with which smuggling operations were able to circumvent the new restrictions. "The drastic provisions of the present immigration act have led to the creation of a new and thriving industry, if by such a term it may be dignified, having for its object the illegal introduction into the United States of Mexican aliens on a wholesale scale by means of organized efforts," Berkshire wrote in a report to Congress. "Steerers and smugglers of the several organizations reside on either side of the international line and include in their ranks Mexican line riders, fiscal guards, professional smugglers, formerly engaged in the Chinese and opium traffic, and amateur smugglers, attracted by the prospect of 'easy money.'"

The new immigration law required migrants to pass a literacy test and pay an $8-a-head entry fee. Those provisions helped establish the smugglers' own fees: they charged migrants attempting to avoid the head tax about half of what they would have paid legally. They demanded that border crossers who would have flunked the literacy test fork over all the cash they carried.

Berkshire complained that his division was understaffed. In requesting additional resources, he became an early advocate of a militarized southwest border. Despite "the vigilance of the officers," he wrote, "the menace persists." Berkshire recommended "the organization of a closely knit border patrol to work in conjunction with the existing immigration officers, with a view to effectively close up the gaps in the line of defense." Seven years later his wish was granted with the creation of the U.S. Border Patrol.

But in the meantime, if government officials worried about breaches in border security, representatives of farmers, railroads, and mines, who needed an easy supply of laborers, worked quickly to widen those "gaps in the line of defense." Major employers, represented by, among others, a young Herbert Hoover, then head of the U.S. Food Administration, worked diligently behind the scenes to convince the Woodrow Wilson administration of a severe labor shortage that could be relieved by lifting restrictions on Mexican labor. Secretary of Labor William B. Wilson (no relation to the president who appointed him), a Scottish immigrant, former miner, and one of the founders of the United Mine Workers Union, heeded the call. Resisting pressure from labor unions, he not only temporarily waived the immigration requirements on Mexicans, he also ordered that more immigration officers be assigned to the border to "facilitate the entry of Mexicans," he extended the suspension of immigration regulations, and he set in motion America's first *bracero*, or temporary worker, program that allowed employers to bring in low-paid Mexican workers for more than two years after the war ended.

Subsequent legislation in the 1920s, which tightened restrictions on European migrants, only added to the demand for Mexican laborers and for the smugglers who supplied them. In 1924, Congress not only established the Border Patrol, it added a $10 visa fee to the $8 head tax. Once again, tightened enforcement gave the smuggling business a shot in the arm.

"The origin of illegal immigration is to be found in the farmers and ranchers, and railroad, mining, and other enterprises to which Mexican labor is indispensable," wrote the educator and anthropologist Manuel Gamio in 1930. Some coyotes worked with "big commercial, industrial, or agricultural enterprises in the border states and even in the interior of the United States, which have need of Mexican labor," Gamio reported.

The smugglers' payments varied according to the need. During times when labor was plentiful, the companies kept coyotes on retainer. When labor was scarce, firms paid smugglers by the worker to provide them with an incentive. Smugglers charged their human cargo fees of $5 to $10, more if they had baggage, driving them across the border or taking them across the Rio Grande by boat. The coyotes could be resourceful and sometimes "rented" passports or head-tax receipts to get their charges into the United States.

They were techniques that nearly a century later, Amelia would have found familiar. "I used *mica* cards [the Spanish slang for laminated immigration cards]," she explained. "I bought them from my sister in Los Angeles for eighty dollars each."

Amelia believed the cards were authentic, although most likely they were forgeries, easily obtainable on the streets. The cards came with photographs of people already on them. So Amelia set about doing the opposite of what most counterfeiters do. Instead of forging documents to match their owners, she worked with makeup and hair clippers to alter the appearance of her customers. "I made up the migrants to look like the picture on the visas," she bragged.

Although investigators have broken up a number of well-organized, top-down smuggling rings, the enterprises are, for the most part, decentralized, fragmented, and like Amelia's operation, family-run. They operate in much the same way as a general contractor who builds or remodels houses does business with individual specialists and small businesses.

A two-year investigation into one organization headed by a husband-and-wife team based in the tiny Arizona town of Bowie, near Tucson, resulted in the 2006 indictment of fifty-five people. Authorities said that over a ten-year period the ring had smuggled in hundreds of migrants from Mexico, El Salvador, and the Dominican Republic. But overall, if the results of law enforcement investigations are any indication, most smuggling rings have fewer than a dozen members.

As a federal investigator, Armando Garcia spent nearly twenty years tracking down human smugglers, even going so far as to transport migrants across the southern border and run drop houses for rings he infiltrated. But asked about the component parts of smuggling groups, Garcia, the assistant special agent in charge of the Phoenix office of the Bureau of Immigration and Customs Enforcement (ICE), described a shifting mosaic of independent business operators.

"The different cells are just opportunistic," he explained. "Whoever has the money to pay them to transport is who they deal with. We often have difficulty in identifying organizations, because everybody has contact with everybody. You check their phone records. They talked to this transportation cell, this cell that houses them in Phoenix, and they're just using them at the time because they're either cheaper or available."

Researchers have found that the majority of migrants coming over the Mexican border use hired smugglers, but Matthew Allen, a veteran human smuggling investigator, who in 2008 became the head of the ICE office in Phoenix, told me he has no idea of how many groups there are. "If you're looking for a number of smuggling organizations, that's a very big unknown," he said.

Getting a handle on the size and scope of the smuggling trade is virtually impossible. In 2006, authorities estimated that migrant smuggling across Arizona's U.S.–Mexico border was a $1.7 billion-a-year business. The same year, the writer Alex Kotlowitz reported that smugglers sneaking Chinese into the United States, often through Mexico, were charging their customers "upward of $70,000" per person.

What is clear is that the industry generates hundreds of millions of dollars a year. Social scientist David Spener tried to break it down. He estimated that migrants took 660,000 coyote-assisted trips across the southwestern border each year between 1965 and 1986. Multiplied by the going rate for smuggler services, he calculated that the industry took in $381.5 million to $478.5 million annually, expressed in 2004 dollars.

The corporate structure of the coyotaje industry is both fractured and hierarchical, according to researchers Fuentes and García. At the top of the chain are the *patrones*, the chief executives such as Amelia. They oversee divisions and departments with specialists in transportation and logistics, bribery, surveillance, marketing, banking procedures, and real estate. Travel packages usually involve the trip to and across the border, a stop at a safe house, then transportation to the ultimate destination.

At the bottom of the pyramid is the *baquetón* (a term for someone who is basically idle), a freelance marketing agent who hooks up would-be migrants with smuggling organizations for a finder's fee.

The patrone often organizes charter buses, which hold as many as sixty passengers, to pick up clients from the interior of Mexico and transport them to the border, where they stay in hotels connected to the smuggling organization. There, the migrants are handed over to *guías* (guides), who physically escort the travelers across the border. The guides often work with *chequeadores* (spotters who monitor inspection points), sometimes using infrared night vision scopes and cell phones, the same technology used by the U.S. Border Patrol.

Once over the border, other company divisions take over. The *levantón* picks up the migrants and drives them to a drop house. Members of the smuggling groups often pack migrants into rented homes and make arrangements for clients to pay off their smuggling fees by having family members wire payments or make deposits in the coyotes' bank accounts. Once the money has been received, it's time for the final leg in the smuggling itinerary. Escorts take migrants from drop houses to bus stations or airports to travel to their final destinations.

For smuggling businesses, overhead costs add up. Homes have to be rented, bus and plane tickets paid for, subcontractors compensated.

Amelia paid baquetónes about $200 for each migrant delivered to the border, another $300 for each person the guías successfully transported across, and $200 to the levantónes for each client picked up.

The tanking economy and the bursting housing bubble provided a financial break for smuggling companies. In late 2008, Phoenix, Arizona, investigators discovered that smugglers looking for drop houses were able to make inexpensive rental deals with homeowners eager to stave off foreclosures.

Not all the costs of running a smuggling business are financial. Being associated with a black market enterprise and an outlaw culture is a risky undertaking. The cops who promised to assist Amelia after her husband was killed later turned against her and demanded a piece of the action. Smuggling is illegal in Mexico, and officials who allow it want to be paid for looking the other way.

"We are any easy target for corrupt officials, more than drug dealers," she said. "They don't ask fees from drug smugglers. If they did, they'd be killed. With us, it's like taking lollipops from a baby."

As we talked, a handsome man in a goatee and wearing shorts walked from the back of the house into the living room. He was Amelia's second husband, "Marco," the thirty-nine-year-old father of her toddler. Marco used to work for Amelia as a guía. He had firsthand experience with corrupt officials who would extort him, and he was justifiably afraid of them.

More than once, he said, Mexican cops apprehended a group of migrants as he started to escort them across the border. The goal of the police, Marco explained, was to rob the guide. But unsure of who among the group was in charge, they beat people up until they figured out that he was the escort. They put him in a patrol car and called Amelia, his boss. Amelia drove to where they were being held and paid the police $1,000 a head.

Then, said Marco, the police would release everyone, point them toward a safe area to cross the border, and wish them luck, saying, "Go through here. Be careful."

The full extent of bribery and corruption at checkpoints and international frontiers is unknown, but reports from humanitarian and human rights agencies indicate it is common. Around the world, border guards ask for "expediting fees." Cash payments often are folded into passports. Criminal networks have put migration control officials on their payrolls. In the United Kingdom, according to a parliamentary report, between 2000 and 2005 more than 700 allegations of corruption in the immigration system led to 409 investigations.

Along Europe's eastern borders, where security has been beefed up, Slovakia and Poland have raised the pay of frontier police to make them less vulnerable to bribery. Slovakian guards have been provided with mountain-crossing motorbikes and motorized skis. But Interpol and other international police agencies suggest that the syndicates that smuggle migrants also might traffic in drugs, giving them deep pockets to reach beyond low-level border patrol agents to middle management and above. Their efforts seem to be paying off. Migrants at the Beregsurány refugee camp in northern Hungary told reporters that for each one caught crossing the border, five to ten get through.

On both sides of the U.S.–Mexico border, drug and migrant traffickers have paid off law enforcement officials, from small-town cops all the way up to the head of an FBI division. Border corruption is a growth enterprise. Between 2004 and 2006, American prosecutors charged at least two hundred public employees with helping to move narcotics or illegal immigrants across the U.S.–Mexico border, a rate double that of previous years. By the summer of 2008, officials had at least two hundred open investigations into law enforcement employees working along the border.

Senior U.S. Border Patrol agents Mario Alvarez and Samuel McClaren helped launch a California program that jailed dozens of human smugglers. But when they showed up at headquarters, believing they were to receive an award, they themselves were arrested, and charged with releasing illegal immigrants from federal custody in exchange for cash. A fellow agent uncovered their scheme when he found their telephone numbers on a list in possession of a captured smuggler.

The take can be rewarding. Prosecutors believe Alvarez and McClaren received $300,000 from smuggling networks. Another corrupt official, Richard Elizalda, a nine-year veteran of the Border Patrol, would wave through cars carrying migrants at his inspection lane at the San Ysidro port of entry near San Diego, earning as much as

$1,000 per illegal immigrant, according to authorities. He would text-message human smugglers to let them know which inspection lane they should come through. At the time of his arrest, agents found $36,760 in currency at Elizalda's house, valuable jewelry, and expensive cars—a 2005 BMW and a 2000 Lexus.

With the stakes so high, human smuggling has become literally a cutthroat business. Not long ago I accompanied Benny Piña, then a lieutenant with the Phoenix, Arizona, Police Department, when he rolled out to a crime scene on the outskirts of town. By the time he arrived, other members of the homicide squad had cordoned off the area, set up an air-conditioned command post as shelter from the 103-degree desert sun, and were ready to brief the boss.

The burly Phoenix cop, who was later promoted to the rank of commander, finished the remains of lunch, a Big Mac, and walked the fifty feet to the police trailer, where eight homicide investigators and two civilians—members of the crime scene detail—crowded around to summarize what the police knew.

"The victim is an Hispanic male. Appears to be twenty-five to thirty-five years old. Maybe five-nine. A hundred and sixty to a hundred and eighty. Looks like he's been there a few days," said a sergeant, reading from notes.

A transient looking for metal along the dry riverbed had discovered the bloated corpse. The dead man was lying on his back, his arms pinned underneath him, his wrists bound together by handcuffs.

A detective suggested that a helicopter be called in to survey the scene from the air and take pictures. Two plainclothes officers from Immigration and Customs Enforcement, wearing the uniform favored by many federal agents—blue jeans and casual, untucked shirts—stood in the circle taking notes on white tablets. Because a third of all murders committed in Phoenix involve migrants as either victims or perpetrators, the Phoenix Police Department had ten ICE agents embedded with them, working violent crimes.

The basic facts noted, the group left the cool comfort of the trailer and hiked a hundred yards or so over hot rocks to where the body lay at the bottom of a short, sandy rise. The dead man wore a white shirt, his chest area soaked with blood. Two investigators stepped over the yellow tape marking the crime scene and carefully walked around the body looking for footprints, noting a nearby shell casing and blood splattered on nearby shrubs.

Piña deduced what had likely happened. There was no evidence of a struggle. Nothing to indicate that the body had been dragged. The man's wallet was untouched. Credit cards and cash remained inside it. So rule out robbery as a motive. ICE files showed the victim was a Mexican citizen who had been a onetime driver for a human smuggling ring. The victim had been walked out to the spot and shot. This was an execution. Another one.

"Probably feuding smugglers," Piña told me before heading off to another homicide scene. "Who knows if he's dabbling in drug operations as well? Clearly someone wanted him dead for retaliatory purposes because he wasn't robbed."

The old Wild West lives on. Northwest of Phoenix, in the one-time gold mining town of Wickenburg, an old mesquite tree just behind the Circle K downtown is supposed to have once served as a city lockup. According to legend, nineteenth-century outlaws would be chained to the tree before being carted off to the big city jail in Phoenix. In the new Wild West, the intersection where the tree stands has become a well-traveled route by today's lawmen and lawwomen, patrolling roads commonly used by smugglers moving their human cargoes from stash houses in Phoenix to Las Vegas or Los Angeles.

Sheriffs' deputies and federal agents are on the lookout for vans or cars filled with people; the cops call them "loads." But in recent years, law enforcement has been competing with other hunters of vehicles that fit the profile—a new breed of highway robbers known as *bajadores*. Bandits from rival smuggling organizations are kidnapping migrants and extorting money from their relatives.

In one eighteen-week period in early 2007, police and federal agents came across seventy cases in which smugglers tried to rip off competitors.

"We're seeing that the smugglers in the desert will try to hijack a load. They shoot first, they'll shoot the driver," explained ICE official Alonzo Peña.

"We've had them involved in attempting to do carjackings at gunpoint," he said. "We've had them forcing them off the road, causing accidents. We've had them involved in home invasions. And these drop houses, we've had everything from where they pull people's fingernails out to make them—to force them to make phone calls to their families to send money, to putting guns to people's heads and in their mouths, to pistol-whipping them, to forcing some of the women that are being held to have sex with the smugglers."

Peña described a case in which migrants had been held for a month.

"When the officers arrived to make entry, the people were in the kitchen getting food. The officers were telling them to drop everything and put their hands up. People wouldn't let go of the food because they hadn't been fed. One person said he had been in the house for over thirty days and all he was given while he was there was bean broth and a tortilla a day."

Similar heartrending stories about smugglers and their human freight are repeated throughout the world. Many of the trips end in tragedy. Smugglers stuff their wares into dangerous boats, trucks, and vans, often abandoning them at any sign of trouble. Migrants smuggled across the U.S. border with Mexico and from France to England through the Channel Tunnel have suffocated in the backs of trucks. Hundreds of migrants have drowned in ramshackle boats attempting to cross the Strait of Gibraltar, trying to make it from the coast of West Africa to the Spanish-owned Canary Islands, or to the tiny Italian island of Lampedusa, midway between Sicily and North Africa. Smuggling routes vary according to where obstacles are placed. When Moroccan officials aggressively moved to prevent sub-Saharan migrants from coming through their country, smugglers used alternative pathways farther south, in Mauritania or Senegal. As enforcement tightened around the Canary Islands and off the coast of Italy, increasing numbers of migrants, with the help of smugglers, have tried to make it to Europe through Greek Islands in the Aegean Sea or Evros in northwestern Greece.

The stories of persistent migration in the face of tragedy highlight the desperation many migrants feel. Nigerians who made it to Spain told me they and their families had sold everything so they could make the trip. They had put their lives in the hands of smugglers who along the journey handed them off from one gang to another.

In Madrid, the Spanish capital, many were living on the streets or in shelters, relying on charity. One man, Emmanuel, said it had taken him almost five years to make the two-thousand-mile exodus from Nigeria through the Sahara and across the Strait of Gibraltar. He seemed pained to remember what he had witnessed coming through the desert.

"I hear many story and I see many bones," he said. "Human bones that die. Their skeletons, there on the ground. Many, many people died. I cried."

Some of the Africans were walking investments. They had been given money by relatives who had raised it by selling off family plots of land. The understanding was that once the migrants had made it to Europe and found jobs, they would send back cash payments. The cash they had been given went for smuggling fees. The going rate in 2007 for a dangerous, twenty-four-hour-long trip on a fishing boat across the Strait of Gibraltar was about $1,500 per person.

For centuries, the narrow band of water has been an intersection of culture and warfare. It now marks a front line in Europe's struggle against illegal immigration. At Europe's southwestern tip, near an ancient fortress once used to ward off invaders, Spanish border police now use high-tech surveillance systems to look toward Africa and specifically to Morocco, on the continent's northwestern corner.

From the industrial Moroccan port city of Tangiers, regular ferries shuttle back and forth. It takes about an hour for the nine-mile crossing, a popular day trip for tourists who can leave Europe in the morning, spend the day in Africa, then return. For European-bound Africans, visa requirements make travel much more problematic.

In 2007, a Moroccan human rights activist took me and my associates to a forest near Tangiers. He asked us not to reveal the exact location. On the way, we stopped to pick up supplies of medicine, cigarettes, and food. We drove from the coastal route inland, then up a mountainous road. We pulled over and parked. My colleague Saul Gonzalez agreed to stay with the car. Cameraman Jim Van Vranken and I hiked uphill about a quarter of a mile into the woods. Waiting for us was a man in his thirties named Hamidou, who greeted me as if I had come to a meeting in his home, which in a sense we had. Hamidou was hiding out from border police with fifty-seven other people. Moroccan gendarmes were making sweeps through nearby areas, and Hamidou was worried that he and his compatriots would be arrested and deported. All of them had trekked, with the help of smugglers, from the impoverished African nation of Mali. Hamidou's clothes were ragged, his shoes almost detached from their soles. He and the others, waiting for a chance to cross into Europe, fed themselves by looking for scraps in a nearby village and by begging.

He told us, *"On n'oublie dés fois que nous sommes des humains."* (Sometimes we forget that we're humans. We're in the forest like animals.)

Hamidou said they were stuck, afraid that if they went home, they'd be killed.

He said, *"Y'a pas de solution."* (There's no solution.) "Everywhere in Africa, there's war, famine. We're trapped."

Returning to his homeland was out of the question, and he couldn't get into Europe because of stepped-up border enforcement. When we returned down the hillside to the car, Jim and I found Saul being interrogated by the gendarmes. He had told them that his associates had hiked away, and the cops had sent a search party to look for us in the direction he said we'd gone—downhill.

My guess was that Hamidou and his friends would soon be discovered and probably deported. The Moroccans, with European assistance, were improving their ability to seal the border, but they were not stopping illegal migration. Migrants were simply adopting different strategies and planning alternate routes. As long as the potential rewards at the end of the journey seemed even remotely possible, the lure of the promised land was encouragement enough for the exodus to continue.

CHAPTER 7

"We Rely Heavily on Immigrant Labor"

Lindsay, California, a dusty speck of a town equidistant between Los Angeles and San Francisco, may seem like an unlikely destination for a modern-day Exodus. But for the past couple of decades, this quiet, rural community, bumped up against the foothills of the Sierra Nevada, has been the chosen destination for migrants arriving from the same tiny Mexican village of Las Tortugas (The Turtles) in the western Mexican state of Michoacán. Relatives and friends have followed one another north, stealthily crossing the border to find work in the packing sheds and groves of olive and citrus trees that ring the area. Many of the former residents of "Turtleland," as some of the younger Lindsay inhabitants refer to their parents' hometown, have settled, bought homes, raised their own families, and in some cases started businesses. The new colonizers contributed to Lindsay's population growth, which, between 1990 and 2007, increased by 28 percent, to a modest 10,652.

Lindsay life is based on the citrus industry. Drive by the groves, and as you enter the town, you pass the Orangewood Manor trailer park, next to the Orangewood Apartments, not far from the local watering hole, the Orange Bar. At the end of each April, as the deliciously sweet aroma wafting from thousands of acres of orange groves scents the air, Lindsay stages its Orange Blossom Festival and parade.

During harvest times, tractor trailers loaded with containers brimming with tangelos and oranges lumber through the country roads toward the packing houses, staffed mostly by Latinas, women who grade and box the produce for shipment around the world.

Located at the southeastern end of California's agriculture-rich four-hundred-mile-long Central Valley, the counties around Lindsay—Tulare and Fresno—are the most prolific producers of agricultural commodities in the United States. That distinction is made possible by two precious and plentiful resources that come to the area from far distances—water from the north and workers from the south.

Migration is nothing new to Lindsay. On an outside wall of a Lindsay packing shed owned by the LoBue Brothers, a citrus company started by Italian migrants in 1934, a colorful mural shows a group of grim-faced men hoping to get work as orange pickers. They are stand-ing next to a hand-lettered sign reading TRAMPS WANTED. The men depicted in the painting were "Arkies" and "Okies," the so-called fruit tramps of the Great Depression and Dust Bowl era. During the 1930s, Harvest Gypsies, as John Steinbeck called them, swarmed into California farmlands looking for work. They were among succes-sive waves of itinerant laborers—Mexicans, Irish, Chinese, Japanese, Filipinos, Armenians, and others—who over the past 150 years have passed through California's great Central Valley, working to put food on America's tables and on their own.

"The Border Patrol used to hit the Mexican theater every week-end!" recalled Maggie Cerros, a former farm worker who moved to Lindsay from Arizona in 1966. Cerros, a resident of the once-grand Mount Whitney Hotel, now a retirement home, said migrant farm-hands would come into town to go to the movies and the nearby Laundromat. Knowing where to find them, immigration authorities would park their buses and conduct raids. "They used to just hit Lindsay," she said.

Adjacent to the old LoBue Brothers packing house and mural is the new Sweet Brier Plaza. Most of the time, the plaza is a pleasant, open space and promenade. But each Friday evening, as the site of a farmers' market and community street fair, it is transformed, as if a Mexican village square has been transported to central California. Stalls offer bags of roasted *cacahuetes* (peanuts), CDs of Mexican ballads, jewelry, T-shirts, balloons, pizzas, nachos, and enchiladas. Ranchero music blares from loudspeakers. Farm workers out for the evening, many of them wearing white cowboy hats, stand around watching children run into and out of water fountains.

Despite the agricultural bounty it produces, seasonal work and low pay make Lindsay one of the poorest places in the country. In 2000, a third of its population lived below the poverty level. Boarded-up stores and vacant lots mark Lindsay as a waypoint for transient farm workers. They can send money home to Mexico from the cheap jewelry and furniture shops that also wire cash through the Ria Envios, AFEX, or Giromex currency exchange networks that store owners run as franchises. And when work dies down in the orange groves, farm-hands head north to Watsonville and Stockton to pick berries, then up to Washington State for the apple harvest.

Lindsay is a perfect example of the industrialized world's reliance on migrant workers. Not only for the food, nutrition, and sustenance their labor provides, but also as raw materials for the economic engines that drive the gross domestic product and international trade. For each agricultural employee (who is more likely than not to be a migrant) at least one other job is created, not to mention the direct business benefit to the firms that use the migrants. In the grocery stores of the United States, some 80 percent of the fresh oranges are grown, packed, and shipped largely by migrant workers in California.

María de Lourdes López is small, so it takes her longer than some of the other workers to move her aluminum ladder from one orange tree into the next, climb up, clip the fruit, fill the sack hanging from her neck, then back down, empty the bag into a field bin, and repeat the process. The harvest techniques have changed little over the decades. The bags are vinyl instead of canvas, the ladders are metal not wood, the large wooden bins have been replaced by plastic ones, and the migrants tend to be Mexicans like María instead of Okies.

Harvesting citrus is labor-intensive, and the pace can be exhausting. Timing is everything for growers and workers. The farmers want to get fresh products to market. For their employees, the faster they empty their sacks, the more money they make. So pickers move quickly, climbing up and down, cutting the green stalks with tiny blades wrapped around their gloved fingers. Some workers can make up to $100 in a seven-hour day. María is lucky if she clears $30.

In 2008, at age twenty-eight, María de Lourdes López left Las Tortugas in Mexico to get to Lindsay. Her goals were simple: to reunite with aunts, uncles, and brothers, and to find a job—picking oranges or working in a packing house.

María lives adjacent to an orange grove on the outskirts of town in a trailer she shares with her thirty-four-year-old brother Antonio (also a farm worker), his wife, and their three children.

In risking her life to seek a new one, María left behind friends and relatives. She quit a dead-end job at a Mexican plastics factory and left a poor, rural area whose chief exports are U.S.-bound migrants. The state relies heavily on the production of corn, which, like other farmers in the area, the López family used to grow on their small plot of land. They sold the corn locally, but in the 1990s, corn prices plummeted, and the family couldn't make a living.

"We couldn't sell the corn, so we just grew it for our own family," explained Antonio. "There was so much competition. Corn was coming in from other places, and we couldn't compete, so we stopped growing crops to sell."

Family members moved north. María's own trip was harrowing. A representative of a smuggling business arranged for her to take a two-day bus ride along with forty other would-be migrants from Las Tortugas to Sonoyta, a border town on the edge of the Sonoran desert. At a hotel, the group met a guide who escorted them to the border and had them climb over the fence. "We walked in a line very fast," she said. "There were lots of bushes and cactus needles. We walked all night."

When members of the group heard U.S. Border Patrol agents, the guide told them to hide under trees and behind rocks. But when they emerged from their hiding place, the guide was nowhere to be seen. He'd run away. Eventually, she and the others were picked up by the Border Patrol, taken to Nogales, Arizona, and deported back into Mexico.

They quickly met up with another guide who took them across the border and through the desert. "I was scared," she said. "We walked for five days. There were snakes." They made it to a country road, where a van picked them up and drove them to a safe house in Phoenix. Her brother met her there, loaned her $1,400 to pay off the coyote, and drove her to central California.

Of all the migrant-dependent industries, in the consciousness of many Americans, coal mines, garment factories, and farms are close rivals for first place in their historic mistreatment of immigrant laborers. Edward R. Murrow's scathing depiction of farm workers' lives in his 1960 documentary "Harvest of Shame" set a standard by which subsequent exposés of working conditions came to be judged. "Workers in the sweatshops of the soil," Murrow proclaimed.

The treatment of migrant farm workers is a global issue. The use of migrants in agriculture has increased with the dramatic flight of people from rural to urban areas. That mass movement reached a momentous milestone in 2008, when, for the first time in the history of the world, more people lived in cities than in the countryside. The departure of potential working-age farmhands raised the demand for migrant workers. To perform seasonal labor, European fruit and vegetable growers, faced with stiff international competition, turned to increasing numbers of what the United Nations has called "semi-legal foreigners" from North and West Africa and the poorer countries of eastern and southeastern Europe. Often, workers are hired for the day and paid by the piece with housing and transportation costs deducted from their wages.

In the United States, farmers worry that if immigration crackdowns intensify, they won't be able to rely on people like María to pick their crops. In 150 years of industrial agriculture, fears about the consequences of immigration politics are as much a part of the business as concerns about weather and pests. And although they've fought hard battles, farmers have maintained the upper hand in preserving the supply of cheap labor.

Even according to official reports by the U.S. Department of Labor, America's vast army of migrant farm workers consists mostly of illegal immigrants from Mexico.

"Nobody's trying to argue that we want to bring in illegal aliens, make them stay, and put them into forced indentured servitude. That's not the objective of an industry like ours," explained Joel

Nelsen, president of California Citrus Mutual, a trade association that bills itself as the "voice of the citrus grower."

California farmers say they have little choice in hiring because only migrants apply for farm work at the wages they offer. They insist they can't pay more because they have to compete with the low food prices of foreign competitors.

"Our average payroll runs about $10 to $13 an hour. It's a good-paying job. These people want to come in here and work and then go home. We simply want to give them that opportunity," said Nelsen, explaining that few legal residents apply for the jobs. "The domestic California individual is not willing to work in agriculture harvesting oranges."

Not surprisingly, immigrants are overrepresented in the U.S. labor force. While more than 37 million foreign-born residents accounted for 12.5 percent of the population, they made up 15.4 percent of the labor force, according to 2008 Census Bureau figures. Even though the survey was compiled before October 2009, when U.S. unemployment rates officially hit double digits, the statistics nonetheless reflect the tremendous workload shouldered by migrants—as part of a labor force in which nearly one in six workers was foreign-born. The numbers also reflect the comparative industriousness of the foreign-born: of all migrants over age sixteen in the United States, the vast majority (63.4 percent) was working in 2008. That compared to less than half—49.4 percent—of native-born American adults who were in the U.S. labor force. The census figures have no separate category for illegal immigrants, but do distinguish between citizen and noncitizen migrants. Noncitizens are more prevalent than either native-born or naturalized citizens in America's farming, fishing, service, construction, and transportation industries. Foreign-born U.S. citizens are more likely to have professional and management jobs than noncitizen migrants. As for their region of origin, migrants from Europe and Asia are nearly twice as prevalent in white-collar jobs as workers from Mexico and Latin America, who are more likely to be engaged in manual labor.

Until fairly recently, businesses that rely heavily on illegal migrants were reluctant to go public about the issue. The most outspoken industry has long been agriculture because of farmers' strong belief, rooted in experience, that politicians sympathize with their need for ready access to cheap migrant labor. In 2001 I interviewed Bob Vice, an avocado grower from Fallbrook, near San Diego, who at the time was president of the National Council of Agricultural Employers. Vice was candid about illegal migrants working in the fields.

"Well, our best guesstimate based on a lot of different information is somewhere around 80 percent," he said. "It could be 85 percent. But we believe that there's at least in that neighborhood of people that are currently working in agriculture who are working with fraudulent documents."

Since then, increasing numbers of employers in various industries have come out of the closet to join their agricultural brethren. Regulatory filings contain stark admissions. Public companies required to disclose annually to the U.S. Securities and Exchange Commission (SEC) any "risk factors" they face include worries about immigration laws.

"In Texas, we rely heavily on immigrant labor," reported the Sterling Construction Company in 2008. Sterling builds roads, bridges, and water systems in Texas and Nevada. In 2007 it grossed $306 million. "Any adverse changes to existing laws and regulations or changes in enforcement requirements or practices applicable to employment of immigrants could negatively impact the availability and cost of the skilled personnel and labor we need, particularly in Texas."

Infosys Technologies, which imports high-tech workers, mostly from India, was equally blunt: "Restrictions on immigration may affect our ability to compete for and provide services to clients in the United States, which could hamper our growth and cause our revenues to decline."

And a garment manufacturer in Los Angeles, American Apparel, whose owner, Dov Charney, an eccentric Canadian who has advocated looser immigration rules, similarly told the SEC, "American Apparel relies heavily on immigrant labor, and changes in immigration laws or enforcement actions or investigations under such laws could significantly adversely affect American Apparel's labor force, manufacturing capabilities, operations, and financial results." The March 2008 filing also disclosed that the company, with fifty-six hundred workers in its Los Angeles factory, had been under investigation by the Bureau of Immigration and Customs Enforcement (ICE), a fact that could scare off workers and "result in manufacturing and other delays." In late September 2009, the company announced the firing of eighteen hundred workers after U.S. immigration authorities found irregularities in the identification documents they presented when they were hired. One of the laid-off employees told a reporter, "I'm going to have to go to one of those sweatshop companies where I'm going to get paid under the table."

One visible symbol of America's reliance on its migrant work-force has particularly riled modern-day restrictionists. On any given day around the country, street corners and sidewalks outside home improvement stores become outdoor labor markets. Men, most of them illegal migrants from Mexico and Central America, stand around hoping to get picked up by contractors or homeowners and be put to work painting, putting up drywall, or mowing lawns. Dozens of communities have even established official worker centers where laborers can gather. In 2006, a nationwide survey indicated that more than 117,000 workers either had or were looking for day labor employment.

As the economy sank and the demand for their services diminished, many migrant day laborers gave up and returned home. Still, even in places where anti-immigrant tensions were rising and laws were mul-tiplying, many employers were undeterred. In 2008, as I interviewed workers at a day labor center in Phoenix, Ken Hanish drove up in an SUV and hired a man for landscaping work. Hanish was offering $10 to $12 an hour, no papers needed.

"They're good workers," Hanish told me, the engine idling after his new employee had climbed into the back seat. "They're Christian people. I want to support their families and so on. I don't get involved in the immigration issue. That's for the politicians to wrangle about. All I'm concerned about is getting what I want done." Then he drove off.

The casual employment of plentiful migrant workers is an American mainstay. Disregard for such niceties as obeying hiring laws, checking documents, and filling out Employment Eligibility Verification forms has been a recurring source of embarrassment for a number of people in public life who have demonstrated that expe-dience, habit, and hypocrisy so often trump immigration regulations:

- In 1993, President Clinton's nomination of Judge Zoe Baird for attorney general was derailed after it became known that she hired illegal immigrants as household employees. Clinton then nominated lawyer Kimba Wood, who also withdrew because of an illegal migrant-babysitter issue.
- Commentator Linda Chavez, former president George W. Bush's pick for labor secretary in 2001, backed out after revelations that she had provided free room and board to an illegal immigrant.
- In 2004, the former New York police commissioner Bernard Kerik withdrew as Bush's pick for homeland security secretary after it turned out that he had hired an illegal immigrant.
- Michael Chertoff, the man who got the homeland security secretary job, hired a Maryland cleaning company that used illegal immigrants to clean his house.
- One of Chertoff's top deputies, Lorraine Henderson, a federal official responsible for immigration law enforcement in three New England states, resigned after being accused of hiring a Brazilian maid whom she reportedly counseled, "You have to be careful 'cause they will deport you."
- President Obama's Treasury secretary, Michael Geithner, employed a housekeeper whose legal status expired while she worked for him.
- Even Tom Tancredo, the bombastic former Colorado congressman whose aborted 2008 campaign for president was based on ridding America of the "scourge" of illegal immigration and the "cult of multiculturalism," was accused of using illegal immigrants for home renovations in 2002. Tancredo said he was not responsible for checking the immigration status of people who worked for the company he hired. "I haven't the foggiest idea how many people I may have hired in the past as taxi drivers, as waiters, waitresses, home improvement people . . . may have been here illegally, and it is not my job to ask," he insisted.
- Then there was the case that epitomized irony, a particularly juicy example of a double standard. In 2007, executives with the Golden State Fence Company, which had built fences at immigration jails, a Border Patrol station, and the U.S.–Mexico border, were fined and sentenced to home imprisonment for hiring at least fifteen illegal immigrants.

Not to be outdone, across the pond, British officials admitted that they had found thousands of illegal immigrants working in government jobs as janitors and as security guards. One illegal immigrant managed a team of cleaners at the U.K. Border Agency. "How can the agency in charge of border security lecture business about employing illegal immigrants when it cannot even get its own house in order?" questioned the opposition spokesman after one 2008 occurrence.

Perhaps the answer to the question is best reflected in official statements that reflect the priorities and attitudes of both countries' employers. Consider two parallel declarations, the first from the George W. Bush White House, the second from the government of former British prime minister Tony Blair:

- "Immigrants are a critical part of the U.S. workforce and contribute to productivity growth and technological advancement. They make up 15% of all workers and even larger shares of certain occupations such as construction, food services, and health care."
- "The Treasury estimates that migration contributed around 15–20 percent to growth between 2001 and 2005. Migration increases investment, innovation, and entrepreneurship in the UK and is central to developing a high-value economy. Similarly, the ability to hire workers from abroad is important in making the UK an attractive business environment for firms."

Significantly, neither statement made any distinction between legal and illegal immigrants. The declarations were simply unvarnished pro-business, pro-migrant axioms.

Since ancient times, warfare, international trade, commerce, and banking have helped create an ever-growing global marketplace for labor, beginning with the first systems of international labor migration, slavery. Often captured as wartime bounty by conquering raiders and pillagers, on every continent slaves were essential building blocks of empires and societies.

For the early European colonizers of the New World, particularly the English, settling America was, in large part, a business venture. Many colonies were established as private corporations.

But landowners needed workers, a need they filled by importing indentured servants from the old country. Their timing was ripe. With Europe in turmoil, wracked by war and economic dislocation, peasants and serfs were being driven from their lands. Selling themselves into bondage to become America's first migrant laborers was an escape. Of all the colonial white immigrants between 1580 and 1775, more than half came as indentured servants who had agreed to provide several years of labor in exchange for passage, food, protection, and eventual landownership.

Colonial development was a labor-intensive undertaking. The increasing production of such commodities as tobacco, cotton, sugar, rice, and indigo required a growing workforce. As the needs of colonies rose, landowners found themselves with a labor shortage. Their solution was to turn to the world's first multinational corporations, slave trading companies owned by British, Dutch, Portuguese, and American interests. They could deliver captive African slaves who would be much cheaper than European servants.

The new American nation saw little other recorded migration until about 1820, when European industrialization, combined with the end of feudalism, unshackled peasants. No longer were they tied to the land. They could seek new opportunities in a rapidly globalizing world. Within decades, millions of people who had never before ventured beyond their villages traveled on new railways, roads, and canals. Instead of risking their lives aboard sailboats, they could cross oceans on steamers. Through new methods of communication—newspapers, mail, and telegraph—they learned that land was relatively cheap and that America's own Industrial Revolution was creating increased demands for workers in factories and mines, in construction, and on farms and railroads. The scale of emigration from Europe between 1846 and 1924 was enormous. Substantial proportions of the European population moved away. The British Isles lost 41 percent of their population. Thirty-six percent of Norwegians left their country. Twenty-two percent of the Swedish population emigrated.

The dramatic numbers of migrants to the United States prompted angry reactions from nativists, who looked down on "inferior races" and who felt that cheaper immigrant workers were depressing labor rates. The most notorious of the anti-immigrant crusades was the

Know Nothing movement of the 1850s, which had a strong dislike of migrants in general and Catholics in particular. Although it fell apart as a result of factions fighting over slavery, its spirit lived on toward the end of the century in the form of powerful anti-Asian forces. They had so much political muscle that they were able to persuade Congress in 1882 to enact the Chinese Exclusion Act, which banned immigration from China and prevented Chinese residents of the United States from becoming citizens.

Migration to the United States peaked at about the turn of the century. Between 1891 and 1920, twenty-seven million people came from Europe, particularly from southern and eastern Europe.

At the same time, a custom of migration from Mexico was beginning. We tend to think of Mexican migration as a contemporary phenomenon, but it has a long tradition, spurred to a large extent by the expansion of railroads. In the decades spanning the nineteenth and twentieth centuries, railroad companies developed extensive networks throughout the United States and Mexico. By 1890, all forty-eight U.S. states or territories had been linked up to the Mexican rail system. Not only were American railways sources of employment for many Mexican migrants, they also carried job seekers from the countryside and villages of Mexico to the fields, mines, and factories of the United States. In particular, the rapid economic development of the Southwest created a growing demand for cheap labor.

At the same time, political changes in Mexico also stimulated migration. President Porfirio Díaz, intent on industrialization, worked to dismantle an ancient system of landownership. His efforts left 97 percent of rural peasants landless by 1910. As the tides of opportunity dropped in Mexico and rose in the United States, Mexicans began crossing the border in large numbers. Between 1880 and 1929 as many as three million Mexicans migrated to the United States.

The U.S. reliance on Mexican labor has been persistent. Many of the children of early migrants crossed the border decades later to work in the United States under the bracero program (from the Spanish word *brazo*, meaning arm). On a 1993 trip to a Mexican village to report on illegal migration, I spoke to one person after another who told me how migrants from the town were following a pattern established by uncles, fathers, and grandfathers.

(The custom has had dramatic consequences. Fully a tenth of Mexico's population—that is, people born in Mexico—resides in the United States. Of the approximately 12.7 million Mexicans living in the United States in 2008, the Pew Hispanic Center estimated that 55 percent were in the country illegally.)

Many of the same forces that propelled migration to the United States played out elsewhere around the globe. Western Europe became an attractive destination after World War II with the rise of a consumer society and high economic growth. The United Kingdom drew hundreds of thousands of settlers from Commonwealth countries in the West Indies and the Indian subcontinent. France and Germany made fateful decisions to import workers from Algeria, Turkey, and Yugoslavia. Migrant laborers (known by the Germans as *Gastarbeiter*—guest workers) were expected to return home when the work was done. But things didn't quite turn out that way, and instead, hundreds of thousands of Muslims settled in.

In the Middle East, the recession that followed the oil shock of 1973 altered migration patterns. Oil-rich Persian Gulf states brought foreign workers from Arab and Asian countries. In southern Europe, nations such as Greece, Portugal, and Spain, which had long exported workers, became more prosperous after joining the European Community in the 1980s and also started attracting migrants.

In the United States, the number of immigrants as a percentage of the population more than doubled in four decades. In 1970, migrants made up just 4.7 percent of the total population, the lowest share since 1850, when the United States census first asked about birthplaces.

In 2008, foreign-born residents of the United States constituted 12.5 percent of the population, even though many Americans were under the mistaken impression that it was much higher. Asked what proportion of the U.S. population were immigrants, the average estimate of a thousand Americans surveyed in a 2009 national poll was 35 percent. The actual percentage of immigrants is lower than it was 1890, when the foreign-born constituted 14.8 percent of the U.S. population. To put that into perspective, to reach the equivalent of the 1890 foreign-born population today would take an increase in the number of migrants equal to all the inhabitants of the cities of Los Angeles and Chicago.

As the debate over immigration has intensified, think tanks, official number-crunchers, and activists of various stripes have issued reports and argued over the value of migrants, trying to calculate whether they are financial burdens or benefits to society. That terrain is well plowed, and beyond the parameters of this book. However the figures add up, there can be little argument that on the plus side of the ledger, their value is immense.

"The absence of the estimated 1.4 million undocumented immigrants in Texas in fiscal 2005 would have been a loss to our gross state product of $17.7 billion," wrote Republican Carole Keeton Strayhorn, a former Texas comptroller, in December 2006. "Undocumented immigrants produced $1.58 billion in state revenues, which exceeded the $1.16 billion in state services they received."

A think tank at Rutgers, the State University of New Jersey, took a similar tack, but in a more lyrical way—and it didn't differentiate between legal and non-legal migrants: "New Jersey's immigrants are so essential to its economy that if you did the thought experiment of subtracting their work, you'd find that New Jersey itself would grind to a halt."

Similarly, in New York in 2007, the Fiscal Policy Institute, a liberal think tank backed by public employee unions, issued a 121-page report, "Working for a Better Life," as part of a project titled Truth about Immigrants. Intending to "portray realistically the overall role of immigrants in the New York economy" during what it described as a time of "political frenzy" around immigration issues, the report rather unglamorously declared that (1) "Immigrants contribute broadly to the New York economy," and (2) "Over time, immigrants become part of our communities."

But going beyond the obvious, the report also offered statistical snapshots, finding that in New York City, where 37 percent of residents are foreign-born, immigrants "make up a quarter of all CEOs, half of accountants, a third of office clerks, a third of receptionists, and half of building cleaners." The survey showed that in the downstate suburbs of Nassau, Putnam, Rockland, Suffolk, and Westchester counties, nursing was the occupation with the largest number of immigrants, and that in upstate New York, immigrants accounted for

20 percent of college professors and an estimated 80 percent of seasonal farm workers.

Those numbers may not be surprising in the state where the Statue of Liberty, dubbed by the poet Emma Lazarus as the "Mother of Exiles," has stood since 1886 as a welcoming beacon and a symbol of mass migration.

In the monument's shadows are the brick and limestone buildings of the old Ellis Island Immigration Center, a fitting emblem of America's inconsistent immigration policies. Opened in 1892 during the era of mass European migration, it processed millions of passengers. After restrictive laws were enacted in 1924, it served as a migrant prison and deportation center. In September 1990, thirty-six years after it had been abandoned and fallen into disrepair, Ellis Island was reopened as a museum after a fund-raising drive championed by Ronald Reagan who, as president, had signed a milestone immigration bill. Many modern-day conservative idolizers of the late president do not like to be reminded of what they consider Reagan's "big mistake," enacting a 1986 amnesty program that set some 2.7 million illegal migrants on the road to citizenship. Such is America's love-hate relationship with its migrant history.

The millions of curious visitors who have toured Ellis Island since it became a tourist attraction vastly exceed the number of migrants who passed through its storied doors. Its online databases of ship records have become repositories of information for family researchers immersing themselves in the growing leisure pursuit of genealogical exploration. Americans of European descent tend to romanticize their immigration history, in a way mirroring the exaggerated images and expectations migrants brought with them of streets paved with gold. European immigrants looked forward with rose-tinted lenses; their descendants inherited those glasses to look backward.

The raw reality is a story mixed with rags-to-riches fairy tales as well as accounts of exploitation. There are many faces of immigration. These days, in a global economy where migration has become so much easier, determined migrants are finding ways and places to move—out of desperation or ambition. But history is also repeating itself. Today, ruthless employers are taking advantage of migrants, depending on them to build economies, and are recycling systems of indentured servitude.

CHAPTER 8

Servitude and Cash Flows

Forty years ago, the United Arab Emirates was an inhospitable desert. But the intersection of oil money, trade, massive borrowing, and a seemingly endless supply of cheap, foreign labor turned the Persian Gulf state and its most populous emirate, Dubai, into a surreally prosperous center of commerce and glitz poised between the East and the West.

Migrant workers in Dubai have built a jungle of skyscrapers rising from the sand as monuments to conspicuous affluence and extravagance. Think over-the-top opulence, Donald Trump on steroids, unabashed grandiosity. Combine with modern-day feudalism. Throw in visions of the pyramids and the people who built them, and you begin to get an idea of the forces that have shaped this phantasmal urban landscape.

The UAE is more than simply a study in indulgence and excess. It also is the quintessential migrant-dependent economy. Foreigners are everywhere. In a nation of 4.5 million residents, more than 90 percent of the private-sector labor force consists of expatriate workers. The wealth they create doesn't all remain in the UAE. Most expatriates do little else but work to send money home, spending little of what they actually earn in the country. In 2008, migrants transferred more than $10 billion out of the UAE.

Taken together, the United Arab Emirates, on the one hand, and the global remittance industry on the other provide vivid illustrations of dynamic, migration-fueled economic engines. Both are utterly dependent on migrants. Both stand accused of exploiting them. Yet both provide services and jobs that are indispensable and that, like them or not, migrants have come to rely on.

By the end of 2009, the global economic contagion had finally caught up to Dubai. The sheikdom's years of exuberant expansion slowed dramatically, as hubris and one-upsmanship proved little match for the sobering reality of massive debt and the rush of air escaping from the deflating property bubble. Prices plunged in the overblown real estate market as construction projects were halted or delayed. With the frenetic pace of development slowing, many migrant workers were sent home. But the crisis did not alter the fundamentals of the UAE economy. While Islam may be the UAE's official religion, the sheikdom's true and unabashed devotion is to greed, wealth, and ostentation, with migrant workers as the essential fuel.

Migrants work at almost every level of UAE society, except the very top one, which is occupied by the ruling sheiks and their families. The vast majority of foreign workers perform menial jobs—as construction workers and servants, office clerks and janitors, taxi drivers and cooks—but many have white-collar employment as corporate executives, bankers, accountants, business owners, and bureaucrats. At the Dubai hotel where I stayed, an Indian manager barked instructions to a meek Nepalese porter named Sherpa, whose previous job had been hauling luggage for Western trekkers in the Himalayas. Here, he was lugging bags for tourists. Behind the desk, Filipino clerks checked guests in and out.

In 2008, Filipino workers in the UAE sent home more than $584 million. Among them was Rolando Decena, a forty-one-year-old carpenter from the city of Cainta, just outside the Philippine capital of Manila. Decena is a slight, intense, and devoutly religious man who had worked in the Middle East twice before. He felt that leaving his country was his only option.

"In the Philippines, I had no permanent job," he told me. "I'm the father of three children. So I have to provide for my family, but

Philippines not so well, their economy, so I try to go overseas and work abroad."

Decena applied for a carpentry job after seeing an add in a Philippine newspaper. A company representative interviewed him at a hotel in Manila, and, to his delight, offered him work. In 2007, he left his pregnant wife, teenage son, and twenty-year-old daughter to take a job as a foreman in a furniture factory in Dubai. Things did not work out exactly as Decena planned, a story I'll come to later, but his family was relying on him. That's the way it is for the armies of migrant workers who have established the shimmering city-state of Dubai as a commercial and trading hub of the Middle East.

Like other businesspeople, Tariq Ramadan, a suave developer and money manager, was in awe at the stunning pace of development. The Kuwaiti-born, Canadian-educated Palestinian named one of his companies Richville.

"The growth of Dubai—we sometimes make jokes about this, but it's actually a reality," he said, describing a formula for more or less instant prosperity based on relentless construction. "They've sold desert sand, seawater, and the air," he explained. "Because the land is sold by gross floor area, so we sell the air. We sold the sand and the water, which is the Palms, and everybody made money."

The Palms are a series of artificial islands in the shape of palm trees. One is the site of the Atlantis, a fifteen-hundred-room resort complex built at a cost of $1.5 billion and which opened in September 2008. It has an archipelago with the contours of the globe. And on one island, all to itself, is the iconic Burj Al Arab Hotel, built in the shape of a billowing sail. At 1,053 feet (321 meters), it is the world's tallest hotel building and Dubai's only seven-star resort, where a suite for the night will set you back $2,000 to $60,000.

One poster in a glitzy mall could serve as the nation's motto: "Indulgence That's Simply Out of This World." One outlandish symbol of the UAE's cherished lifestyle is Ski Dubai, the largest indoor ski resort in the Middle East, with five ski slopes covered with real snow, year-round. Despite the often blazing desert heat outside, an area the size of three football fields is kept below freezing.

To try to understand the official mind-set, I went to the center of Dubai, to the International Financial Center, whose imposing entrance is redolent of the Arc de Triomphe. In the building's palatial lobby, I met Nasser Al Shaali, who at the time of my visit in late 2008 was the center's chief executive officer. A few months later, the suave businessman became the CEO of his family's luxury yacht construction company, reportedly the largest of its kind in the Middle East. "The roots of the glitz and the glamour and the glass that is Dubai were planted almost fifty years ago, when the previous ruler of Dubai, Sheik Rashid [bin Said al-Maktoum, the cofounder in 1971 with his brother, of the United Arab Emirates] installed the beginnings of the excellence in infrastructure that we see the fruits of today," Al Shaali told me. The goateed businessman is an unapologetic booster of the vision of obsessive and unbridled gigantism laid down by the ruling sheiks.

"The culture in Dubai is that we want to be on top of the world. Being number two is not enough. For us, whether it be the airline industry, or aluminum industry, or the financial industry, or what have you, we want to reach for the top, and that is the vision of His Highness [Sheikh Mohammed bin Rashid Al Maktoum, Dubai's current ruler, a son of the late Sheik Rashid]. That's his drive. As he said it, 'The word "impossible" is not in a leader's dictionary.'"

What Dubai's rulers see as the impossible coming true was made possible by the legions of foreign laborers. Close to a million of them—construction workers, most from South Asia—are at the bottom of the economic ladder.

"Amid all the material progress in the country, it's quite clear that it's the foreign migrant workers that have paid the price and continue to pay the price for the tremendous boom," Sarah Leah Whitson told me. Whitson is an executive director of Human Rights Watch, which since 2006 has been documenting abusive conditions faced by the UAE's migrant construction workers. "It's really through the exploitation of these workers that the UAE has financed its property boom, its development boom, and it's not even in circumstances where that was necessary. It's just a race to the bottom, and construction companies and development companies exploiting and trying to make as much profit as they can."

Without their docile, mostly compliant caste of subservient immigrants, the emirates' feudal rulers would have remained lords of sand instead of imperial majesties of commerce. But while Western democracies might consider themselves more enlightened and empathetic in their treatment of migrants, they do share a basic if unstated assumption with the UAE: migrant workers are a disposable commodity to be managed in the service of the host country. It's just that in the UAE, that core principle rises to a whole new level.

A common justification for the mistreatment of migrants is that their lives, no matter how pitiful, are an improvement over whatever squalor and poverty they may have endured back home. Notwithstanding the moral failings of this rationale for abuse, that sad reality cannot be denied. Faced with lousy alternatives, migrant workers choose the ones that will earn them money, and then suffer the consequences. On the surface, it would seem like a "win-win" outcome. As migrants improve their lot and send money home, employers boost their own personal and national economic circumstances by renting their labor. But the trade-off is uneven, and, as the UAE demonstrates, the costs of its lavish prosperity are immense. Since no enforced international standards govern the treatment of migrant workers, their fate is in the hands of rulers and their minions, intention being "on top of the world," even if that means standing on top of those at the bottom.

The sumptuous shopping malls and hotels created by migrant construction workers in Dubai are a far cry from their own living arrangements. Ubiquitous white buses ferry workers back and forth from construction sites to company-run labor camps. A half hour's drive outside of town, but a world away, is one workers' colony named Sonapur, a labor camp stretching for blocks and blocks, housing tens of thousands of migrants, mostly from India, Bangladesh, and Pakistan. Sonapur means City of Gold in Hindi or Urdu. But the teaming, dusty outpost doesn't live up to its name. Crowded apartment buildings, one after the next, serve as dormitories.

On Fridays, workers have the day off and can find a taste of home. Street vendors sell *jilapee*, sweets made of deep-fried flour and sugar. The day I visited, teams of men who work at different construction companies, Al Muhairi Builders and Modern Contract Systems, played cricket, competing against each other on a vacant patch of dirt.

Conditions inside the housing blocks vary. In one, rows of rooms, six bunk beds to each, reminded me of a prison complex. Hindus and

Muslims ate in separate cafeterias, according to their dietary preferences. Bathrooms were communal. In one more primitive complex,
the outside courtyard had been flooded by sewage.

Investigators from Human Rights Watch documented a variety
of problems. "In a number of housing centers that we visited, the conditions were quite poor, with sixteen men to a room, sometimes no
air-conditioning, not very sanitary facilities, not enough access to
bathing facilities and certainly recreational facilities," said Whitson.

But, she explained, the housing conditions are not the chief
issue for human rights advocates. "Our main concern is the system by
which labor is imported and employed in the UAE, which, when you
add up the conditions, we believe amounts to indentured servitude,"
she said.

As they stood around watching their friends play cricket, a
number of laborers and bricklayers, some of them from Shangla,
one of the poorest areas of Pakistan, spoke to me. They were earning
about $300 a month. But the jobs didn't come for free. To get them,
they had to pay off middlemen back home as much as $2,000, a for-
tune for most of the men. Many wound up borrowing the money
from loan sharks charging high interest rates.

Yusuf Oman, a thirty-five-year-old electrician from Bangladesh,
signed a contract obligating him to work for his UAE employer for
three years. Like others, it took him one year to earn enough to pay
back the loan he obtained to land the job. But he seemed resigned
to his fate, even grateful. He works so he can send money to his
family back home. He has three children, ranging in age from nine
to thirteen. In Dubai, he was able to make more than four times
what he earned in Bangladesh, where he earned the equivalent of
$73 a month.

Some workers said they had been lied to—promised jobs and
salaries that never materialized. Sayid Mohammad Monir thought he'd
be coming to work in an office, only to be given a job as a bricklayer.
He didn't want to complain because he was afraid of getting deported.

To me, the workers seemed trapped, stranded without much re-
course. Desperate conditions in their own countries had forced them
here. They needed to work to pay off debts, and they were contractu-
ally obligated to remain with their employers. Other than Western
human rights groups with little influence in the UAE, no one was

looking out for them. Labor unions don't exist, and strikes are banned. On top of everything, even though they were only about a thousand miles away from home, the laborers couldn't leave without the consent of their employers. Their bosses were keeping the men's passports, a violation of international and UAE laws.

Mohammad Khan, a lanky construction worker on a crew building a twenty-eight-story Radisson Hotel, pulled out of his pocket the Ministry of Labour work permit that his employer, a building contractor, had given him when they took his passport.

"Can you leave the country with this?" I asked as he showed me the card.

Khan knew the answer as well as I did. He just shook his head.

Sarah Leah Whitson ticked off the ways in which workers' rights are being grossly violated. "Employers routinely hold two months of wages as a so-called security to keep the workers from leaving. They're confiscating their passports. The law in the UAE forbids workers from going to work for another employer without their current employer's consent, which they can't even ask for unless two years have passed. You can see that a worker who is working on a construction job in the UAE doesn't really have the freedom to leave, and that's really what the definition of indentured servitude is. You don't have the freedom to walk away. You don't have your passport, and the money you're earning is not yours; you're paying it to someone else."

I asked the developer Tariq Ramadan how employers justify the confiscation of passports. He replied that the practice is so common that when he worked for someone else, as a noncitizen, even his passport was taken.

But, he said, the law is clear. "You cannot keep the passport of somebody working with you whether it's a director or a manager or a laborer. However, sometimes it's in their best interest to keep their passport at the company. They live in crowded accommodations and they can easily lose their passports," he explained, not very convincingly.

When I brought up the question of human rights with Nasser Al Shaali, then with the International Financial Center, he took a different tack: "I would point out that the situation of day laborers and other blue-collar workers in the country compared to their home jurisdiction is often an order of magnitude in terms of improvement."

Whitson from Human Rights Watch was unimpressed by the argument. "That's not the standard," she said angrily. "The notion that you should exploit workers as much as possible, but maybe one iota better than the conditions that they might otherwise be in, is a morally bankrupt and legally bankrupt proposition to make."

Government officials in the UAE have not completely turned a blind eye to criticism. Like scolded children caught in repeated acts of misbehavior, they have issued statements of contrition accompanied by promises to shape up. But they are inveterate recidivists.

In 2003, asked about oversight of the conditions of migrant workers, a government official pleaded guilty with an explanation. "I would like to mention here that the ministry has nearly 80 inspectors to monitor more than 2.5 million laborers," Khalid Al Khazraji of the UAE Labor and Social Affairs Ministry told a reporter. "With such a small number of inspectors, we cannot play a proactive role in the market," he explained, insisting more were being hired.

But three years later, in 2006, the government still employed only eighty labor inspectors, as Minister of Labour Ali Kaabi acknowledged when he was confronted with subsequent allegations of worker mistreatment. He trotted out the same excuse for lax enforcement. "Our laws are tougher than anyone else's in the Mideast," Ali Kaabi told the Associated Press. "But the lack of inspectors means sometimes we don't see these problems."

In May 2009, Human Rights Watch acknowledged that the government had taken steps to address prior complaints, but said in a report that "the abuse of workers remains commonplace." The government responded indignantly, asserting that it was committed to better housing and health care programs. It announced the hiring of additional inspectors and said it was moving to prosecute recalcitrant employees. But once again, a UAE official admitted there was room for improvement.

"Respecting workers' rights is a moral, cultural, and economic imperative for the UAE," declared Anwar Mohammad Gargash, the UAE minister of state for foreign affairs. "The government is proud of its steady progress in transparently achieving its objectives and remains committed to doing much more on a priority basis in future."

Construction workers in the UAE are not the only ones suffering abuse. Hundreds of household employees have complained of ill treatment, long hours, sexual assaults, and being stiffed on pay. Many run away and are taken in by their embassies or consulates. The problem is so prevalent that the embassies of the Philippines, India, Indonesia, and Sri Lanka have established safe houses for runaway maids. At the time of my visit to Dubai, the Philippine consulate's labor attaché was sheltering about seventy women who had left their employers.

In Dubai, each week on average, the consulate arranges transportation home for half a dozen domestic workers. Each day, two or three live-in nannies or maids come to consulate offices in Dubai complaining about abuse and overwork. Consul General Benito B. Valeriano told me it was common to hear complaints about twenty-hour workdays and low wages.

The Philippine government has set a wage minimum of $400 a month for Filipina maids working abroad. But in the UAE, domestic workers are often paid less than half that amount. Given the fact that his government places such a high premium on overseas workers, one of the main official responsibilities of the Philippine diplomatic posts is to look after their interests. But Valeriano confessed his government couldn't do that effectively and was embarrassed about being interviewed on the subject by a foreign reporter.

"I have to protect the image of the Philippines," he said. "What does it say about my country that overseas workers have to leave and come here?"

The problem is not confined to the UAE. In 2007, the Philippine government repatriated a total of 3,032 migrants from around the world.

As for Roland Decena, the Filipino carpenter who got a job in a Dubai furniture factory, his sad story turns out to be unusual only in the details. When he arrived from the Philippines, his employer confiscated his passport and told him, to his surprise, he had to live inside the factory along with twenty other men. In addition, his boss unexpectedly started deducting a third of his $270-a-month salary, telling Decena to his shock that he owed just over $2,000 in "expenses."

"They said I have to pay all expenses," he said. "The air ticket and the employment expenses I have to pay. So every month, I have to pay them expenses. So it takes almost more than a year to pay the money."

Things went from bad to worse after a fire swept through the building. "The fire broke out to our workshop and our accommodations. Everything was lost except the pair of clothes that I am wearing at that time."

His employer gave him the equivalent of only $50 for everything he had lost. Incensed, Decena, who has a high school diploma, figured out how to negotiate the Dubai court system. He filed civil suits demanding his employer pay him back wages and return his passport. He quit the factory job but couldn't work elsewhere legally because his boss wouldn't grant him permission to take another job. He stayed at a friend's apartment and borrowed money for living expenses. Eventually Decena won his legal cases, but he was so much in debt, he couldn't afford a plane ticket home. He was trying to figure out how to scrape together some money, with little to sustain him but his faith.

"I only pray for our sake that He will not forget us," he said earnestly. "God will help us stand for what is right. Even if you're standing alone, God will be behind you if you're a right man."

Waiting for him back in the Philippines was a new addition to his family, a baby boy, born six months after he left for Dubai. Talking about the prospects of being reunited with his family and meeting his youngest child, Decena smiled anxiously.

"I am so excited to see my baby," he said. "To see my baby."

Starting in late 2008, the UAE's dizzying pace of real estate deals and speculation became less frenetic as the global economic slowdown cast a pall of uncertainty over future and existing projects. Some migrant workers were laid off and sent home, but most stayed. Economic growth was down but by no means out, and officially no one was reconsidering the dependence on migrant labor or the glories of property development.

"It doesn't matter how imaginative or crazy you think your idea is, chances are you can find ways of making it work in Dubai," said Nasser Al Shaali, echoing the ruling sheik's vision of Utopia. "Whether it be the world's largest man-made island in the shape of a palm tree, or the world's largest and second-largest towers, or the world's largest shopping mall, and so on and so forth. Or if you want to build the Pyramid of Giza, but bigger than the real one, or build the

Statue of Liberty, but bigger than the real one, or an Eiffel Tower that's bigger than the real one. It's all possible in Dubai. It's a place where dreams really do come true."

Hyperbole aside, unquestionably many migrants fare better than they would have back in their home countries. But their status in the UAE as a throwaway underclass is enshrined in policy. Migrants cannot become citizens or qualify for their privileges. Emiratis, as the citizens are called, receive free education, health care, and other subsidized benefits. Emirati men can obtain free land and no-interest loans to build homes. They receive $19,000 government handouts for wedding costs. Even though they are a shrinking minority, natives remain at the top of the pyramid, living in villas behind high walls, often segregated from foreigners. Meaningful interaction with the hired migrant help is virtually nonexistent, and in public places such as shopping malls, Emirati men often stand out immaculately clothed in well-pressed *dishdashas*, their flowing white robes.

Not surprisingly, the distance and disparity have built resentment. I asked an Indian taxicab driver what he thought about the locals. He was disdainfully crude, referring to them by sliding his thumb and forefinger over the creased arm of his shirt.

"All they do is eat, pray, and fuck," he said.

The gap between the lives and rights of migrants and those of native Emiratis makes the UAE a *Gulf* state in the true meaning of the word. The yawning divide guarantees a high living standard for a lucky few, but the luxuries come at a high price for those who make them possible.

The resentments, indignities, and injustices often endured by migrants are all part of individual and collective calculations that go into decisions about leaving home in the first place, and about whether to remain in their destinations. The questions are variations of "Am I better off staying or leaving?" or "Will I be more able to provide for my family here or there?"

Families and economies around the world are dependent on money sent home by migrants working abroad. Toward the end of 2008, as economic shock waves rebounded across the world, remittances sent home from abroad started dropping in some places and leveling off in others. Nevertheless, they remained a mainstay of the global economy. Even as markets slumped, job losses mounted, homes were lost, and businesses went under, the world's migrants sent home 15 percent more than they did in 2007, according to the World Bank economist Dilip Ratha. Ratha, who has become the worldwide authority on remittances, put the 2008 total at $338 billion—a conservative estimate because it is based on official reports. He believes that, in general, unrecorded sums sent home by migrants could be at least 50 percent higher than the official tallies.

In 2009, as the economy worsened, there were scattered stories about "reverse remittances," reports that residents of developing countries were sending money to migrant relatives struggling with unemployment. Instead of providing support to family members back home, migrants who had crossed borders in search of opportunities were on the receiving end of the remittance pipeline. The *New York Times*, for example, reported on a farmer in southern Mexico who had sold a cow to raise funds for a nephew in northern California. But there was scant data to suggest a trend, and experts agreed that the trickle of "reverse remittances" was minuscule compared to funds moving in the opposite direction.

Nonetheless, as a result of the recession, global remittances in 2009 dropped by an estimated 6 percent compared to 2008. The decline was less than had been predicted earlier in the year. The World Bank's Dilip Ratha concluded that resourceful migrants were demonstrating resilience. "[E]ven though the job market has been weak in many destination countries," he wrote on his blog, "they are staying on longer and trying to send money home by cutting living costs. New migration flows are lower due to the economic crisis, but they are still positive." Throughout much of the developing world, signs that absent breadwinners may be sending home earnings are evident in the partially completed houses one sees everywhere. Bare, vertical rebar bars protrude from roofs until there's enough money to continue the building. Lacking access to credit, poor families pay for construction when the cash is available.

In the sandy dunes on the outskirts of the fishing town of Kayar in Senegal, West Africa, rows of gray cinder blocks dried in the sun outside a house under construction. On the second floor, up the crude stairs, laborers quickly scooped mortar from a wheelbarrow and spread the cement on a low wall, gradually adding layers to the sprouting brick framework. Soon this phase of the construction project would end, and Medoune Diop, his brothers, and his friends would be out of work until more money came along.

"It goes step by step," Diop explained. The owner of the property bought the land before he left on a wooden fishing boat for Spain. Unlike hundreds of other would-be African migrants, he made it safely and got a job.

"Since he doesn't have papers in Spain, as he makes money, he sends it home as soon as he earns it," said Diop. "Because he doesn't know if the police will arrest him."

So the building of the seven-room, $30,000 house goes in stages. At the time of my visit, the structure was more of a shell than a home, with no floor and no roof. Diop's plan was to continue working as long as he received the money, and stop if the flow of funding stopped. There was a chance that the project would come to a halt. "If they deport him, the house won't be finished," Diop said.

In Senegal, remittances in 2007 accounted for 8.5 percent of the gross domestic product. In the Philippines, the percentage was even higher, amounting to 11.6 percent of its GDP. In at least eight developing countries, remittances accounted for more than 20 percent of the national income. Topping the list was the poor nation of Moldova, in Eastern Europe. In 2007, remittances sent home by migrant Moldovans made up 45.5 percent of the country's income. Its most profitable exports are its people.

To put the scope of global remittances into perspective, in 2007, migrants sent home about thirteen times more than the United States spent on foreign aid, and two and a half times as much money as all the foreign assistance contributed by developed countries to poor nations.

Migration experts and scholars have studied the role and value of remittances sent home from abroad. Is there a multiplier effect? Do economies actually grow as a result of the money migrants send home? A study from Bangladesh found that the top four uses of remittances sent from abroad were, in descending order, food and clothing, home construction or repair, land for farming, and repayments of loans that financed the migration itself.

Remittances keep many families afloat financially and finance domestic consumption, but to what extent they foster economic development is a matter of debate. Generally, remittances flow directly from migrants to their families. But there have been efforts to harness the financial power of remittances for economic development. In the United States, Mexican migrants and their families have formed "hometown associations," banding together to pool resources and raise money for public works projects in Mexico. They are often encouraged to do so by Mexican federal, state, and municipal governments, which have set up funds (so-called Three for One or Two for One programs) to match contributions sent by the migrant clubs.

The funds moving around the world not only are a mainstay of the migrant economy, they also fuel global financial enterprises whose fortunes, in turn, rely on human mobility.

Migrants transfer remittances using a number of methods. Intermediaries range from the Western Union Company, the Goliath of the money transfer industry, to networks of families and friends who hand-carry cash or merchandise from migrants in one country to relatives back home.

Money transfer companies make their money two ways: by collecting transaction fees and by charging currency exchange rates. The fees can be hefty and the exchange rates unfavorable to consumers. No remittance firm even approaches the dominance of Western Union, whose history, well-being, and business model are intimately tied to the global movement of people. The company controls about 17 percent of the global market, light-years ahead of its closest competitor, Moneygram International, with roughly 4 percent.

"We are very, very confident in our future," crowed the Western Union company chief executive Christina A. Gold in February 2009. At a time when other financial business leaders were seeking government handouts or exercising cautious restraint in bleak public pronouncements, Gold was telling analysts of her bullishness about the migration industry.

"The mobile workforce will continue seeking employment opportunities throughout the world," she said. "There are an estimated 200 million cross-border migrants, as well as an estimated 300 million people who have migrated within . . . [countries]."

In March 2009, a Western Union official gleefully predicted that despite the global financial slowdown, UAE remittances would nonetheless see double-digit growth. "Even if, of 100 construction projects 70 remain, they still need laborers who will fuel remittances," said Jean Claude Farah, Western Union's regional vice president.

Western Union has long stood at the intersection of globalization and migration, having entered the business of wiring money by telegraph in 1871 as immigration to the United States was soaring. Today, its distinctive gold-on-black logo reaches from remote villages to crowded metropolitan centers. In 2008, the firm boasted of having 375,000 locations in more than two hundred countries, a reach that to the company's aptly named CEO, Gold, translated into bright prospects even in a sour economy. "As you look at GDP and you look at what's going on in different countries," she told financial analysts in early 2000, "it's really pushing our customers and they're looking for jobs. In the end it will create great opportunity for us because people will have to migrate to different geographies or to different jobs and we'll be able to pick that up."

Western Union is facing increasing competition from smaller companies that specialize in transferring funds along regional corridors such as North America to Latin America and the Caribbean, and from Western Europe to North Africa. In addition, banks, credit unions, ATM firms, phone companies, and check cashing operators also compete for the migrant remittance business, often using new technologies.

Remit2India, for example, a partnership of financial institutions and India's largest media conglomerate, the Times Group, allows nonresident Indians or NRIs (a commonly used term for members of the Indian diaspora) in twenty-two countries to send money online to 141 banks in India or have funds delivered by courier.

Credit and debit card companies also are providing money transfer services. iKobo Money Transfer, a Texas company founded in 2001, enables customers to transfer funds using credit cards or bank accounts. The firms send the recipient a Visa debit card via FedEx to be used to withdraw the transferred money from an ATM at the other end or to make purchases.

Banks also have also been jumping on the migrant money train. Bank of America's SafeSend program allows people with B of A checking accounts to transfer funds to one of forty-five hundred agents throughout Mexico. Wells Fargo has a similar service, called ExpressSend. Its U.S. customers may send money to Mexico, El Salvador, Guatemala, India, the Philippines, and Vietnam.

For financial institutions, offering migrants, regardless of their legal status, the ability to transfer money abroad was an opportunity to tap into a new source of customers, a base that traditionally has been outside the banking system.

"It meant a significant increase in our checking accounts," Brenda Ross-Dulan, a Wells Fargo senior vice president, told me in late 2003. Her bank, along with other U.S. financial institutions, had successfully pressed the U.S. Treasury Department to allow customers to use identification cards issued by foreign consulates to open bank accounts and use the remittance services. "Aside from our being able to help the individual person, it [a checking account] is probably the cheapest form of funding that any financial institution has," said Ross-Dulan. She estimated that within a few months of receiving permission to use consular ID cards, the increase in new checking accounts had been in the "double digits."

Banks in India and the Philippines also have aggressively targeted migrants. A number of Indian banks allow customers who maintain a minimum balance to transfer funds without cost from a foreign branch to one in India. Philippine banks have also been forming partnerships to grab the migrant remittance market, particularly in the United States. Eight of the ten largest Philippine banks have remittance operations in the United States, and one, Metrobank, partnered with the California-based Internet company Xoom.com to let overseas Filipino workers remit money via the Internet.

The latest entry in the global remittance industry is the mobile phone business. One international trade association, GSMA (Global System for Mobile communications Association), representing more than 750 mobile operators, estimated optimistically that once the technology is in place, and the regulatory hurdles cleared to allow cell phones to be used for transferring funds, the costs of money transfers could plummet and the formal global remittance market could more than triple in three years.

In Kenya, Safaricom teamed with Vodafone and the Commercial Bank of Africa to roll out what it called its M-Pesa service in 2007, and within eighteen months some four million people had signed up. The phones work as portable ATMs. Users deposit money with

M-Pesa agents, who earn commissions for the transactions. Using menus in English or Swahili, the agents send a text message with a code confirming the deposit. To transfer money, the mobile phone user sends another text message to the recipient with the code and amount to be withdrawn. The recipient goes to any M-Pesa agent and withdraws the funds.

South Africa and the Philippines have similar systems in place. Two rival Philippine services—GCASH, operated by Globe Telecom, and Padala, run by Smart Communications—allow overseas Filipinos to send home money. Using GCASH, customers can send money using the social networking site friendster.com. GCASH also has outlets in twenty-five countries, including fifty-two locations in the United States, most of them in partnership with the Philippine National Bank.

At the other end of the technological spectrum are informal money transfer networks such as the *hawala* (used in the Middle East and parts of Asia and Africa) and *hundi* (common in Pakistan and Bangladesh) systems. These are arrangements in which operators take money on one end, then instruct relatives or colleagues in another country to hand a like amount to someone else. Billions of dollars are channeled through these systems, to the dismay of governments. Not only does this form of exchange dodge taxes and money laundering laws, it also escapes scrutiny, making it difficult to track payments and cash flows of terrorist networks.

Other comparatively low-tech money transfer systems simply use guys in vans. Rubén Hernández-León, a professor at the University of California at Los Angeles, has written about how Belle Street in downtown Dalton in northern Georgia turned into a kind of "remittances row" on Saturday mornings. Vans lined up to accept parcels, goods, and cash to deliver to homes in towns and villages in Mexico. Making regular round trips, the vans carried cargoes including shoes, stoves, washers, televisions, and stereos as well as money.

One customer told Hernández-León the van services beat commercial services. "It doesn't take long, they arrive quickly, and it arrives like you sent it: in dollars. That's how it gets there. And if you use the companies and you send a hundred dollars, they're going to charge you like ten. But over there where they go to get the money, they set the price, how much they'll pay. . . . Let's say I send a hundred dollars from here [Georgia] by Western Union or to the bank they have over there [Mexico]. Right now the dollar's at 9.10 [pesos], but over there they'll pay them 8.80 [pesos]. I lose out!"

Such grievances are common. International financial organizations such as the World Bank and the International Monetary Fund have complained about high costs charged by money transfer companies as well as their lack of accountability. The prices can be steep and wildly variable. Western Union's high margins and its prominence have made the company a target. In 2007, migrants' rights groups launched a boycott of the firm. The political action had little effect. In 2008, Western Union grossed nearly $5.3 billion, an 8 percent increase over the previous year.

The massive sums moved by the remittance industry are a reflection not only of the numbers of migrants but also of the significant sacrifices they often make to send money home. One survey of two hundred Bangladeshi migrants indicated that they had sent back 61 percent of their incomes over a five-year period. The Chamber of Commerce and Industry in Abu Dhabi, the United Arab Emirates capital, reported in 2007 that migrants "remit home nearly 80 percent of their income, as their spending in the UAE is restricted to essential needs." In the United States in 2006, the vast majority (73 percent) of adult Latin American immigrants were regularly sending money home in amounts averaging about 10 percent of their earnings.

As money transfer operations, banks, phone companies, and development organizations vie to control the remittances circulating through the veins and arteries of the migration economies, governments are under pressure to better manage the global movement of people. A global marketplace, dependent on the flow of goods, capital, and information, also needs people in the right places and at the right times. Dubai, as extreme as it might be, is the perfect example of an economy whose very existence relies on its ability to control the mobility of its workforce. In the United Arab Emirates, there are few checks on the sheikdom's power to place its own economic interests above all others. But even in Western democracies, such nonmaterial considerations as civil rights and dignity often take a backseat to economic dictates of market forces. And in the age-old quest to manage human resources, too often the need *for* labor trumps the needs *of* labor.

CHAPTER 9

"Help Wanted" or "No Trespassing"

To environmentalists, the steep canyon on the U.S.–Mexican border about two miles from the Pacific Ocean near San Diego was a natural treasure. On a summer afternoon, the fragrances of native shrubs and laurel sumac bushes would combine with the bouquet of black sage in bloom. Kestrels dipped and soared. White-tailed kites hovered.

To border officials, the ravine was something else—a treacherous corridor for illegal aliens and criminals bringing contraband into the United States, a gully that richly deserved its forbidding sobriquet, Smuggler's Gulch. For more than a century, the notorious canyon had been used as a passageway for traffic in people, drugs, and—during Prohibition, when, according to local lore, it got its name—booze. During the 1990s, border control advocates recommended a drastic solution to eliminate the ongoing intrusions: fill it in and cover it up.

"Smuggler's Gulch is an area which is, I believe, posing a very serious threat to our stability in this country and in California," California congressman David Dreier proclaimed during a 2005 congressional floor debate.

Over the protests of the Sierra Club, the Audubon Society, and the Mexican government, in 2008 the U.S. Department of Homeland Security hired the Kiewit Company to bring in bulldozers and earthmovers to shove thirty-five thousand truckloads of dirt into the ravine and construct a 150-foot-high berm. The result was an eight-hundred-foot-wide dam, topped with a Border Patrol road, stadium lighting, three layers of fencing, and video surveillance cameras. The massive barricade stands as a $59 million monument to the strong-willed and persistent determination of immigration hardliners who successfully launched their ambitious project during the Clinton era, saw it championed by the Bush administration, and watched it completed during the Obama presidency.

Moving enough dirt to cover a football field to a height equivalent to a fifty-story building may have been a drastic measure, but to organizations that have long protested that even with record expenditures on immigration control, not enough is being done, it was a necessary one.

"Look at the policy decisions being made by the nation's political leaders, and the inescapable conclusion is that their priority is cheap labor above all else," Dan Stein of the conservative Federation for American Immigration Reform (FAIR) has repeatedly complained.

In that respect, advocates of tougher border enforcement make an undeniably valid point. That's not to say proponents of immigration control don't wield influence. The topographical rearrangement of a California canyon is testament to how restrictionists, motivated by varying degrees of politics, xenophobia, racism, fear, or self-interest, have managed to influence immigration strategies. Nonetheless, the overall trajectory of national policies, actions, and inaction has been to manage human mobility for the benefit of business and industry. The evidence of porous borders and national priorities is compelling. Look no further than the presence of the estimated 11.9 million illegal migrants in the United States. More than 8 million of those illegal immigrants are part of the U.S. workforce. The numbers tell the story: America's "Help Wanted" signs overshadow its "No Trespassing" notices.

This is far from a recent development. Even though we might think of visas, passports, and border controls as more or less natural conditions of travel, the desire of nation-states and sovereigns to control the movements of their subjects has historically been linked to the quest to manage human resources.

During the medieval ages in Western Europe, serfs were tied to manors and obligated to work the fields. If the real estate was sold, they were included as fixtures, part of the deal. Russia's Ivan IV (aka Ivan the Terrible) forbade internal migration as a way of preventing peasants from fleeing estates and causing labor shortages.

King George III's lame effort to control human mobility spawned America's first migrant rights movement, even before the nation was born. In 1763, the monarch ordered American settlers not to move west beyond the Appalachian Mountains. "We do hereby strictly forbid, on Pain of our Displeasure, all our loving Subjects from making any Purchases or Settlements whatever" of land outside the influence of the British government, he decreed.

The king's "loving Subjects" did not return the affection. Angry colonists made freedom of movement one of their justifications for self-government. Eager to move farther afield to engage in commerce such as the fur trade, they recorded their displeasure as one of the charges against the king in the Declaration of Independence: "He has endeavoured to prevent the population of these States; for that purpose obstructing the Laws for Naturalization of Foreigners; refusing to pass others to encourage their migrations hither . . ."

In nineteenth-century Europe, the spread of industrial capitalism also involved battles over migration control. A plentiful workforce would not only keep industry humming, it also would help owners avoid making concessions to labor unions. But there was a problem. Peasants inclined to *Landflucht* (rural flight) or *Heimatlosigkeit* (uprootedness) were shackled by powerful agrarian interests who maintained a quasi-feudal form of social control over them. "The first objective of the landlord class," in the words of historian Perry Anderson, was "to arrest the mobility of the villager and bind him to the estates." The Chamber of Commerce in Breslau (now called Wroclaw and part of Poland) made an appeal for unfettered labor migration, declaring, "It is not enough that freedom of movement be introduced in one state. It is necessary that in general, every citizen of a German state be free to apply his energy wherever in his opinion he can do so most advantageously, that industry take its workers where it can find them, and that the various regions transfer their labor force or temporary population surplus without hindrance and in accordance with their needs."

In the rapidly urbanizing Ruhr area in the west, owners of mines, factories, railroads, machine shops, and foundries wanted to recruit massive numbers of migrant workers from rural areas in the Prussian east. The business owners appealed to Otto von Bismarck, then president of the Prussian government, who was intent on uniting the German states and creating an empire. Bismarck was sympathetic. A unified Germany, he felt, required the unconstrained promotion of a capitalist, industrial economy. Bismarck not only promulgated uniform business regulations, and common systems of weights, measures, and currency, he also agreed that industrialists needed a ready supply of labor. So, to make sure the population could be redistributed to provide for the demands of a new economy, he relaxed controls on mobility. In 1867 he enacted the Gesetz zur Freizügigkeit (Law on Freedom of Movement), providing that "No citizen of the [North German] Confederation may be denied abode, residency, the pursuit of an occupation, or the acquisition of real estate on the basis of religious confession or because he lacks citizenship in a given state or municipality." Factory owners were able to meet their increasing need for labor, and workers won the right to move where they wanted.

The freedom to travel came as new railroads and sea-crossing iron steamships made moving more efficient and faster, providing supply chains of workers for nation-builders and industrialists across the Atlantic Ocean. One consequence of international mobility on both continents was the emergence of new, nationalist political movements. Newcomers with foreign languages and different cultures were often seen as eroding new national identities and competing for jobs. In both Europe and the United States, immigration became a highly volatile issue as restrictionists campaigned to control the flow.

In 1996, Ron Henley, then a supervisory agent with the Border Patrol, took me for a ride along the border near San Diego to point out its vulnerabilities. At that time the rudimentary fence consisted of steel matting used by the military to build temporary landing strips for aircraft. But it was pretty much a token gesture. Slats in the fence ran horizontally, acting as virtual ladder rungs for climbers. As we bounced along the dirt road in his Bronco SUV, Henley said the barrier presented no challenge to serious border crossers. "I've seen some very old women get over that fence," he said. Its main purpose, he explained, was to prevent what the Border Patrol called "drive-throughs" of vehicles carrying drugs and migrants.

Over the next decade or so, the picture changed drastically. Modern fencing along the border ran for forty-four miles, reinforced by a second layer along ten of those miles. In addition to the fences, there was a gradually widening "no-man's zone," improved stadium lighting, more night vision equipment, a larger force of Border Patrol agents, and embedded motion detectors that, when they work, alert monitors to the presence of people (or animals) crossing through.

In late 2008, the Lightning Fence Company finished installing concertina wire along four and a half miles of fencing between San Diego and Tijuana. The Border Patrol had been very specific about its requirements for the new razor wire. There had to be three coils with three-foot-wide loops of stainless steel Supermaze, designed, according to its manufacturer, with 2.4 inches between the barbs and intended "for high-density maximum security applications."

The militarized border is a stark contrast to the much more tranquil appearance of the boundary during most of its existence. The political line was established in the 1848 Treaty of Guadalupe Hidalgo, which ended the war between the United States and Mexico.

For most of the nineteenth century, with labor in high demand, the new United States had virtually open borders with few legal restrictions. The federal government didn't even regulate migration. It left that job to the states, a policy that remained in place until 1864, when Congress passed the first comprehensive federal immigration law, An Act to Encourage Immigration.

The federal foray into migration management came during a period when a growing economy needed more workers and consumers. It was the beginning of a series of immigration laws and policies in the United States that often have tracked national fortunes and business cycles, opening and closing the doors as the demand for labor increased and dipped. The 1864 law established the U.S. Immigration Bureau, which was supposed to *increase* the supply of migrants to American industry to meet its production needs during the Civil War. (Because the law allowed recruiters to require workers to sign contracts pledging their wages for a year, organized labor and their supporters attacked the legislation for creating a "species of servitude." It was repealed in 1886.)

In the late nineteenth century, America shifted from an agri-cultural to an urban and industrial power. The growth of railroad companies, mines, steel, meatpacking industries, and industrial farming required more and more migrant workers. Railroads—among them Illinois Central, the Burlington, and the Northern Pacific—sent agents to Europe to entice migrants to move. Owners of mines and factories also sent emissaries abroad on recruiting expeditions.

The captains of enterprise found migration to be as great a boon as the expansion of industry: "Were the owners of every gold and silver mine in the world compelled to send to the Treasury at Washington, at their own expense, every ounce of the precious metals produced, the national wealth would not be enhanced one-half as much as it is from the golden stream which flows into the country every year through immigration," wrote the industrialist Andrew Carnegie.

During the 1860s and 1870s—years of post–Civil War Recon-struction, territorial expansion, and rapid industrialization—new settlers were in great demand. So much so that twenty-five of the thirty-eight states provided migrants with economic incentives, includ-ing good deals on property and real estate tax exemptions. Southern states were part of the scramble. They desperately needed cheap labor to replace emancipated slaves.

Between 1880 and 1914, some 22.3 million people arrived in the United States. The peak year for migration was 1907. The spring of that year saw a virtual traffic jam of steamers at Ellis Island. On two days alone—Tuesday, April 16, and Wednesday, April 17—a total of thirteen ships pulled in from Belgium, England, Germany, France, and the West Indies, carrying a total of 16,121 immigrants. Among the vessels was the *Nieuw Amsterdam*, a new, block-long steamship packed above capacity. Built to accommodate 2,200 passengers in steerage, it carried 2,300. The trip across the Atlantic from Rotterdam lasted eleven days. As they entered the main building, prepared for an inspection process that could take up to five hours, the newcomers, speaking a cacophony of languages, including Dutch, German, Polish, Yiddish, Turkish, and Hungarian, made their way three abreast up the steps and into the Registry Room to be questioned and tested. They had arrived at an opportune time, when an expanding economy craved labor. That year, railroad companies, mines, and banks all posted record levels of business.

• • •

In the southwestern states, economies were expanding rapidly, but sparse populations could not fill the rising demands of labor-intensive industries. Pulled by available jobs in the United States and pushed along by Mexican government policies that displaced farmers from communal farms, workers from Mexico came by the thousands to work in fields, mines, fruit orchards, packing plants, and on the railroads.

Loose controls accommodated industry's needs, allowing Mexican laborers to travel freely back and forth across the border. The policy was essentially "easy come, easy go." The U.S. Commissioner-General of Immigration, an agency then under the Department of Commerce and Labor, did not even bother to get an accurate count of the number of incoming Mexicans, estimated at more than fifty thousand a year. Labor contractors and recruiters fanned out throughout the border areas to ensure a steady stream of Mexican workers, disregarding an1885 federal law that specifically prohibited American employers from signing contracts promising jobs to migrants before they arrived in the country.

Unregulated migration served both countries. Mexico had an escape valve for its poorest citizens, who were unemployed and potentially revolutionary. U.S. industries were provided a ready source of cheap labor. Representatives of large industrial enterprises told Congress that they were so dependent on Mexican labor that immigration restrictions would leave them on the verge of bankruptcy.

A 1910 U.S. congressional commission reported that Mexican railroad workers were not only plentiful, they also were cheap, at least compared to "the English-speaking races formerly employed by most of the railroad companies." Railroad companies paid nearly all their Mexican track maintenance workers less than $1.25 a day, compared to the daily rate of $1.50 or more (a 20 percent difference) earned by just about every English, Greek, Irish, and Norwegian employee. The report noted that in addition to their low pay rates, the railroads prized Mexicans for their docility, finding that they were well suited to the hot climate "and regarded as being very tractable; in fact, they are noted for their passive obedience." A Texas cotton grower said, "They are content with whatever you give them. [T]hey're more subservient, if that's the word."

• • •

Mexico wasn't the only source of cheap labor in the West. In the latter part of the nineteenth century, migrants from China poured into the country to work in fields, mines, and on the railroads.

Some fifteen thousand Chinese miners joined the California Gold Rush in the 1850s. Over the next thirty years, nearly 250,000 Chinese migrants, many recruited by U.S. companies, crossed the Pacific. But after the gold boom went bust and an economic depression took hold, many Americans blamed Asian immigrants for the decline. The United States was entering a prolonged period of economic contraction, a downturn that lasted almost as long as the Great Depression. An increasingly virulent restrictionist movement argued that migration laws needed to be adjusted accordingly.

Anti-Chinese hatred was motivated by a combination of unbridled racism and the fear by organized labor that the pool of cheap Chinese workers was depressing wages. The xenophobia started in the West in the 1870s and rippled through national politics.

Mobs attacked Chinese businesses and homes in San Francisco. The California Workingmen's Party adopted the slogan "The Chinese Must Go!" and rallies decrying the "Chinese curse" were held around California. At an 1882 mass meeting in Los Angeles, some three thousand people in attendance passed a resolution blaming Chinese migrants for driving down living standards, declaring that "centuries of abject slavery have endowed the Chinaman with an almost supernatural power of enduring privation low wages and an existence truly devoid of anything that is not embodied in a machine." Newspaper publisher J. J. Ayers condemned "these heathen bloodsuckers," and banker John G. Downey, a former California governor, asserted, "The great founders of the Republic had clearly in view the happiness of a white race." (Downey, an Irish immigrant, would take little comfort in knowing that by 2007, the Southern California city named in his honor was 8 percent Asian and 66 percent Latino.)

With political pressure mounting, in an effort to bring a halt to most legal immigration from China, Congress passed the Asian Exclusion Act of 1882, ending what had been a policy of virtually free access by migrants. It was the first time that federal law had been used to control and limit migration to the United States by nationality.

As a result, the first "illegal immigrants" to the United States were Chinese.

Comparatively little attention was focused on Mexicans. The racial calculations of the political establishment held Asians, and later, eastern and southern Europeans to be "undesirable" but did not include Mexicans. Mexicans were considered inferior to whites, but the U.S. government did not categorize them by race. Definitions became complicated in 1848, when the United States annexed part of Mexico following the Mexican-American War. Since, at the time, only whites were legally able to become naturalized U.S. citizens, conferring automatic citizenship on residents of the newly acquired territory meant that de facto Mexicans would be recognized as "white." Their new standing was not seen as a racial promotion. "Rather," as the historian Mae Ngai has written, "it indicated Mexicans' new status as a conquered population."

The vitriol that spewed forth against migrants who had crossed the Pacific was replicated by denunciations of those who were arriving in increasing numbers from southern and eastern Europe to America's eastern shore. Restrictionists saw newcomers as an unwelcome, untidy flood. Virulent anti-Catholics assailed Irish migrants. Others saw dangers in the arriving Italians, Russians, Ukrainians, Slovaks, Poles, Croatians, Serbs, Slavs, Greeks, and Jews. Conservative political figures and intellectuals were in the forefront of an influential movement advocating greater migration controls, not only because of the extent of the influx but because the newcomers' diversity represented "races most alien to the body of the American people and from the lowest and most illiterate classes among those races," as Congressman (later Senator) Henry Cabot Lodge, a blue-blooded Republican politician from Boston, put it.

Quoting the observations of U.S. consuls general stationed in Europe, Lodge categorized by nationality what for him were the odious qualities of the most undesirable migrants—Austrians ("ultra-socialists and anarchists"), Bohemians ("illiterate and ignorant in the extreme"), Slovaks (known for their "love of whisky"), southern Italians (given to "brigandage"), and Russians (belonging to the "lowest classes").

By 1907, immigrants from southern and eastern Europe outnumbered northern European arrivals by four to one. Congress appointed a commission to study the issue, and in 1911, the Dillingham Commission, named for its chairman, Senator William P. Dillingham, a Republican from Vermont, published a forty-two-volume report on the threats posed by large-scale migration across the Atlantic.

Two commission staff members summarized the commission's conclusions in a 605-page book whose findings were telegraphed in its title: *The Immigration Problem*. Jeremiah W. Jenks and W. Jett Lauck reported that compared to Americans born in the United States, immigrants were more inclined toward insanity. They had failed to assimilate or to learn English, contributed to overcrowding, were unsanitary, unskilled, illiterate, imperiled job safety, displaced workers, and retarded wage increases.

Nativists found support from prominent academics and pseudo-scientists who championed the dubious cause of eugenics, which tried to limit the population of so-called inferior races. One proponent, Madison Grant, chairman of the New York Zoological Society, described the "Nordics" of northern and western Europe who settled America as "a pure race of one of the most gifted and vigorous stocks on earth."

New immigrants from Europe, Grant wrote in 1921, included "a large and increasing number of the weak, the broken and the mentally crippled of all races drawn from the lowest stratum of the Mediterranean basin and the Balkans, together with hordes of the wretched, submerged populations of the Polish Ghettos. Our jails, insane asylums and almshouses are filled with this human flotsam and the whole tone of American life, social, moral and political has been lowered and vulgarized by them."

The pressure for immigration controls was part of a powerful political movement, which crescendoed with three landmark laws. The Immigration Act of 1917 established a literacy test, added a head tax, excluded "idiots," alcoholics, anarchists, and contract laborers, and extended an Asian "barred zone." It was followed by the Immigration Acts of 1921 and 1924 which established a system of national preferences and quotas. Numerical limits were based on the number of people from each country who had been in the United States before 1890. The system, designed to favor migrants from the north and the west of Europe, all but shut the "golden door" of the United States to future "huddled masses" from eastern and southern Europe.

At the southern border, the U.S. government continued its more laissez-faire attitude. In 1917, when America entered World War I, the agriculture industry complained of a labor shortage. Working-age men were either entering the military or going into factories engaged in war production. Growers wanted to import Mexicans but faced restrictions due to the Immigration Act passed that year. They turned to a friend in Washington, Herbert Hoover, then the U.S. food administrator, who was responsible for increasing wartime agricultural production. Joined by representatives of railroad, mining, and industrial interests, the future president successfully persuaded the secretary of labor to exempt Mexicans from the act's restrictions.

Even following the establishment of the Border Patrol in 1924, a hands-off policy toward Mexican migrants persisted. The new agency was poorly staffed and underfunded. Border Patrol agents earned half as much as brick-layers and had to supply their own horses and saddles. The U.S.–Mexico border was, for all practical purposes, an imaginary line. Industries competed for Mexican laborers, since quota laws had made fresh European workers more difficult to obtain. Labor agents from the northern United States went into Texas and recruited Mexican workers, spiriting them out of the state in crowded, canvas-covered trucks.

But with the onset of the Great Depression at the end of the decade, there was little tolerance for migrants. Once again, seeking to manage migration, Herbert Hoover sprang into action. Years earlier, during World War I, he had responded to the needs of agribusiness by pressuring Washington to open the migration valve and allow in more Mexican workers. But that was then. Elected president in 1928, he was grappling with an economic freefall and was faced with breadlines, soup kitchens, and mass unemployment. The Hoover administration resolved to not only stop the flow of migrants from Mexico, but to reverse it. Local officials (particularly from Los Angeles), anxious to relieve swelling welfare rolls, implored Hoover's secretary of labor, William Nuckles Doak, who was responsible for overseeing the Immigration Service, to "get rid of Mexicans," in the words of scholars Francisco E. Balderrama and Raymond Rodríguez. Doak was happy to oblige and undertook a mass deportation program that continued into the administrations of Franklin D. Roosevelt. Immigration agents were ruthless in their raids, chasing down Latinos, ignoring due process, and failing to distinguish between legal and nonlegal residents of the United States. Authorities deported as many as one million people.

They decided "these are the ones that are easier to get rid of," Maria Acosta told me in 2003. She was two and a half years old in 1932 when her father, Alfredo, a legal U.S. resident born in Mexico, was swept up in an immigration raid as he worked with other laborers on a federal public works project near their home in northern California. Her father later told her about the cold efficiency of the immigration agents who arrived at the work site to process her father and the other workers who were about to become deportees.

"They said, 'We decided to send you to Mexico. So, line up and come one by one and get your tickets.'" The agent asked, "'How many are you in the family?' And my father says, 'Five.' He says, 'Here are five tickets.' He says, 'Be ready tomorrow. The bus is going to go by about eight o'clock. Be on the sidewalk. And one suitcase per person. One for you, one for your wife, and one for the three children.'"

The family was bused to Los Angeles and then put on a train to the northern state of Chihuahua, Mexico, where Acosta, who had been born in the United States, lived until she was a teenager.

"My parents couldn't understand why they were kicked out. Just—'They don't want you anymore; there's no room for you.' They were humiliated." Acosta lived in a house without running water or electricity until age fifteen, when she returned to the United States to work as a seamstress in a garment factory.

During the 1940s and 1950s, U.S. immigration policies were fickle and situational—varying according to changing politics and the requirements of businesses. Mexicans were considered alternately dependable and expendable. The Bracero or Mexican Farm Labor Program, begun in 1942 as a series of agreements between the U.S. and Mexican governments, lasted twenty-two years. Even though the program was begun to address World War II labor needs, the vast majority of workers imported under its auspices came after the war ended. The plan did little to deter illegal migration.

If anything, the program served only to increase it. Many farmers preferred to circumvent the agreement. Hiring illegal immigrants freed them of obligations to meet wage requirements and to provide their workers with housing, food, and medical care.

With the end of the Korean War, an economic downturn combined with McCarthy-era anti-immigrant hysteria brought yet another crackdown. In 1954 President Dwight D. Eisenhower's new immigration chief, retired General Joseph "Jumpin' Joe" Swing, launched Operation Wetback. Government personnel rounded up migrants in border communities and deported them by bus, truck, train, and ship, transporting them into the Mexican interior. By the time the deportations ended a few months after they began, the Immigration and Naturalization Service claimed to have forcibly removed 1.1 million Mexicans. Many of them, of course, turned right around and returned.

Over the past six decades, United States immigration policies have been influenced by an assortment of factors: changing economic needs, Cold War politics, civil rights movements, and the mass influx of Mexicans.

The 1952 Immigration Act created a preference for the admission of professionals whose skills were valued and whose services were seen as needed for the Cold War race against the Soviet Union. The precedent-setting law opened the door for the entry of temporary workers and for a visa program still in existence. The law once again linked the Department of Labor to immigration management by allowing the granting of visas unless the department determined that the supply of labor was sufficient. Over several decades, Congress passed laws (in 1976, 1990, 1998, and again in 2000) incrementally increasing the number of employment-based visas.

The rise of the civil rights movement helped usher in the landmark Immigration and Nationality Act of 1965. By finally abolishing the discriminatory system assigning preferences on the basis of national origins, the law was a milestone for racial equality.

"This bill says simply that from this day forth those wishing to immigrate to America shall be admitted on the basis of their skills and their close relationship to those already here," explained President Lyndon B. Johnson at the signing ceremony on Liberty Island, where the Statue of Liberty is located. The 1965 law gave preference to reuniting family members (74 percent of visas) and to skilled migrants (20 percent of visas).

"This bill that we will sign today is not a revolutionary bill. It does not affect the lives of millions," said LBJ. Johnson was repeating the assurances of the bill's proponents, chief among them Robert F. Kennedy and Edward M. Kennedy, who, in response to critics, had predicted that the act would not cause immigration levels to rise nor change appreciably the composition of the migrant population. But they were wrong on both counts. As a result of the act, legal immigration from Asia and Latin America soared, while European migration was hardly affected.

There were three main reasons for the increase in the number of Asians and Latin Americans. First of all, as had been the case in Europe a century before, modernization and industrial change spurred people to move from the countryside to the cities. Immigration was the logical next step. Another factor was the changing U.S. economy. America's manufacturing base was sliding, and demand was growing for workers at both ends of the job skills spectrum—well-trained experts and service employees. Finally, the 1965 law encouraged migration based on family ties, so migrants who moved to the United States were allowed to send for relatives—a process known as chain migration.

The changing U.S. economy also was a lure. In the 1970s, both legal and illegal migration from Mexico increased.

"We're facing a vast army that's carrying out a silent invasion of the United States," declared Immigration and Naturalization Service (INS) commissioner Leonard Chapman in 1978.

The United States had come through a period of high inflation and unemployment. As a result, public opinion surveys showed support for measures to decrease legal migration levels. In Mexico, the government was coping with an economic crisis. As the nation entered an economic recession, officials there devalued the peso. In the White House, members of the National Security Council monitoring the growing crisis tried to anticipate its effect on migration levels and politics.

"[W]e can expect that as things get tougher for poorer Mexicans and the dollar earned abroad buys even more for the family back home, the U.S. labor market will become even more attractive to 'illegals,'" economist Robert M. Hormats wrote to his boss, Brent Scowcroft, President Gerald Ford's national security adviser, in a 1976 memo. "This will result in additional calls to end the displacement of U.S. workers by cracking down on immigration laws," Hormats predicted.

• • •

It's an ironic but obvious fact: even when the economy sours in the United States, Mexicans still move north, driven by the relative differences between the countries. During the first quarter of 2009, emigration from Mexico declined 27 percent over the same period in 2007. Nonetheless, even with the sagging U.S. economy, from April 2008 to the end of March 2009, 636,303 people left Mexico, according to the Mexican government. (Government figures don't record where they moved, but it is a safe bet that most wound up in the United States.) That represented a huge drop compared to previous years, but it pointed to a degree of confidence in the perceived benefits of crossing the border.

Current debates over immigration have their roots in the 1980s. As migration from Mexico increased, the subject became an increasingly pressing political item as well as a hot potato for policymakers, legislators, and lobbyists. Proponents of tighter immigration controls, particularly in the Southwest, were alarmed by an unprecedented influx of migrants and by the massive cultural and demographic changes under way. By 1980 it was clear that the number of Latinos in the United States would soon outnumber blacks.

The four hundred Border Patrol agents were no match for migrants able to cross over from Mexico into the United States practically at will.

"Invited and uninvited, rich and poor—but mostly poor—foreigners are pouring into the U.S. in greater numbers than at any time since the last great surge of European immigrants in the early 1900s," *Time* magazine reported in 1981.

"This country has lost control of its borders, and no country can sustain that kind of position," declared President Ronald Reagan.

With proposals for federal immigration legislation stymied, Reagan decided to address the issue through the budget process, beefing up the staff of the U.S. Border Patrol and supplying the agency with new equipment. In 1985, I looked on as Harold Ezell, the western regional commissioner of the INS, welcomed a crop of newly trained and freshly deployed agents to the San Diego office. Ezell was a showman who relished the opportunity to make a point for a visiting reporter.

"You're doing this for the salvation, in my opinion, of our entire nation," he told the assembled agents, dressed in new khaki green uniforms. "If we don't gain control of these borders within the next five years, the America that we know today is not going to be the America of tomorrow."

Ezell was a strong supporter of the Immigration Reform and Control Act (IRCA), which Reagan signed the following year. But the new regulations did nothing to alter the migration trajectory that the INS commissioner had inelegantly described as a "silent invasion" seven years earlier. If anything, IRCA ended up accelerating the trend. The legislation was a compromise that ended up providing amnesty for some three million previously illegal migrants, far more than the program's backers had anticipated. And that was just for starters. Once new legal residents had become citizens, they became eligible to bring in relatives under the family reunification provision of the 1965 law.

Moreover, the political centerpiece of IRCA proved to be ineffective. Under the law, for the first time in U.S. history, it became a crime to employ an illegal migrant. The idea was to reduce unlawful migration by cutting out the bait: jobs. Proponents had gone along with amnesty figuring that the big stick of employer sanctions would accomplish their long-range goal. As a trade-off, it seemed like a sound plan.

But employers had managed to push through a huge loophole in the law. IRCA made it unlawful to hire a migrant "knowing the alien is an unauthorized alien." The word "knowing" was the key. The law required employers to inspect documents provided by job applicants, but it didn't obligate them to check the authenticity of the paperwork. If employers accepted identity documents on "good faith," as the law provides, they could easily plead ignorance if the paperwork ended up being bogus. IRCA spawned a boon for the counterfeiting industry, which provided legitimate-looking but fraudulent documents to illegal migrant workers. As a result, the law did little if anything to stop migration.

In recent decades, the economy has again played a role in immigration policy and debates. The end of the Cold War and job cuts in the aerospace industry led to a recession in the early 1990s that was felt particularly hard in California. At the same time, a rise in the service economy created a need for low-skilled jobs and acted as a magnet for migrant workers. The combination of continued migration and economic uncertainty made for a volatile political brew. In 1994, anti-migration activists campaigned for a California ballot initiative, Proposition 187. The "Save Our State" measure was designed to eliminate public social services for illegal migrants. Politicians seized on an emotional issue.

"They keep on coming!" an announcer ominously intoned over black-and-white video of Mexicans rushing across the border near San Diego. Latino activists quickly denounced the commercial for Republican governor Pete Wilson of California, then running for reelection, as racist, xenophobic, and fear-mongering. But Wilson's ad tapped into popular sentiment. He won the contest easily, beating his Democratic rival, Kathleen Brown, by 15 percentage points.

However, stepped-up border enforcement was hardly a partisan issue. The buildup of the U.S. Border Patrol, begun by Ronald Reagan, continued on President Bill Clinton's watch. Operation Blockade in El Paso, Texas, was followed by Operation Gatekeeper in San Diego. The Democratic administration's militarization of the border—the fencing, high-intensity floodlights, and intensive patrols—was unprecedented.

Congress's focus on deterrence continued with the Illegal Immigration Reform and Immigrant Responsibility Act of 1996, which further expanded the Border Patrol, a cause President George W. Bush advanced during his administration. In eight years, Bush more than doubled the staff of the Border Patrol, raising the total from about nine thousand to twenty thousand agents. In the last four years of his administration the combined budgets for the main agencies responsible for immigration issues (U.S. Customs and Border Protection, U.S. Immigration and Customs Enforcement, and U.S. Citizenship and Immigration Services—all under the Department of Homeland Security) jumped by 50 percent.

But the effects of border enforcement on the extent of illegal migration were hard to gauge. Even though the Mexican government reported a more than 50 percent decline in the number of migrants leaving during 2008 compared to the previous year, analysts suggested that the economic downturn may have had as much to do with the drop as stepped-up enforcement.

Regardless of the numbers, more vigorous border controls have affected the travel patterns of illegal migrants. For one thing, they have chosen more risky, less guarded routes through the desert and mountains to enter the United States. As a result, more have died making the journey. In addition, the increased difficulties in crossing the border have had the unintended consequence of bottling up migrants who have made it to the United States. Instead of coming and going (a practice called "circular migration"), as migrants often used to do when cross-border travel was easier, many have decided to stay in the United States, fearing that if they leave, they won't be able to return.

In addition to policing at the border, the Bush administration stepped up enforcement of immigration laws inside the country. It increased deportations and prosecutions of illegal migrants wanted for crimes. Cooperation between local law enforcement and federal immigration agencies became routine. Acknowledging "[e]mployment as a primary driving force behind illegal immigration," the Bush administration also substantially increased its enforcement of immigration laws at work sites. The office of Immigration and Customs Enforcement (ICE) made close to seven thousand arrests in 2008, a nearly fourteenfold increase since 2002. The highly publicized raids drew the wrath of migrants' rights groups and lawyers, complaining about heavy-handed tactics. But the work-site enforcement program made a negligible dent in the illegal migrant employment picture. For one thing, of those arrested, only 135 were owners or managerial staff. For another, the number of people arrested amounted to less than 1 percent of the illegal workforce and was about equal to the number of traffic tickets issued by the New Haven, Connecticut, Police Department in the last six months of 2008. If there was any message in ICE's work-site enforcement program, it was that in general employers had little to worry about.

By contrast, the Obama administration embarked on a sterner and more strategic approach to immigration law enforcement. The administration aimed to walk a fine line. One ultimate goal, as the president had defined it, was to bring illegal immigrants "out of the shadows." But, as they pushed off efforts to enact comprehensive immigration reform until the second year, administration officials worked to establish their immigration enforcement bona fides. Within a year of taking office, Janet Napolitano, the U.S. secretary of homeland security, expanded a program to allow law enforcement officials to act as immigration agents, mandated the use of a worker verification system (E-Verify) by employers with federal contracts, and stepped up a program to audit the hiring records of businesses "to determine compliance with employment eligibility verification laws."

"ICE [Immigration and Customs Enforcement] is focused on finding and penalizing employers who believe they can unfairly get ahead by cultivating illegal workplaces," declared John Morton, the head of the investigative arm of the Department of Homeland Security. "We are increasing criminal and civil enforcement of immigration-related employment laws and imposing smart, tough employer sanctions to even the playing field for employers who play by the rules."

The Obama administration also continued the buildup of border fortifications, even as questions persisted about their cost and effectiveness. In September 2009, the Government Accountability Office issued two in a continuing series of reports highlighting problems in the development of the Secure Border Initiative (SBI) program. The system, combining radars, sensors, cameras, and 661 miles of fencing, was seven years behind schedule and plagued by technical snafus as well as cost overruns. With much of the fencing (303 miles) designed only to prevent vehicles from crossing, the GAO said the government had not established a method to evaluate the system's effectiveness. Investigators found also that in three years, "there had been 3,363 breaches in the fence, with each breach costing an average of $1,300 to repair."

At the time of the review, the SBI program had cost $3.7 billion in four years. It had been criticized by the left for being a waste of money and inhumane and by environmental groups for endangering wildlife habitat. Critics on the right complained that it didn't go far *enough*. Napolitano decided to split the difference—to proceed with existing plans and to defer any decision about whether to expand the project.

As the administration's top official responsible for immigration law enforcement, if Janet Napolitano had any doubts about a border fence, she did not let it show. "The Border Patrol has increased its forces to more than twenty thousand officers, and DHS has built more than six hundred miles of border fencing," she boasted during a November 2009 speech. "Both of these milestones demonstrate that we have gotten Congress's message." In truth, she was actually taking credit for continuing the policies of President George W. Bush.

Before landing the job that made her responsible for the border fence, she famously questioned its effectiveness in the face of the jobs magnet. "Show me a fifty-foot fence, and I'll show you a fifty-one-foot ladder," she repeated as Arizona governor, when the fence project got under way.

By promising to get tougher on recalcitrant employers of illegal immigrants, Napolitano demonstrated a degree of consistency, but only up to a point. Her priorities were reflected in her funding. The Department of Homeland Security's 2010 fiscal year budget allocated more than $779 million to "Border Security Fencing, Infrastructure, and Technology," compared to $6 million allotted to the "Worksite Enforcement" program.

If the allocation of resources is any indication, most businesses using illegal immigrants have little to fear. For all intents and purposes, an employer-friendly status quo continues, and, in the end, for all the words, money, and passion, devoted to migration control, for all the expenditures on border patrol agents, high-tech security, watchtowers, sensors, infrared cameras, patrol aircrafts, raids, roundups, prisons, deportations, and concertina wire, the fact remains that in 2008, the estimated number of illegal immigrants in the American workforce (about 8.3 million) equaled the entire population of New York City. (To be fair, not everyone in the country illegally sneaked across the border. Between a third and half of illegal migrants are believed to have entered on valid temporary visas but neglected to leave.)

Nonetheless, no matter how they arrived, the vast majority of illegal immigrants are here to stay. There is no political will, let alone a humane or practical way, to deport them. The upshot is a massive underground population servicing a large part of America's labor needs.

The absence of a lucid immigration policy may seem dysfunctional. Quite the contrary. By default, as the numbers indicate, employers of illegal immigrants have won the day. And as all sides flail around, arguing over a more coherent national policy, a main priority of the corporate community is to ensure that the gates are kept open or at least ajar.

CHAPTER 10

Politics, Influence, and Alliances

The 2008 May Day demonstration in Los Angeles, timed to coincide with other pro-migrant rallies around the country, was a noisy affair. South Broadway, which cuts through downtown L.A., is a bustling place anyway. The street is a popular shopping area for working-class Latino migrants. Ranchero music blasting from storefront shops gives it the feel of a commercial neighborhood in Latin America. As May Day demonstrators moved up Broadway, heading toward a gathering spot at a blocked-off intersection, conga drums and bullhorns competed with the racket of a low-flying police helicopter. Many marchers walked behind a slow-moving sound truck carrying the immensely popular, Grammy award-wining *norteño* band Los Tigres del Norte. Standing on the flatbed, the musicians performed selections from their politically charged repertoire about the migrant experience. A new release, "*El Muro*" ("The Wall"), urged the president to build bridges instead of fences.

Vendors yelling "One dollar! One dollar! One dollar!" hawked small plastic flags of Mexico, the United States, and El Salvador. Others sold T-shirts stenciled with the image of Che Guevara. Pushcarts featured grilled hot dogs, shaved ice, and *deliciosos helados* (delicious ice cream).

Along the route, banners and signs read "No More Separating Families," "Stop the Raids," "Legalize LA!," "Today We March. Tomorrow We Vote." One man carried a hand-lettered poster that said "Army vet and son of illegal immigrants." The rally had a somber undercurrent. The economy was fading, and attendance was lower than organizers had expected because people had been reluctant to leave work. Business at money transfer operations along the route was down. "It's less people and less money this year," a manager told me.

One man, a thirty-four-year-old construction worker, said he was considering returning home to Mexico with his wife, a flower seller. He said if he got work twice a week, he was lucky. "Sometimes there's nothing," he lamented.

One by one, speakers at the microphones denounced high-profile immigration raids and deportations, calling instead for a legalization program. The lineup at the podium included politicians, labor activists, and migrant rights advocates. But one major supporter of the cause was an organization not represented at the dais or in the streets, one generally not given to participation in boisterous political demonstrations, particularly not at International Workers' Day events: the Los Angeles Area Chamber of Commerce.

Nonetheless, the voice of the L.A. business community, with a membership of fifteen hundred companies, did make a quiet gesture of solidarity timed to coincide with May Day. Although he was not in attendance to hear cheers from the ten thousand demonstrators in the downtown streets, chamber president Garry Toebben picked up their mantle by calling on the federal government to suspend its immigration raids on businesses.

Noting that the California "economy is largely dependent on immigrant labor and has been for more than a century," Toebben told a reporter, "the status quo is no longer good enough. . . . As a business community, we call on our California [congressional] delegation to take the lead to pursue immigration reform."

The pursuit of business-friendly immigration policies has been a priority for companies that have come to rely on migrant workforces. Although the language is often couched according to circumstances and political currents, the overriding objectives of employers have been consistent. The immigration laws they favor would have the effect of providing a cheap, disposable, compliant labor force by authorizing additional work visas. They would like the current illegal workforce legalized, and, beyond gathering paperwork and consulting computer records, employers do not want to be held responsible or penalized for hiring immigrant workers with the wrong identification documents.

Advocates for business groups pushing at both the federal and state levels to ease immigration restrictions have often formed alliances with migrants' rights organizations, sometimes joining with them to pursue lawsuits that challenge attempts to inhibit the use of migrant labor.

The convergence by business interests and civil rights groups involved in immigration politics has made for strange bedfellow coalitions. The public side of the pro-immigration debate is more likely to feature a representative of the National Council of La Raza than of the Chamber of Commerce. Nonetheless, marriages of convenience have been forged between organizations that under different circumstances are generally on opposite sides.

One organization, the National Immigration Forum, has established itself as the go-to group for journalists wanting the liberal take on immigration issues. Its representatives, such as the executive director Ali Noorani, the son of Pakistani immigrants, speak out at rallies and on TV talk shows. But behind the scenes, the forum's less visible leaders have expressed more concern for the value of migrant workers than for their rights. In 2009, its board, claiming to "collectively reflect the broad pro-immigrant community," included the chairman John Gay, at the time the chief lobbyist for the National Restaurant Association, and Randel Johnson, a vice president of the U.S. Chamber of Commerce.

In 2007, the U.S. Department of Homeland Security announced plans to implement a "no match" rule to prosecute employers for hiring workers who presented Social Security numbers that don't match those on file with the Social Security Administration. Civil rights groups such as the National Council of La Raza and the AFL-CIO predictably and immediately cried foul. Their lawsuits were backed up by the U.S. Chamber of Commerce, the American Nursery and Landscape Association, and the National Roofing Contractors Association—the latter groups all representing employers normally at odds with unions.

The odd political groupings also have played out in immigration disputes at the local level. For instance, after Hazleton, Pennsylvania, enacted its anti-illegal immigrant ordinance, such usual suspects as the American Civil Liberties Union and various Latino organizations quickly mounted court challenges. Less noticed were the business groups that joined them. High-powered lawyers filed amicus curiae (friend of the court) briefs on behalf of the U.S. Chamber of Commerce as well as chambers representing the states of Arizona, Colorado, Florida, Illinois, Indiana, Kansas, Kentucky, Missouri, New Jersey, North Carolina, Oklahoma, Tennessee, and West Virginia.

The business community's political message about the need for migrant workers has remained consistent, with its arguments for easy access and looser regulations tailored to fit the occasion. During periods of prosperity, the case made by business leaders and their allies is that bringing in or legalizing migrant workers helps the economy grow and gives the nation an edge in a globally competitive environment. When downturns or threats emerge, they contend that migrants will assist in getting the economy back on track. To the business community, migrants are like aspirin, magic potions, or keys to a successful marriage—to be used in sickness and in health.

In 2006, when the United States was preoccupied with terrorist threats, the Washington, D.C.–based American Immigration Law Foundation (AILA), funded in part by business groups, argued, "Legalizing undocumented workers, coupled with a large guest worker program, is . . . in the interest of our national security and constitutes a step that would aid our country in its efforts to combat terrorism."

Three years later, the Immigration Policy Center (IPC), the AILA's research arm, reported that a legalization program was the perfect remedy for a new ailment: "Legalizing Undocumented Immigrants a Key to U.S. Economic Recovery" read the subtitle of a March 2009 IPC report. "Legalizing undocumented workers would improve wages and working conditions for all workers and increase tax revenues for cash-strapped federal, state, and local governments."

A business-backed national lobbying group, ImmigrationWorks USA, delivered the same message in a February 2009 "Action Alert" issued to members. "Even in a recession, even with unemployment rising, many employers still need foreign workers to keep our businesses open and keep Americans employed," it argued.

With the economy in the doldrums, ImmigrationWorks USA prepped its members with a list of "Talking Points for Congressional Visits." Even as the American jobless rate rose, the pitch relied on an old business bromide about worker shortages.

"I'm an employer in your district," read the suggested script. "My company [makes, does, provides, equips—fill in the details of what you do], and I'm here to talk to you about immigration. Even now, even in a recession, I have trouble finding workers to do [fill in with concrete details about your business]."

ImmigrationWorks USA was founded in 2008 by conservative activist Tamar Jacoby, who has long sparred with fellow conservative Republicans over immigration issues. She advocates a compromise policy that combines border security, more visas for migrant workers, and a form of legalization or amnesty for workers who are in the United States illegally.

The organization has a key principle: "At a time of labor shortages, American employers should not face a choice between growing their businesses and obeying the law."

For business owners in labor-intensive industries, lobbying for worker mobility has a long history, dating back to the times of the industrial revolution in Europe when business owners argued that restrictions on peasants be lifted so that laborers could move to cities to take factory jobs. Since then, businesses have persistently complained about labor shortages, suggesting they could be resolved if only immigration regulations were eased. Labor organizations, of course, have questioned the motives of migration-friendly businesses, pointing out that an excess of willing workers gives employers the upper hand when it comes to determining wages and working conditions. If one person won't accept the terms of a job, someone who is needier might. Industry pleas for the ability to import foreign workers because of labor shortages have continued in both good times and bad. Often the loudest voices have come from agriculture. Where borders have prevented workers from getting to the jobs, time and again employers and their advocates have fought for impediments to be removed or boundaries erased. Take the case of Germany's industrial revolution some 140 years ago.

In 1917, with the approach of the summer harvest season, the *Los Angeles Times* lamented that as the national government was busy furnishing "men, money and munitions" for World War I, California ranchers were figuring out how to cope with "a shortage of many thousands of men" to work in the fields. But the *Times* also reported that the farmers had brought the "acute labor shortage" on themselves.

"One of the anomalies of the situation is that there are thousands of men not now at work," the paper found. Quoting investigators from the State Council of Defense, a disaster preparedness organization, the *Times* said, "One of the large factors in keeping farm labor away from California has been that some of the farmers have been in the habit of treating their help more like peons than self-respecting American citizens." Officials suggested that improved working conditions would attract more workers. The notoriously antilabor newspaper had another idea. "One of the causes of the labor shortage," it later editorialized, is that "there has been a cessation of arrivals of settlers from foreign countries. . . . The *Times* has hopes that the shortage in farm labor may be supplied by Chinese, when Congress in its wisdom shall repeal or suspend for a period the operation of the exclusion law."

American industrialists voiced similar complaints about labor shortages in their factories and offered corresponding solutions. In the summer of 1917, Elbert H. Gary, whose namesake Indiana city was the headquarters for United States Steel Corporation, the company he founded, traveled to Chicago to present his own plan to alleviate the problem. Addressing the Commercial Club, a business group, Gary, then the chairman of U.S. Steel, declared that the United States should import workers from Puerto Rico and the Virgin Islands as well as "from Oriental countries."

The drumbeat from the "employing class" about worker shortages prompted the American Federation of Labor to create its Committee on Alleged Shortage of Labor to investigate the issue.

In the fall of 1917, the committee issued its report. Not surprisingly, it found no lack of available workers "with the exception of a few classifications brought into existence through war conditions." To the contrary, union representatives around the country reported unemployment of skilled workers, "situation wanted" ads, and a high turnover of laborers. The AFL said farmers had experienced no problems harvesting crops and reported that many employers were having difficulty finding workers because they were not providing decent housing. The federation concluded that Americanized immigrants had become less willing to endure harsh working conditions and low pay and that the "employing class is awake to the fact . . . [that] the teachings of trade-unionism are spreading." The result has been "the shifting of the common labor supply from economic slaves to relatively free men."

A subsequent union report on the labor shortage quoted an anonymous government official: "My experience," he wrote, "has taught me that the average large employer of labor figures that in order that wages may be maintained to the point of his satisfaction, there should be two workers for every job."

Nearly a century later, American business owners seemed to be channeling the old claims of their grandparents' generation. In 2006 and 2007, as the U.S. Congress tackled the subject of immigration law reform, a spate of news stories featured dire warnings from farmers complaining about the difficulty of finding workers and warning that fruit would rot and fields would lie fallow. Reporters unquestioningly broadcast their pronouncements.

"If the migrants don't show up for the next harvest, Nick says he'll have to destroy entire orchards that were planted more than a century ago," reported ABC News correspondent John Quiñones after interviewing a pear grower in Lake County, in northern California. "Most of his crop, almost two million pounds, lies on the ground, rotting away. Thanks to increased security along the Mexican border, thousands of migrant workers who harvest the nation's fruits and vegetables never showed up to work."

Across the country, an apple farmer in upstate New York had the same lament, "We need to import this labor to pick crops or we're going to be importing our crops," John Teeple, told a newspaper reporter.

The flurry of apocalyptic-sounding news reports prompted a sober analysis of the claims by the migration expert Philip L. Martin, a professor of agricultural economics at the University of California, Davis. Examining the pear industry, Martin found not only that the business was in decline anyway, but also that the Lake County pear harvest actually increased in 2006 over the previous year. "These reports of farm labor shortages are not accompanied by data that would buttress the anecdotes, like lower production of fruits and vegetables or a rise in farm wages as growers scrambled for the fewer workers available," Martin pointed out.

"Economists evaluating claims of labor shortages look not to what employers *say*, but to what they *do*," he wrote, concluding there was no evidence of a worker scarcity. "Fruit and vegetable production is rising, the average earnings of farm workers are not going up extraordinarily fast, and consumers are not feeling a pinch—the cost of fresh fruits and vegetables has averaged about $1 a day for most households over the past decade."

Farmers were not the only employer group to invoke a labor shortage as a reason for wanting looser immigration laws. Executives in healthcare, engineering, and computer businesses were also seeking to import workers. But even in 2007, with low unemployment and an economy that seemed to be going great guns, it was hard to make the case for an actual shortage of workers. As former Merrill Lynch economist David Rosenberg told *Business Week*, "While it makes for nice cocktail conversation, the data aren't saying there is an acute labor shortage in this country." In a market economy, he explained, if you want more of something, you can pay more and have it.

In other words, just as in the early twentieth century, modern-day complaints by employers about a scarcity of workers are more likely to mean either that there's a shortage of *cheap* labor or that employees are simply unwilling to take jobs with unacceptable wages.

The common wisdom that Americans won't do certain jobs falls apart under the right circumstances. In late 2008 and early 2009, as unemployment soared, Colorado farmers, used to hiring migrant workers, found that increasing numbers of American residents and citizens were willing to take jobs in the fields. "A lot of the American workers are now applying for farm jobs that maybe they may not have applied for in the past," Olga Ruiz, an official with the Colorado Department of Labor and Employment, told a Denver television reporter. And, by the end of 2009, there were reports of U.S. citizens standing on street corners and outside home improvement stores soliciting day-labor jobs more commonly done by illegal migrants.

The list of business groups advocating looser immigration laws and regulations represents a *Who's Who* of corporate movers and shakers. At the top, in terms of reach, is the U.S. Chamber of

Commerce, the world's largest business federation, whose chief pro-immigration/probusiness argument, through thick and thin, has been, "We need the continued contributions of these immigrants to grow and remain competitive."

In addition to seeking changes in federal immigration laws, the chamber has filed lawsuits challenging state and local efforts to crack down on illegal migrants, spoken out against "ill-advised enforcement-only bills," opposed measures to verify the legal status of job applicants, and lobbied to raise the caps on work visas so that American companies could import more foreign employees. The chamber also has lent support to two major industry groups, Compete America and the Essential Worker Immigration Coalition (EWIC).

The focus of EWIC (headquartered at the chamber's own offices in Washington, D.C.) is "lesser skilled and unskilled" labor. Cofounded by John Gay, formerly a lobbyist with the National Restaurant Association, EWIC's membership roster includes trade organizations representing meatpackers, restaurants, hotels, builders, agribusiness, outdoor amusement parks, flower growers, and home care agencies. The organization's mission is to support "policies that facilitate the employment of essential workers" through programs that bring in "guest" workers and allow "hardworking, tax-paying undocumented workers to earn legal status." EWIC, along with other business groups, law firms, and multinational companies, has provided funding to the American Immigration Law Foundation, the advocacy group referred to earlier, which proposed that legalizing illegal immigrants would both combat terrorism and provide the "Key to U.S. Economic Recovery."

Compete America represents companies in need of workers at the other end of the skills spectrum. In pursuit of its cause that "U.S. employers must have timely access to highly educated foreign nationals and have the ability to keep that talent in their workforce permanently when economically beneficial," the organization's priority has been to boost the number of highly skilled visas issued under the H-1B program. Its members are high-tech and computer companies ranging from Google, Inc., Microsoft, Oracle, QUALCOMM, Inc., and Hewlett-Packard to manufacturers including Motorola, Inc., the National Association of Manufacturers, the

Semiconductor Industry Association, Texas Instruments, Boeing, and Coca-Cola.

At a 2007 House subcommittee hearing, Laszlo Bock, Google's vice president of people operations, who came as a child with his parents from Communist Romania, made the case for accepting more skilled migrant workers into the American workforce. Choking up over the privilege of speaking before a congressional committee, and with his refugee mother in the audience, Bock explained that 8 percent of Google's employees were in the United States on H-1B visas. "We believe that it is in the best interest of the United States to welcome into our workforce talented individuals who happen to have been born elsewhere, rather than send them back to their countries of origin," Bock told the panel. "Hiring and retaining the most talented employees—regardless of national origin—is essential to the United States' ability to compete globally."

During the Bush administration, the push for what's come to be known as "comprehensive immigration reform" (or what those involved in the debate refer to as "CIR") was expensive and sustained. The Center for Responsive Politics listed some 450 organizations and companies that lobbied for immigration issues in 2007 alone. They spent millions of dollars and represented a broad spectrum of interests. Exactly how much was spent and on what is difficult to tell because reporting requirements allow room for substantial fudging of specific figures and activities. A handful of organizations, such as the Federation for American Immigration Reform (FAIR) and NumbersUSA, argued for more restrictive policies, but the vast majority of lobbyists represented companies, trade organizations, and interest groups pushing for more permissive legislation to allow for greater importation or for the legalization of migrant workers.

Companies lobbying for looser immigration rules spanned the corporate spectrum and included hotel and restaurant chains such as McDonald's and Marriott, farm bureaus and dairy associations from around the country, and meatpackers such as Tyson Foods. Financial service companies, including Citigroup, Ernst & Young, Lehman Brothers, and Goldman Sachs, urged Congress to allow them to bring in more foreign workers, as did construction firms and landscapers, manufacturers, and hospitals.

Universities and colleges lobbied to allow more foreign students into the country under the DREAM (Development, Relief, and Education for Alien Minors) Act, which would have provided immigrant children in the country unlawfully the opportunity to become residents. Many immigrant advocates argued for passage of the DREAM Act on humanitarian grounds, showing, for example, how accomplished youngsters brought to America as infants would suffer if they were deported. The College Board, a group of fifty-six hundred colleges and universities, agreed with that assessment. Skipping over the obvious self-interest in gaining more tuition-paying customers, it made another fiscal argument, concluding, "In strictly economic terms, the contributions that DREAM Act students would make over their lifetimes would dwarf the small additional investment in their education beyond high school, and the intangible benefits of legalizing and educating these students would be significant."

To business-minded advocates of immigration reform, the economic justifications for admitting migrants are ample, whether they be illegal immigrant students, pear pickers, bricklayers, or computer programmers. To those categories, add another one: fashion models. Under current law, foreign models wishing to work temporarily in the United States must compete against computer experts and accountants for a limited number of H-1B visas. Unfair? Definitely, according to a coalition of modeling agencies, which in March 2006 formed the Fashion Model Fairness Project and hired the Washington, D.C., lobbyist Bruce A. Morrison to represent them. Morrrison, a former Democratic congressman who helped write immigration policy, was called on to push for a proposed new visa category for models. His argument: the economy, stupid.

"When a model who is selected by someone who is doing a production is outside the country and is not in America, and needs to come into the country, if they can't get here, it's American workers who get hurt," Morrison told an interviewer. "Because the production then moves out of the country, and all the jobs that are associated with the production that would otherwise be American jobs turn into foreign jobs in places like Milan and Buenos Aires."

Besides working on behalf of modeling agencies, Morrison represents the American Hospital Association (AHA), which represents some five thousand hospitals and health care systems and which has hired Morrison to lobby for visas to allow trained nurses into the country. Experts say there are about 135,000 unfilled positions for registered nurses across the United States. The AHA wants the federal government to invest more money in nurses' training to solve the long-range problem, but for the short term, it has supported bills authorizing the issuance of thousands of temporary work visas for foreign nurses—up to twenty thousand a year in one bill promoted by Morrison, the Emergency Nursing Supply Relief Act, and up to fifty thousand in another, the Nursing Relief Act of 2009.

"They [the AHA] have no bias in favor of foreign trained nurses," Morrison told me. "If anything they have a bias in favor of domestic nurses. Most of all, my clients want there to be more nurses in order to fill slots that are going unfilled all over the country."

"Although significant nurse recruitment initiatives have been adopted," a Texas hospital executive told a congressional committee, "they cannot overcome a shortage of this magnitude. . . . When local solutions fail to address the workforce challenges, hospitals must be able to have the option to recruit qualified foreign nurses to provide care to our patients."

Nurses' unions such as the American Nurses Association have said the industry's reliance on foreign nurses avoids the real problem, maintaining that instead of looking overseas for workers, by improving pay and working conditions, hospitals could find employees domestically. Investments in training programs also would lure more people into nursing jobs.

President Obama has also expressed skepticism about a need for foreign nurses. "The notion that we would have to import nurses makes absolutely no sense," he told a health care forum.

"For people who get fired up about the immigration debate and yet don't notice that we could be training nurses right here in the United States—and there are a lot of people who would love to be in that helping profession and yet we just aren't providing the resources to get them trained—that's something that we've got to fix. That should be a no-brainer."

Similarly, U.S. computer programmers and engineers have opposed efforts by the high-technology industry to open more doors for foreign high-tech workers. They have tried to convince successive U.S. administrations to curb the numbers of H-1B visa holders, but with little success. Their cause has been championed by two veteran senators, Charles Grassley, a Republican from Iowa, and Democrat Richard Durbin of Illinois. In 2007, the two tried unsuccessfully to require employers to make a "good-faith effort" to require employers to hire American workers over H-1B visa holders.

In 2009, with the recession bearing down, Grassley upped the verbal wattage, describing abusers of the high-tech visa program as "H-1B pimps." Teaming with Vermont's socialist senator Bernie Sanders, the Iowa Republican authored a measure, the Employ American Workers Act, to ban the use of H-1B workers by banks receiving bailout money under the Troubled Asset Relief Program (TARP).

Probusiness commentators swung back, declaring the proposals anticompetitive.

"America must compete in a global economy," editorialized the *Wall Street Journal*. "And if U.S. companies can't hire these skilled workers—many of whom graduate from U.S. universities, by the way— you can bet foreign competitors will."

Forbes writer Megha Bahree sounded the same theme in a commentary headlined "Chuck Grassley Hurts America." She wrote, "By sending non-U.S.-born employees packing, the government is ensuring the growth that does happen will be in Beijing and Bangalore."

By the time President Obama signed the economic stimulus legislation on February 17, 2009, the Grassley-Sanders language had been softened from an outright ban on using H-1B visa holders to a condition that required bailed-out banks to take "good-faith steps to recruit U.S. workers . . . using industry-wide standards and offering compensation that is at least as great as those offered to the H-1B nonimmigrant."

The compromise did little to stifle outrage from the promigration business community. One prominent immigration attorney from a global law firm that describes itself as "the leading provider of corporate immigration services and solutions" predicted the provision would make it "more difficult for American banks" and would lead financial institutions that obtained TARP funding to discontinue hiring workers with H-1B visas.

"You are giving them a lot of new hoops to jump through that competitors, both in the U.S. and abroad, don't have to face," Austin T. Fragomen Jr., the head of Fragomen, Del Rey, Bernsen & Loewy, told the *American Banker*. "Global banks need to have a global work-force," he said. "The idea of hiring just American workers is shortsighted. If you hire a percentage of foreign nationals, then you have a stable of people developing with the banks that can then return to their home country and have an impact on recruiting overseas."

Microsoft Corporation, which has been a heavy user of the H-1B program, acknowledged that the recession had led to a reduced need for foreign computer experts, but made it clear that Microsoft would yield no ground in any battles over visa restrictions or limits: "Given the economic downturn, we are filing substantially fewer H-1B appli-cations than we filed last year," wrote the company general counsel Brad Smith in April 2009 on a Microsoft blog.

"[To] succeed and continue adding jobs in the highly competitive global technology business, Microsoft and other U.S. companies must be able to hire top talent wherever it is located," he added. "The number of H-1B visas remains very limited. . . . Because of these lim-its, many very valuable employees may not be selected for H-1Bs this year. For many, this means that they will have to leave—taking their skills, innovation, inspiration, and valuable economic contributions with them, at a time when America needs them the most."

When it comes to economic interests and the politics of immigration, the story has been pretty consistent, with one exception: organized labor. For much of its history, the goals of organizers—to safeguard worker rights and protect wages—put American labor in the antimigrant camp. But changing demographics and diminishing union member-ships spurred labor leaders to adjust their outlook. Their shifted stance has broadly aligned labor with promigration business and civil rights groups, albeit with different and sometimes conflicting emphases.

For more than a century, up until the late 1980s, the American labor movement was at the forefront of efforts to banish or restrict migration. Labor leaders led violent anti-Chinese mobs in the late nineteenth century, and in the twentieth successfully lobbied for a literacy test.

Union organizers showed little regard or concern for migrant farm workers, whom they saw as undercutting their own organizing efforts. In 1951 the National Farm Labor Union charged that "California agriculture is being flooded with thousands upon thousands of Mexican illegals." It recommended that AFL unions police their ranks to eliminate illegal migrants.

In the early 1970s, the United Farm Workers union (UFW), led by César Chávez, ran a "wet line" at the Arizona border to discourage Mexicans from coming across to work in the fields as strikebreakers. Law enforcement officials investigated UFW members whom they suspected of intimidating Mexican migrants and setting fire to their cars.

In 1979, Chávez complained that the Immigration and Naturalization Service (INS) wasn't doing enough to deport migrant laborers working during a UFW lettuce strike. He called enforcement efforts a "farce." In response, Leonard Castillo, commissioner of the INS, reportedly replied, "This is one of those cases where the poor are demanding the deportation of the destitute."

During the 1980s, as union membership declined and migration increased, labor's attitudes toward migrants changed appreciably. The "Justice for Janitors" campaign, begun in 1985, became a civil rights issue as sympathizers and religious leaders conducted sit-ins and demonstrations.

By 1999, with labor union membership at its lowest point in fifty years, at a meeting of the AFL-CIO convention in Los Angeles, proimmigrant organizers in unions representing janitors, garment workers, and employees of restaurants and hotels argued for a change in policy. Four months later, the leadership declared, "The AFL-CIO proudly stands on the side of immigrant workers." In a turnaround that union brothers and sisters of a century earlier, and even César Chávez, could hardly have imagined, labor went on record (in both English and Spanish) to support amnesty for illegal migrants and a lifting of employer sanction laws.

In April 2009, the labor federation took yet another step away from its historical opposition to temporary worker programs. Joining with the union coalition "Change to Win," labor leaders adopted the position that temporary worker programs should be improved, not expanded, and should be limited to temporary or seasonal rather than permanent jobs.

"The labor movement is not opposed to temporary workers coming in the future," union leader Eliseo Medina told a Senate committee. "It's a question of how many, how do they get here, and what rights they have when they get here."

Chávez's own United Farm Workers union also had undergone a transformation. In 2000, seven years after Chávez's death, his successor and son-in-law Arturo S. Rodriguez, himself a farm worker rights activist, began quiet negotiations with growers on proposed changes to farm labor and immigration laws. At the same time, officials from the administrations of the U.S. and Mexican presidents, George W. Bush and Vicente Fox, were conducting talks about an immigration deal. (Those plans were derailed by the September 2001 terrorist attacks, which pushed the United States to harden border controls rather than ease them.)

By 2003, advocates for growers and farm workers had hammered out a compromise that eventually resulted in legislation, the Agricultural Job Opportunity, Benefits, and Security Act (AgJOBS for short), introduced by Democrats—U.S. senator Edward M. Kennedy and Rep-resentative Howard Berman—and Republicans—Senator Larry Craig and Representative Chris Cannon. AgJOBS provided for a program of legalization for existing employees and a temporary worker scheme, one that provided that labor rights would be monitored by the U.S. Department of Labor.

"I think we both realize that neither one of us would achieve what we'd want to happen unless we came together and sat down and worked out something that made sense for all the parties," Rodriguez told me as we sat outside his office, a few steps from the burial place of César Chávez at the UFW compound in central California. He laughed when I asked him if, given the stormy history of the UFW's relationship with growers, he ever thought he'd be sitting down with adversaries trying to work on legislation.

"We're in a new millennium," he said. "We want to ensure that workers are given the opportunity to improve their standard of living, however that happens."

Farm labor unions have made such a U-turn that they are actively helping growers recruit temporary migrant workers from abroad.

The Ohio-based Farm Labor Organizing Committee (FLOC) maintains an office two blocks from the U.S. consulate in Monterrey.

A steady stream of United States–bound workers recruited by FLOC comes into the two-story building to be briefed by the union's Mexican staff members about the rights of migrant farmhands working in the United States. The union represents some seven thousand migrant workers as part of a collective bargaining agreement with a growers' association in North Carolina. The seasonal workers enter the United States under the H-2A temporary farm worker program. The union arranges for their transportation and placement, and then monitors their housing and working conditions once they start on the job.

The United Farm Workers has a similar program to recruit temporary workers from Mexico and Thailand to U.S. farms. The migrants work under union contracts.

"The trick is that first of all we never displace workers in this country that want to work in agriculture or any other particular industry," the UFW's Rodriguez explained. "Secondly, if they are brought in, that they're brought in under a humane situation and treated with the respect and dignity they deserve, like anyone else. And if we can maintain that kind of philosophy and ensure that that happens, then I think we've done our job."

One goal of the UFW recruitment program, said Rodriguez, is to promote the survival of the U.S. farm industry. "We want to ensure that agriculture continues in the United States. It would be a sad day for consumers to become dependent on foreign agricultural products in this country. And unfortunately, that's the direction we're moving."

Growers also are worried about the threat of foreign competition. But they have additional concerns about immigration proposals and policies. If a new amnesty program were to be implemented, workers provided with legal status would be more likely to exercise the freedom to seek better-paying jobs off the farms. At the same time, increased border security has the effect of cutting off the flow of migrant labor.

"As the border tightens," explained Joel Nelsen, president of California Citrus Mutual, a citrus producers' trade association, "it puts us in a major quandary." The solution, said Nelsen, is to permit farm workers to go back and forth across the border according to the seasonal needs of industry.

"The bottom line is we've got to figure out how to allow people that want to work in our industry into this country and send them back home, because that's where the majority of them want to go, back home," he said.

The AgJOBS bill pushed by the nascent alliance between worker advocates and agribusiness was just one of a number of proposed federal immigration laws that sputtered and eventually died between 2003 and 2007.

The Senate debated four grandly named immigration packages (the Secure America and Orderly Immigration Act of 2005, the Comprehensive Enforcement and Immigration Reform Act of 2005, the Comprehensive Immigration Reform Act of 2006, followed by the Secure Borders, Economic Opportunity, and Immigration Reform Act of 2007). The last one was a compromise for everyone. The proposal was championed by both President Bush and leading Senate Democrats. It promised to increase border security, crack down on companies that employ illegal immigrants, establish a more robust temporary worker program, and offer legal status to most illegal immigrants. It was that last provision—labeled "amnesty" by its critics and euphemistically soft-pedaled by others as "a path to citizenship"—that doomed the bill. Egged on by the conservative blogosphere as well as by TV and radio talk show hosts, opponents deluged politicians' inboxes, receptionists, and phone answering machines with hate mail and angry messages.

"The assault on lawmakers in Washington was relentless," reported the New York Times. "Technologically enhanced grass-roots activism is what turned this around, people empowered by the Internet and talk radio," Colin A. Hanna, president of Let Freedom Ring, a conservative group that sponsors the Web site WENEEDAFENCE.com, told the paper.

In 2008, with the presidential campaigns consuming the attention of serious politicos, any hope for changes in immigration policy rested with a new administration. Both major candidates, Senators Barack Obama and John McCain, advocated a combination of border toughness, temporary worker programs, and an avenue to legal residency for illegal migrants.

By the summer of 2009, it was clear that both the proposals and the prospects for immigration reform were a lesson in continuity. Once again, legislators pressed for AgJOBS, pressing a familiar theme, labor shortages.

"With an inadequate supply of workers, farmers from Maine to California, from Washington State to Georgia, have watched their produce rot in fields, and have been forced to fallow close to half a million acres of land, and billions of dollars are being drained out of our economy as a result," proclaimed California senator Dianne Feinstein on the Senate floor.

As dramatic as Feinstein's claim sounded, the president of the California Farm Bureau Federation contradicted it the following week while offering his own reasons for supporting the bill.

"Even though growers are not suffering labor shortages now, we know that as soon as the economy improves we will be back with the same kind of problems we had before," Doug Mosebar told his federation's news-letter, *Ag Alert*. "AgJOBS is important to our nation's economy."

Mosebar's message reflected a subtle shift in emphasis among promigration business advocates. "Right now the need is less acute," ImmigrationWorks USA's Tamar Jacoby acknowledged in a conference call with reporters. "But when the recovery kicks in," she said, "we will need those workers."

The slight change in tone—away from current needs to prospective migrant labor requirements—was reflected in a shorthand buzzword that came to be favored by immigration reform advocates. "Future flow" became the vogue term for temporary migrant worker programs. As in, "Only by moving immigrant workers through legal channels . . . and developing a sensible system for future flow will immigration become manageable."

President Obama's immigration policies differed little from those of his immediate predecessor, George W. Bush. If anything, they were more hard-line. During the first nine months of the 2009–2010 fiscal year (which overlapped both administrations), immigration prosecutions accelerated and were on track to top the previous fiscal year by 14 percent. Like Bush, Obama advocated a path to legalization, a stance he took as a candidate. To earn citizenship, he said as president, illegal migrants would have "to pay a penalty and pay taxes, learn English, go to the back of the line behind those who played by the rules."

Obama came to office with the overwhelming backing of Hispanic voters, who made up 11 percent of the 2008 electorate. But conservatives, determined not to repeat Ronald Reagan's "big mistake" of enacting any program smacking of amnesty, remained a powerful force. In talks with business and immigrant rights groups, Obama administration officials made it clear that immigration reform needed to be perceived as law and order legislation—with tough border controls and enforcement of hiring restrictions.

As they had in 2006 and 2007, business representatives once again joined migrants' rights and religious groups to push for immigration reform legislation, this time joined by unions that had previously opposed temporary worker programs. Organized labor tempered its opposition, offering a proposal for a commission that would set quotas according to perceived market need.

But making progress on immigration reform seemed to be wishful thinking, despite Obama's campaign promise to make immigration reform "a top priority in my first year" and his pledge to be "a president who isn't going to walk away from something as important as comprehensive reform when it becomes politically unpopular." That assurance seemed to take a backseat to political pragmatism, with the White House giving every indication that the stalemate over federal immigration reform would continue. In mid-2009, some Democratic strategists were telling reporters not to expect any action on the issue until 2011, and press secretary Robert Gibbs conceded "the votes aren't there right now." Immigration became overshadowed by such pressing distractions as the economic crisis, global warming, health care reform, and wars in Iraq and Afghanistan. With hopes of reaching consensus seemingly distant, the decision-making process over immigration policy continued to resemble what might be termed, to use an inelegant but apt phrase, a Mexican standoff.

Washington's long stalemate over immigration had the effect of shifting debates over the issue to states and municipalities. Conservatives in particular, annoyed that the impasse at the national level was leading to a continuation of what they regarded as an uncomfortable status quo, introduced a blizzard of immigration laws. Whereas progress on immigration reform was lethargic in the nation's capital, by contrast, in the states, immigration became the subject of frenzied legislative hyperactivity. In 2006, state governments enacted eighty-four immigration-related statutes, more than twice as many as they passed the previous year.

In subsequent years, the trend picked up speed like a runaway train. Between 2007 and the end of 2009, state legislatures considered approximately 4,370 immigration-related bills and resolutions; they enacted 900. Many of the resolutions honored migrants. Others addressed eligibility requirements for public education and benefits, imposed sanctions for hiring illegal immigrants, or pertained to identification and drivers license regulations. Face-offs over immigration became particularly intense in the Southwest. As the population of Latinos multiplied, immigration politics grew polarized and spiteful. A symbol and lightning rod was Joseph M. Arpaio, the crusading sheriff of Maricopa County, Arizona. In the late 1990s, Arpaio made a name for himself by imprisoning convicts in a tent city, dressing them in pink underwear and socks, and putting them to work on chain gangs. But as the immigration issue gained traction in Arizona, Arpaio, who refers to himself as "America's toughest sheriff," found a new cause célèbre. He assigned his deputies to stage roadblocks and to conduct sweeps and raids in pursuit of illegal immigrants. Undeterred by repeated accusations of bullying and racial profiling, Arpaio defiantly vowed to press on in what he saw as a war. "[A]s illegal aliens continue to pour into this county from Mexico," he declared, "my deputies will meet them with an equal degree of determination to stop them in their tracks."

The Arizona's lawman's hard-line stance made him a populist folk hero in a state in which anti-immigrant zealotry had been building. The escalating rhetoric in Arizona sounded like bad dialogue from an old-fashioned Western gunslinger movie, but the long-running showdowns were very real, emotional, and pointed. Latino activists fought flurries of legislation directed at illegal immigrants. But even though proposed bills targeted a segment of the population that played an instrumental role in the economy as both workers and consumers, Arizona businesses were slow to react. But, as they came to realize, they couldn't stay on the sidelines for long.

CHAPTER 11

Southwest Showdowns

It was a typically balmy February afternoon in Phoenix, with winter temperatures hovering in the seventies. In hearing room five inside the Arizona House of Representatives, the twelve legislators who comprised the Commerce and Military Affairs Committee took their seats around the horseshoe-shaped desk.

The Republican chairman, Philip J. Hanson, a former executive in the healthcare industry, called the committee to order. With a solid Republican majority, the outcome of much of the legislation the committee considered was predictable. On controversial items, the votes tilted toward business, generally breaking down along party lines—eight to four.

But on February 16, 2004, Democrats on the committee arrived with a plan to surprise and outmaneuver their Republican counterparts. Their ploy was an exercise in political brinksmanship, designed to shake up the Arizona GOP and their allies in the business community. It was a gamble, but Democrats figured it was worth the risk. The immigration issue was simmering. And, although migrants had become an important part of the Arizona economy, business interests had been virtually silent on the issue. It was time to force their hand.

For years, the political climate in Arizona had been getting ugly and racially charged, as the state experienced dramatic demographic changes along with spectacular growth. In the 1990s, Arizona's population jumped by 40 percent—a rate of increase that was second only to Nevada's. The state's booming economy, affordable real estate, warm desert climate, and hospitable lifestyle lured retirees, middle-class baby boomers, and workers drawn by the promise of expanding job opportunities.

The unprecedented growth spurt was felt most in Maricopa County, home to Phoenix, the state's sprawling capital city, its political and financial hub as well as its largest metropolis. While the white population grew by a remarkable 45 percent, the increase in the number of Latino residents was even more phenomenal. The Latino population of Maricopa County more than doubled in ten years, largely as a result of newcomers from Mexico.

So many people were crossing the border into the state that the government of Mexico felt it necessary to open up new consulates in the border towns of Douglas and Yuma. They complemented the existing Mexican consulate offices in Nogales, Phoenix, and Tucson.

Stepped-up U.S. Border Patrol operations to the east (Operation Hold the Line in Texas) and west (Operation Gatekeeper in California) made Arizona's less-secured 362-mile border with Mexico a preferred crossing route. Mexicans, pushed by the plummeting peso and pulled by opportunity and promise, surged across the boundary and helped swell the population. As the state's Democratic governor, Janet Napolitano (later to become U.S. secretary of homeland security) told me, "Arizona became the place in the United States where illegal immigration was funneled by actions of the federal government."

In the late nineties, Napolitano, a former U.S. attorney, was serving as Arizona's elected attorney general and watching the increase in migration with amazement.

"People need to understand the numbers were just astounding," she explained. "We've had a certain amount of immigration, legal and illegal, our whole history. But this was a different number, a different dimension."

By the end of the decade, Latinos accounted for a quarter of Arizona's population. The plentiful and cheap migrant workforce helped transform the landscape, turning scraggly desert plots into manicured settings. Strip malls, subdivisions, and earth-tone homes sprang up to replace desert rocks and shrubs. In some suburbs, Arizona's signature tree-size saguaro cacti—"gigantic sentinels of the desert," as an early explorer described them—were in danger of being supplanted by new homes. Many architects used gravel and drought-resistant plants to try to blend modern developments with the brown, parched environment. But elsewhere, new fountains, lush green lawns, and golf courses only added to the general impression that the place was being transformed.

Arizona's identity had long been shaped by tricultural influences, a Southwest pastiche formed by Native Americans, an Anglo majority, and a population of Mexicans and Mexican Americans. But the mass migration across the border came as a series of jolts to old-timers, as the cultural and business landscape mirrored the demographic changes. As the weekly *Phoenix New Times* put it, among the few things to flourish in the Sonoran desert geography had been the cacti and right-wing legislators. But added to that, the paper reported in its "Best of Phoenix 1999" issue, were new Mexican restaurants, hot places to find *chimichangas, posole,* and *albondigas,* a new radio station— *la nueva ciento cinco punto nueve* ("the new 105.9"), and movie theaters with Spanish subtitles. It was a remarkably swift transformation. Billboards in Spanish, two Spanish-language TV stations, nightclubs, markets, newspapers, newsletters, and churches all catered to new migrants. In 1995, Bank of America unveiled a multimedia advertising campaign it dubbed *Cerca de Ti* (Close to You).

Many Arizona businesspeople saw the growing Latino population as a fresh market to be tapped and as a source of ready labor. But not everyone was buying visions of multicultural cross-pollination. An anti-immigrant backlash was erupting. The surge in migration "fed into a feeling of anger and frustration," said Napolitano.

"Immigration became equated with crowded classrooms and crowded emergency rooms and prison costs that had gone off the charts," she explained. "And the federal government was perceived as not doing much of anything."

Along the borderlands of Cochise County, old-time residents, many of them local ranchers, concluded that the situation was out of control. Among the mesquite shrubs and sandy canyons, they started civilian patrols, rounding up dozens of suspected illegal migrants. In 2000, vigilantes killed at least three immigrants and wounded seven.

The Mexican consul in Douglas, Arizona, counted what he referred to as "twenty-four human rights abuses by Arizona ranchers against Mexicans" in a one-year period.

Alarmed by the violence, in May 2000, then U.S. representative Jim Kolbe of Tucson wrote to President Bill Clinton seeking "personal intervention."

"The situation has reached a crisis point," Kolbe, a moderate Republican, said in his letter. "The absence of hope has created volatility. Antiforeigner sentiment mounts, as does anger with the federal government. Residents, acting in unilateral fashion, are now taking detentions into their own hands."

As vigilante action garnered national attention, political reaction toward illegal immigration in the Grand Canyon State also heated up. In 2001, an earnest, newly elected state legislator, Russell Pearce, placed the issue front and center on the Arizona political chessboard.

Pearce, a law-and-order Republican, was a twenty-three-year veteran of the Maricopa sheriff's office and a former head of Arizona's Motor Vehicle Division. As a newly minted state representative, he quickly became both a spearhead and a lightning rod for antimigrant legislation. His opponents branded him a racist and a bigot, but personal experiences helped shape his rhetoric and his purpose. In 1977, in an altercation with Latino teenagers, part of the ring finger on his right hand was shot off. Later in December 2004, an illegal immigrant shot and wounded one of Pearce's five children, Sean, a Maricopa County sheriff's deputy, after he and a partner, serving a warrant, broke down a door to a mobile home in search of a homicide suspect. The day of the shooting, Pearce was at the Brookings Institution in Washington, D.C, serving as the conservative voice in a panel discussion on migration.

At the podium, he enumerated the costs of illegal immigration. "They're a huge drain on the resources. Like I say, Arizona has a $2 billion deficit. Health care systems are failing. The education system has imploded. The criminal justice system, 80 percent of the violent crimes in Phoenix are involving illegal aliens. Are we going to continue to pay for people who broke into our country, entered illegally?" he asked. Moments later, he received an emergency call from his wife, Luanne, telling him about the shooting.

Within weeks of taking office in January 2001, Pearce introduced two bills aimed at illegal migrants. One proposed to impound their cars. Another required Child Protective Services workers to report suspected illegal immigrants to federal authorities. Those proposals got nowhere, but Pearce and other like-minded legislators were undeterred. He and other lawmakers kept migrants in their crosshairs, churning out a flurry of bills. They sponsored proposals to keep illegal immigrants out of Arizona colleges and universities, to turn college administrators into extensions of the Border Patrol, to prevent immigrants from using identification cards issued by the Mexican consulates, and to send National Guard troops to the border.

"When did it become open season on minorities?" editorialized Tucson's *Arizona Daily Star* in January 2003. "When did it become acceptable to attack the poor and minorities under the guise of fairness and equity?"

In July 2003, Pearce and his allies announced the formation of a new organization called Protect Arizona Now. Its purpose was to gather signatures for an ultimately successful ballot initiative, cowritten by Pearce, which was intended to prevent illegal migrants from voting or getting public services.

"They come here and they're a burden on society," Pearce announced at a state capitol press conference. Opponents immediately labeled the initiative effort racist and bound to cause discrimination. But Pearce escalated his inflammatory rhetoric.

"This invasion is destroying America," he wrote. "Elitist editorial boards, pompous professors, and left-leaning liberals are mounting a final and futile fight against a commonsense measure that is supported by nearly three out of four voters. While the elitists complain that Prop. 200 might (gasp!) offend some illegal immigrants or cause divisions, 74 percent of Arizonans understand that the only division Prop. 200 will cause is the one between lawbreakers and law-keepers."

As the initiative campaign gathered steam and signatures, Pearce and his supporters in the Arizona legislature pumped out even more bills aimed at illegal immigrants. They proposed laws to outlaw smuggling, to require undocumented students to pay out-of-state tuition for state colleges and universities, to prevent them from using drivers' licenses, to charge them with felonies if they carried firearms, and to create a state-sponsored posse of armed volunteers who could patrol the border "immune from civil liability for any act or omission resulting in any damage or injury if the member was acting in good faith."

As if those weren't enough, in January 2004, Pearce reached into his anti-immigrant arsenal and shot off yet another volley. It was a proposal to deprive illegal migrants of their lifeblood—jobs—and it ended up changing the character of the debate.

Until that point, business had been restrained in its reaction to the anti-immigrant legislation. Business leaders had recognized that the proposals were putting many of their workers in jeopardy, but Pearce's House Bill 2448 directly targeted employers. It proposed to lift for six months the state licenses of employers found guilty of "hiring or employing an illegal alien." For a second offense, a company would have its business license permanently revoked. Or, as Pearce later put it to me, "Go find another state to go do business in because it won't be Arizona!"

It was a serious threat. Researchers estimated that immigrant workers made up as much as 14 percent of Arizona's labor force. They were involved in every economic sector, accounting for 278,100 full-time jobs and contributing $29 billion to the economy.

And while federal law makes it illegal for businesses to knowingly hire "unauthorized aliens," enforcement had been a low priority. In the 2003–2004 fiscal year, the Office of Immigration and Customs Enforcement (ICE) assigned only ninety agents to work-site enforcement for the entire country. Their anemic productivity gave little reason for businesses to feel threatened. In the next fiscal year, 2004–2005, federal officials notified just three employers nationwide that they would be fined for hiring illegal migrants or not properly filling out employment eligibility verification forms.

As Pearce saw it, the feds had given businesses that employed illegal immigrants a free pass, but his bill would correct that serious oversight, at least in Arizona.

The February 16, 2004, meeting of the Commerce and Military Affairs Committee started seventy minutes late. From their blue-upholstered swivel chairs, legislators could see facing them in the hearing room some of Arizona's most influential business lobbyists—Robert Shuler of the Western Growers Association, David N. Jones from the Arizona Contractors Association, Michael Preston Green representing the Arizona Restaurant and Hospitality Association,

David Howell from Wells Fargo Bank, Jay Kaprosy on behalf of the Greater Phoenix Chamber of Commerce, and Scott Petersen and Dave Selden from the Arizona Chamber of Commerce.

Selden is an urbane business lawyer, who along with his fast-talking and energetic wife, Julie Pace—both of them partners in a succession of Phoenix law firms—had over the past several years gradually shifted their attention from employment law to the politically fraught issue of immigration.

The business representatives came to the meeting feeling a little wary but confident. Selden expected a close vote, but he anticipated the bill would be killed.

"I thought that Pearce and the more conservative Republicans would vote for it, and that moderate Republicans and the Democrats would vote against it," he said. His reasoning made sense. Democrats were predictable on immigration issues. Moderate Republicans might hold their noses by voting to protect illegal immigrants, but in the end, he felt, business interests would prevail.

Selden was wrong.

In the days leading up to the meeting, prominent Latino legislators, including the then Democratic leader of the Arizona House of Representatives, John Loredo, along with other elected Democrats, had been working on a surprise.

"We'd been fighting these anti-immigrant bills without any help or cooperation from the business community," Loredo told me. "Many of the companies that made a profit off the backs of migrant workers were the same companies donating money to anti-immigration proponents. It seemed hypocritical for them to sit on the sidelines while their workers were being targeted."

"The Chamber of Commerce always gloated at their success record—90 percent," added state representative Steve Gallardo. "And we said, 'We're not going to fight these battles alone.'"

Gallardo, Loredo, and the state representative Robert Meza, a member of the committee, hatched a scheme to gain support by dividing the Republicans. The plan was to drive a wedge between socially conservative legislators such as Russell Pearce and moderates motivated more by pocketbook issues, fiscal conservatism, and probusiness politics.

Loredo saw the split in stark terms: "There was a separation between those legislators who were truly driven by hatred of people with brown skin and those who were anti-immigrant because that was the way the wind was blowing."

At the hearing, the chairman called on supporters of the measure to address the committee. First to speak were leaders of Protect Arizona Now. Kathy McKee, a medical transcriptionist, complained about the failure of the federal government to enforce U.S. employer sanctions. Car dealer Rusty Childress said American workers were being displaced because employers were addicted to cheap labor provided by illegal aliens.

On the other side, Selden did most of the talking for the business interests. He said the bill would give federal bureaucrats "death penalty power" over Arizona companies by making businesses liable for innocent, record-keeping mistakes. Companies, he said, walk a tightrope, often unable to distinguish between phony and real documents, and afraid of being accused of hiring discrimination.

Next, it was time for the legislators to chime in. "From the questioning, it became more apparent that Pearce's point of view would prevail," Selden remembered.

To Selden's surprise, the Democrats voted unanimously to support the legislation, and the bill sailed out of committee on an eight-to-four margin. The "no" votes came from four probusiness Republicans.

The scheme had worked. The Democrats had taught the Republicans a valuable lesson. They could not be taken for granted. If Republicans expected their support on business issues involving immigration, the GOP members should be prepared to reciprocate in matters of migrant rights. Where interests of immigration advocates and business intersected, mutually advantageous alliances should be formed.

"It forced the probusiness people to look at Pearce and try to get him to back off," explained Representative Loredo. "That's what they did."

The 2004 employer sanctions measure never saw the light of day. Even though it got out of committee, Democrats and moderate Republicans united to kill the Pearce bill.

They were not so successful with subsequent anti-immigrant legislation, but they had achieved a goal of galvanizing Arizona employers, who had been hesitant to speak out on immigration issues.

The business community wasn't about to march in lockstep with immigrants rights groups and Latino activists, but 2004 saw the emergence of a new, if reluctant, political movement—employers, seeing their affordable and reliable workforces in jeopardy, were coming out of the shadows.

In March 2004, the Arizona Chamber of Commerce, declaring that "[e]mployers should not be responsible for law enforcement," endorsed a "comprehensive immigration reform" program that would allow illegal migrants the "opportunity to access a fair and equitable process to obtain temporary status with a defined, though not necessarily guaranteed, path to permanent residency that includes their dependents."

Arizona's November 2004 general election was a disappointing one for the chamber and for other supporters of immigration reform. Candidates who had campaigned on promises to crack down on immigration won their races. Republican Andrew Thomas, who had blanketed Maricopa County with "Stop Illegal Immigration" signs, was elected county prosecutor. The Protect Arizona Now initiative passed with 55.6 percent of the statewide vote.

Organized labor had contributed to the losing campaign, as had Latino organizations, chief among them the National Council of La Raza. But big business also played a key role. The Arizona Chamber of Commerce kicked in $479,270 to fight the measure, and Republican attorney Julie Pace, who headed the chamber's immigration committee, helped run the opposition campaign.

Over the next two years, Arizona legislators proposed a stream of bills targeting illegal migrants. Governor Napolitano signed some and vetoed others. But as time went on, her positions on illegal immigration hardened, so much so that in June 2006, she vetoed another Pearce-authored employer sanctions bill because it wasn't tough enough. She described it as "weak and ineffective" by allowing employers to too easily "beat the rap simply by firing the illegally hired employee."

Later that month at the annual awards luncheon of the Arizona Chamber of Commerce and Industry, businesspeople showed noticeable relief that the governor had provided them a reprieve.

"If there was a theme to the awards, it was 'Whew! We dodged that employer-sanctions bullet!'" the *Arizona Republic* reported.

But as everyone knew, Pearce was not out of ammo. He had the baking heat of another Phoenix summer to reload in preparation for the next shoot-out in the following legislative session.

Two states to the east, a parallel drama had played out in Texas, where business interests were similarly provoked into entering the immigration fray.

Frustrated by Washington's inaction on immigration, in December 2005, Governor Rick Perry boosted state spending on border security with Operation Linebacker, a program that increased the local law enforcement presence at the Mexican border. Other Texas Republicans were supporting a barrage of bills to prevent illegal migrants from obtaining benefits, healthcare, and education, to deny U.S. citizenship to children of noncitizens, and to apply a tax on remittances sent to Latin America.

Faced with the onslaught, in April 2006, the Democratic state representative Rafael Anchía of Dallas, a member of the Mexican American Legislative Caucus, decided, in his words, to "reframe the debate" over immigration.

"The noise level and the rhetoric on immigration, primarily among Republicans, had been turned up," he explained. "I saw it coming as a wedge issue."

Although unaware of the ploy used in Arizona, Anchía, the attorney son of immigrants from Mexico and Spain, settled on a similarly provocative playbook.

"In trying to triangulate victory on this, we knew that business had to be a big part of it," he said, using the language of a careful political strategist.

The legislature was considering a tax bill, unrelated to immigration, that would have granted certain deductions to businesses. Anchía tacked on an amendment designed to shake up the business community. His measure would have prohibited companies employing illegal immigrants from getting the proposed tax breaks.

On the floor of the legislature, Anchía made his intentions clear. "The sucking sound is not coming from Mexico. The sucking sound is coming from the United States and it's bringing undocumented workers here," he said. "This is a very cost-effective way; it deals with the demand side and . . . frankly holds businesses accountable."

The proposal sailed through the legislature, and the business community got the rude shock Anchía had intended.

"He was trying to make a point, and he did," explained Bill Hammond, a lobbyist and former Republican legislator who headed the Texas Association of Business, the Lone Star State's largest employer group.

The next day, Hammond, one of the most powerful members of the Texas business and political establishment, went to visit Anchía. The two had become acquainted soon after Anchía's 2004 election. They had been introduced by Anchía's wife, Marissa, who knew Hammond through her work as the executive director for the Southwest region of the U.S. Chamber of Commerce.

Anchía made clear to Hammond that if things didn't change, the business community might see a rocky legislative road ahead. "I suggested unless we wanted the following session to devolve into an anti-immigrant versus employer sanctions free-for-all, then we should really start working together."

The lawmaker declined to describe the scenario as a threat. "It was," he said, "more an overture for collaboration. He [Hammond] knew what would happen, and he had seen an example of it, and we both agreed that was not in the best interest of Texas business or the state."

The meeting paved the way for a series of discussions that led eventually to another strange bedfellows association.

"Immigration Issue Sparks Odd Alliance," headlined the *San Antonio Express-News* in a June 2006 article describing the talks.

"If we can create common ground on some principles for comprehensive immigration reform, then I feel like that would be a good thing for both parties," Hammond told the paper.

With the increasing prospect of immigration restrictionists targeting companies, others in the Texas business community also felt the need to cover their flanks. Independently of Hammond, Houston insurance broker and Republican activist Norman E. Adams, who calls himself "Stormin' Norman," was moving ahead with plans to launch his own probusiness, pro-immigration organization. With the assistance of Pat Kiley, the former executive vice president of the

Associated General Contractors of Houston, he enlisted the support of area construction and contractors associations and in August 2006 created Texans for Sensible Immigration Policy (TSIP).

"There are simply too few American workers to fill the jobs we have," asserted the late Ron Stone, a former Houston TV news anchor in a promotional video he narrated for TSIP. "Without immigration, we cannot begin to sustain the growth and prosperity that we all enjoy and depend upon."

The TSIP solution was amnesty, although the organization did not use that politically charged word. It preferred the term "safe haven."

"We need a safe haven mechanism put in place to encourage current illegals to come forward and be identified with a foolproof verification system so that employers can know for sure who's truly authorized to work."

While TSIP was producing its video, Hammond was thinking more strategically about business, immigration, and politics. Before taking the top job at the business association, he had been a three-year, full-time member of the Texas Workforce Commission, a job he was appointed to by then governor George W. Bush. Previously, he'd served four terms in the Texas House of Representatives, where he'd been a leading force in the 2002 Republican takeover of the state House of Representatives. But in the summer of 2006, Hammond set aside his partisan hat to engage Anchía and other members of the Mexican American Legislative Caucus (MALC)—an organization then composed of forty-one Democrats and two Republicans.

An early gesture of solidarity was "an unprecedented joint statement" opposing a congressional measure seeking to prevent federal funds from being used by illegal migrants for in-state tuition rates. The proposal came from a Houston member of Congress, Representative John Culberson, whose Hammond's own business group, the Texas Association of Business, had endorsed for re-election. But Hammond took on his fellow Republican:

"This is not the time to be closing doors," Hammond wrote. "This is the time to be opening doors!"

By the time negotiations between Hammond and the Latino legislators were completed, they had come to terms on a fifteen-point program that focused on matching foreign workers to employers' needs. It was a plan whose emphasis differed from the immigration perspective then favored by most GOP members of the U.S. Congress, which focused on border security.

"I think unfortunately for a lot of different reasons, they've got it wrong," Hammond told reporters.

As he was hammering out proposals with Latino Democrats, the GOP business leader was lobbying on another front, talking to movers and shakers in Texas industry. He was also working closely with Tamar Jacoby, at the time a senior fellow at the conservative Manhattan Institute, who was in the process of forming the probusiness ImmigrationWorks USA lobbying group.

In late August 2006, Hammond, Jacoby, and about half a dozen business leaders went to Dallas's only five-star hotel, the Mansion on Turtle Creek, once the palatial hillside home of a Texas cotton and oil magnate, to sound an alarm about a worker shortage and to proclaim a solution.

"If we have enough legal immigrants to meet the needs of the employers, a lot of this problem goes away," said Hammond at a press conference.

The group announced the formation of Texas Employers for Immigration Reform, backed by some two dozen supporters, including Adams, the International Bank of Commerce, Pilgrim's Pride Corporation—the largest chicken producer in the United States—and migrant-dependent businesses represented by the Texas Farm Bureau, the Texas Hotel and Lodging Association, the Texas Nursery and Landscape Association, and the Texas Poultry Federation.

Calling for a more robust temporary worker program as well as a way for "hardworking, tax-paying undocumented workers to earn legal status," members of the group protested that nonimmigrant workers were simply not available to perform the menial labor that his and other companies needed.

"How many people can you get to squat down and catch chickens?" asked Lonnie "Bo" Pilgrim, chairman of Pilgrim's Pride.

(If there were any question about Pilgrim's use of foreign labor, it was answered in April 2008 when agents from Immigration and Customs Enforcement [ICE] raided company processing facilities in Arkansas, Tennessee, Florida, West Virginia, and Texas, and arrested migrant workers. According to federal prosecutors, the employees had used false documents to get jobs at the company. Pilgrim's Pride issued a statement downplaying the matter and emphasizing the company's cooperation with federal authorities: "The approximately four hundred employees taken into custody by ICE represent about 4 percent of the ninety-four hundred people employed at these facilities. We share the government's goal of eliminating the hiring or employment of unauthorized workers. Pilgrim's Pride has relied on the ICE Best Hiring Practices in designing its immigration compliance program.")

By January 9, 2007, when Texas lawmakers gathered in Austin to convene the eightieth session of the state legislature, Bill Hammond could look back at a productive few months. He had made new political allies and was in the forefront of what would turn out to be an emerging movement of businesses advocating for immigration reform.

The 2007 Texas legislative session promised to be a stormy one, with immigration taking center stage. But the Democratic state representative from northwestern Dallas had another plan to reinforce the earlier lesson.

Rafael Anchía called reporters to his Dallas law office in early February 2007 to reveal the second part of a one-two punch.

"You hit people where it hurts—in the pocketbook and it gets their attention," Anchía announced. "If none of the anti-immigrant legislation comes to the floor for a vote, I am happy to let HB 351 die."

Anchía was referring to a one-paragraph employer sanctions bill he had introduced. The measure was written to prevent money from the state's Enterprise Fund (designed to bring jobs to Texas) from going to companies that employ "a person who is not lawfully entitled to be present and employed in the United States."

It was a naked threat, just in case the business community had not completely gotten the message the first time around. This time Anchía went after one of the governor's pet projects "because I wanted to make sure we had his attention, too."

Why was it necessary to poke business in the eye one more time? "It may not have been," he admitted. "I just wanted to make sure. It may have been 'belt and suspenders,' but I wanted to make sure everybody was still on board because I figured business is going to get some push back from Republicans, and I wanted to make sure they were as committed as we were."

The tactic pulled Hammond back to the table, and once again, the Texas business representative sat down with a cast of unlikely collaborators. Within a week they had hammered out a deal.

"Diverse coalition pledge [sic] unity and civility on immigration debate," read identically worded press releases from the Texas Association of Business (TAB) and the Mexican American Legislative Caucus.

Also part of what Anchía called "the grand alliance" were the Texas Association of Mexican-American Chambers of Commerce, the League of United Latin American Citizens (LULAC), the Mexican American Legal Defense and Education Fund (MALDEF), the American Civil Liberties Union (ACLU), and Hammond's new group, Texas Employers for Immigration Reform.

Hammond promised that the business community would help kill the immigration bills working their way through the legislature.

"Unless and until the U.S. Congress enacts comprehensive immigration reform, the TAB calls on the Texas legislature to not pass any legislation dealing with immigration, especially in regard to legislation that could add burdens to employers," Hammond grandly declared.

So the most powerful, Republican-led business organization in Texas—on record as opposing labor unions, higher corporate taxes, raises in the minimum wage, mandatory worker compensation, and health benefits—symbolically linked arms with activists who had opposed them on all those issues.

Anchía held up his end of the bargain. "As a symbol of our solidarity and cooperation, I'm withdrawing HB 351 from further consideration in thanks to the business community who is bringing their power, their might, and their heft to making sure the immigration debate is fought on the floor in Washington, not in Austin," he said.

The legislators heeded the call. State immigration laws were off the table at the capitol for the rest of the session—a two-year deal, since the Texas legislature convenes every other year.

It was a marriage of convenience, not of love. To the business community, at stake were the stability and affordability of the Texas workforce as well as the viability of the Texas economy. It was simply a matter of self-interest.

"This is an important part of our economy, and if we sent everyone home, we would suffer tremendously," Hammond acknowledged.

Back in Arizona, the state that helped define vintage American conservatism, disagreements about the immigration issue, and particularly over employer sanctions, were helping to create a Grand Canyon–sized gulf in the conservative movement.

Divisions within the politically active family of the late Barry Goldwater, a five-term U.S. senator and the unsuccessful Republican nominee for president in 1964, mirrored the widening split.

Goldwater took a libertarian approach to social values and advocated minimal government regulation of business—so much so that when President Jimmy Carter proposed employer sanctions in 1978, "Mr. Conservative," as Goldwater became known, wrote, "These employer sanctions are inevitably discriminatory and could raise possible violations of civil rights of potential employees. It is the government, not the employer who should bear the main responsibility of determining who is here legally and who is not."

Those laissez-faire values toward illegal migrants and business had been reflected in the employment practices of a ranch, northwest of Phoenix, partly owned by Barry Goldwater's brother, Robert. The business was highlighted in 1977 in one of a series of articles written by a group of investigative reporters looking into corruption in Arizona.

The story, headlined "Robert Goldwater Linked to Illegal Mexican Aliens," recounted how the operation relied on illegal immigrants.

"A mammoth Arizona citrus farm partly owned by the brother of Senator Barry Goldwater (R-Ariz.) has operated for more than a decade from the labor of illegal Mexican aliens who have been paid cruelly meager wages and forced to live in subhuman conditions," it reported.

Robert Goldwater and his business partner in the Goldmar Corporation denied knowing anything about their employees' living conditions or their immigration status. At the time, it was legal to hire illegal immigrants, but not to harbor them. Six months after the article appeared, the workers went on strike, and the outcome left little doubt about the company's tolerance of illegal migrants.

The labor agreement "is the first negotiated for a group that is almost exclusively composed of 'undocumented workers,' according to Guadalupe Sanchez, who heads the organizing group," reported the *Washington Post*.

"Art Martori, president of Goldmar, said the contract was designed to cover the company's workers regardless of how they came to be in the country. 'It's true everywhere, not just here, that undocumented workers are in the fields,' Martori said, adding that all he could say about his workforce was that it was 'mostly Mexican.'"

Nearly three decades later, the son of the ranch's co-owner, Don—Barry Goldwater's nephew—launched a political career based on a platform that, if enacted earlier, might have landed his father in jail at the time and certainly would have put him at odds with his late uncle's immigration philosophy. In his unsuccessful bid for the Republican nomination for Arizona governor in 2006, Don Goldwater called for tightened border security and strict enforcement of employer sanctions.

"We are at war at this time and we need to start treating the border as if we are in a war," Goldwater said at a campaign stop in Yuma. Goldwater went on to become the director of the Phoenix chapter of the Minuteman Civil Defense Corps, the civilian border patrol group that had endorsed his candidacy.

He also sponsored an initiative for a state law to impose strict penalties on employers who hire illegal workers. The campaign for that ballot proposition led to the public exposure of a rift in *la familia* Goldwater—one that reflects the larger split among conservatives over immigration.

Barry Goldwater Jr., a Republican businessman, former congressman, and son of the iconic U.S. senator, attended a rally for the initiative and was shocked by what he encountered.

"Speeches soaked with hateful, angry racist tones and dialogue. Eyes closed, listening to the roar of inflammatory rhetoric and sermonizing, I could have easily mistaken myself to be at one of David Duke's Ku Klux Klan rallies," he wrote in a column for the *Arizona Republic*.

Barry Jr. took on his first cousin directly, blaming him and his allies for "extreme hysteria," abandoning conservative principles, unfairly targeting immigrants, and tarnishing the Republican Party.

"Our conservative leaders today are rapidly losing the respect of the business community and most rank-and-file Republican contributors," he lamented. In an e-mail to his cousin, Don (and forwarded to a newspaper columnist), Barry got personal, accusing Don of sullying the family name.

"You forget there are other Goldwaters in Arizona. Your actions are trampling on the free market and small businesses struggling to survive and are not what the Goldwater name stands for. You are compromising the conservative cause. Be prepared, Donnie, for honest political criticism."

Cousin Donnie didn't flinch.

"I am surprised that you have taken me on in public. The game is on," he replied in an e-mail.

To Donald Goldwater, foreign invaders were threatening a way of life.

"A lot of these people coming in today, they don't want to assimilate into the United States," Goldwater told me. "A lot of these races back here seem to think that the southwestern part of the United States is their home and it's their country and not ours," adding ominously, "and if the federal government doesn't take control over this thing, somebody's going to light a spark somewhere and the consequences are not going to be good."

Things were certainly not looking good for Arizona businesses that employed illegal migrants. In February 2007, the day after liberal Texan Latino politicos and conservative business leaders announced their "grand alliance," Arizona state representative Russell Pearce introduced a new and improved employer sanctions bill. He dubbed it the Fair and Legal Employment Act.

With the winds of anti-immigrant sentiment at his back, Pearce was confident of victory and determined to choke off the immigrant influx.

"Jobs is the number one lure for those folks," he told me. "It's just like Disneyland or any other theme park. You learned a long time ago, if you want the crowd to go home, you've got to shut down the rides, turn off the lights."

Arizona businesses got the message. After all, they were the ones who ran the rides and kept the lights on, employing an unauthorized workforce estimated to total nearly three hundred thousand. By that count, one of every ten Arizona workers was in the country illegally. And although Pearce's bill set a high bar for law enforcement who, to make any charges stick, had to prove that a "business . . . *knowingly* employ[ed] an unauthorized alien" (my emphasis), the business community prepared for a challenge—both in the courts and on the political stage.

The effort to fend off what businesses regarded as an assault galvanized business executives and led to the formation of a new political movement.

Sheridan Bailey, the bearded and congenial owner of Ironco Enterprises, a Phoenix steel fabrication plant, cofounded one group, Arizona Employers for Immigration Reform (AZEIR), patterned after Texas Employers for Immigration Reform.

For Bailey, this was the discovery of a new cause and a reemergence into politics. He had become disillusioned with political activism after witnessing the chaos of the 1968 Democratic Party convention in Chicago. Bailey had worked as an operative in the presidential campaign of Eugene McCarthy, a maverick Minnesota senator who sought the Democratic nomination on an anti–Vietnam War platform.

With his political spark rekindled, Bailey began talking to other Arizona executives about immigration, discovering that while many were worried that they and their immigrant workforces might be in jeopardy, they intended to keep a low profile.

"We found this conspiracy of silence among employers who had so much at stake and didn't want to go public," he said. "They were afraid they'd alienate their customers or put their bank loans in jeopardy."

AZEIR gave reluctant bosses cover, he explained. Bailey brought in the political fund-raiser Jake Adams to work at his company and on the issue. Adams had raised money for Democratic senatorial candidates and had wanted to get out of politics and into business.

"Sheridan said, 'We have to solve this immigration problem first,'" Adams recalled.

Adams hooked up with other business-oriented advocates of fewer immigration restrictions—among them the Essential Worker Immigration Coalition (an arm of the U.S. Chamber of Commerce) and Tamar Jacoby of ImmigrationWorks USA. Working with Jacoby's organization, Adams not only launched a Web site for AZEIR but also created sites for other similar fledgling groups, among them California Employers for Immigration Reform, Oklahoma Employers for Immigration Reform, Nevada Employers for Immigration Reform, Colorado Employers for Immigration Reform, Oklahoma Employers for Immigration Reform, and New Mexico Employers for Immigration Reform. It was the beginning of a national network that Bailey hoped would advance state by state.

"Grass roots. Get businesses involved, get businesses talking to legislators directly, public information, a whole host of strategies that need to come to the surface for the public to understand what this is about, that it's not just about greedy employers," he explained. "We're an integral part of the fabric of this community, and so if we fail, the community fails."

On July 2, 2007, one week after U.S. congressional proposals for immigration reform died in the U.S. Senate, Napolitano signed Pearce's employer sanctions bill, the Legal Arizona Workers Act, into law. In signing the legislation, Napolitano called it "the most aggressive action in the country against employers who knowingly or intentionally hire undocumented workers," one she said was made necessary "because it is now abundantly clear that Congress finds itself incapable of dealing with the comprehensive immigration reforms our country needs. I signed it too," she added, "out of the realization that the flow of illegal immigration into our state is due to the constant demand of some employers for cheap, undocumented labor."

The new law spawned the creation of another business group, Wake Up, Arizona!, formed by the Phoenix Republican public relations man Gordon C. James, who had worked in the election campaigns for President George W. Bush, former New York mayor Rudy Giuliani, and Arizona senator John McCain.

"The so-called employer sanctions law should really be called 'the job destruction law,' because the ripple effect will touch most of the businesses in Arizona and their employees," proclaimed Marion "Mac" Magruder Jr., chairman of Wake Up, Arizona! at the group's inaugural press conference in July 2007. Magruder is a prominent Phoenix Republican who owns several McDonald's franchises.

"I'll tell you what," Magruder amplified. "When brown people lose their jobs, white people lose their jobs, and that is an absolute fact. . . . Everyone is dependent upon each other. Every business is dependent on each other."

Other members of Wake Up, Arizona! included Steve Chucri, president of the Arizona Restaurant Association; Danny Hendon, owner of a car wash chain; homebuilder Steve Hilton of Meritage Homes; Jeff Moorad, general manager of the Arizona Diamondbacks baseball team; Barry Goldwater Jr.; and Jason LeVecke, a grandson of the founder of the Carl's Jr. restaurant chain, who co-owns 130 restaurants, including 59 Carl's Jr. franchises around Arizona.

LeVecke, a moderate Republican, said he had been angered by the rhetoric coming out of the antimigrant camp.

"If this has been an invasion, it's been the most peaceful, prosperous invasion in mankind's history," he told me, as we sat at a table in one of his Phoenix restaurants.

LeVecke explained that he drew inspiration for his progressive views from the family of his famous grandfather Carl Karcher, who, ironically, was renowned for his support of conservative causes. LeVecke said Karcher's parents were hardscrabble migrants from Germany and Ireland.

"During the Depression, my family were very poor farmers from Ohio. They picked up any job they could get. 'Pay me cash! Pay me, I'll do it,'" he said, tracing a connection that he saw between his relatives and present-day migrants. "We don't understand the history of our immigration. We're saying today we'd rather take the person who waits in line for thirty years, as opposed to taking the person who's willing to risk everything to save their family, the person who's willing to go on foot across the desert, an ocean on a raft. That person we should be embracing as soon as they get onto our shores and say, 'Welcome to America. Good luck and Godspeed.'"

Following up on his convictions, LeVecke helped establish and fund a telephone hotline for migrants in trouble as well as a Web site, both called "Respect/Respeto."

Lydia Guzman, the operation's director and a longtime activist in Arizona's Latino community, said she was pleasantly surprised by the support from the business community. But she also understood that self-interest was part of the motivation.

"In order for a business to thrive and function, you have to have a good team," she said. "And if you have a workforce that is living in fear constantly, if you have a workforce that is afraid to come into work, then it affects business."

For David N. Jones, president and chief executive officer of the Arizona Contractors Association, opposition to employer sanctions was more than a matter of self-interest, it was for the greater good.

"Who's going to make the beds and work in the kitchen?" he asked me. "Are your son and daughter willing to do that? I don't think so."

Like many other employers, Jones is a strong advocate of a temporary worker program. He goes as far as to invoke his own ancestors' indentured servitude in the United Sates during the seventeenth century, as a period that provided migrants with "opportunity." He also suggested that programs could be patterned after ones he experienced in Saudi Arabia as a labor contractor importing Filipinos and Korean workers who lived in compounds.

"They can put monitoring bracelets on the guest workers," he said. "We're going to have to think outside the box in America. If an individual comes in, the employer has the right to know my accountability twenty-four hours a day."

Within weeks of the Arizona sanctions law enactment, Jones and other business leaders went to federal court to challenge it. The first complaint, filed by the husband-and-wife team of Julie Pace and David Selden, argued that immigration law is a federal, not a state responsibility.

Civil rights and immigrant advocate organizations also sued. The cases were consolidated, and, as they made their way through the federal court system and up to the U.S. Supreme Court, a wide swath of business groups entered the legal fray, piling on as coplaintiffs. Wake Up, Arizona!, roofing contractors, landscapers, as well as associations of farm and restaurant owners all joined in. By the time the case went to the U.S. Court of Appeals for the Ninth Circuit, twelve state chambers of commerce along with the U.S. Chamber of Commerce had signed a friend of the court brief. The national effort was coordinated by Julie Pace working with lawyers from the Washington, D.C., office of Sidley Austin LLP, one of the world's largest corporate law firms.

As business groups fought the employer sanctions law in Arizona, they were kept busy in other states with similar legislation that proposed to penalize companies that hired illegal migrants. Pace became an evangelist for the cause, flying around the country to dispense legal advice to employer organizations. And in Washington, D.C., ImmigrationWorks USA, backed by various trade associations and the U.S. Chamber of Commerce, set up shop as a national federation among "state-based business coalitions: employers and trade associations from Florida to Oregon and from every sector of the economy that relies on immigrant workers."

Supporting the ImmigrationWorks campaign was the leadership of the American Immigration Lawyers Association (AILA). "We have your back," Charles H. Kuck, president of the eleven-thousand-strong association, told a telephone conference call meeting of ImmigrationWorks activists. "We can make it happen. Reach out to us."

Migrant-dependent businesses were determined to make sure the flow continued.

CHAPTER 12

Fresh Blood and National Selection

Even the Great Wall of China had gates. Inside of them were centers of trade and commerce. The challenge for the gatekeepers was to make sure that the right people got through.

Part of the tension in U.S. immigration debates has been how to select those admitted through what Emma Lazarus called the "golden door." In the view of many, the "huddled masses" should move to the back of the line.

"U.S. immigration policy should encourage high-skill immigration and strictly limit low-skill immigration," Robert Rector, a senior research fellow at the conservative Heritage Foundation, told a House subcommittee as the debate was unfolding.

"In general," he said, "government policy should limit immigration to those who will be net fiscal contributors, avoiding those who will increase poverty and impose new costs on overburdened U.S. taxpayers."

Rector's viewpoint was echoed not only by the Bush administration and many congressional Republicans, but it also lived on as a bipartisan position within the Obama White House, carrying on from where the previous president's dead-end immigration proposals had failed. Both Bush and Obama supported strengthened border security, worksite enforcement, and the thorniest of all

214

immigration issues—plans to allow millions of illegal immigrants to eventually become citizens. But the other common, underlying motif was one expressed by Obama, that "our immigration policy should be driven by our best judgment of what is in the economic interest of the United States and what is in the best interest of the American worker."

Putting national economic interests in the forefront of the immigration debate is the default cross-party consensus. Doris M. Meissner, an Obama financial contributor who worked as President Bill Clinton's commissioner of the U.S. Immigration and Naturalization Service (INS) for seven years, could have been channeling the conservative Rector during testimony before a spring 2009 Senate committee.

"Perhaps the most broken element of the nation's immigration system is its inability to anticipate, adjust to, or meet future labor market needs," said Meissner, now a director at the Migration Policy Institute (MPI), a Washington, D.C., non-partisan think tank. Meissner advocates a plan advanced by the MPI and some unions: the creation of a government commission to recommend "immigration admissions levels [that] reflect labor market needs, employment and unemployment patterns, and shifting economic and demographic trends."

The April 2009 proposal from the two major U.S. labor confederations, the AFL-CIO and Change to Win (organizations that merged later that year), intended to safeguard American jobs by regulating migration. The plan drew mixed reviews by business lobbyists worried that too much authority vested in government would undercut marketplace forces. The U.S. Chamber of Commerce and ImmigrationWorks USA issued identically worded condemnations of the commission proposal. "The free market is by far the best tool for setting immigration quotas and picking immigrants," they declared.

Short of an outright open-door policy, finding ways to cherry-pick and grant entry to the most useful migrants has been an enduring aspect of immigration debates. Developed nations don't want immigration policies that let in people who become financial burdens. So how should countries calibrate who gets in and who doesn't? The question itself goes to the heart of our values. Selecting migrants based largely on their economic worth may seem like a laudable goal. Certainly, squeezing the fruit is a useful method of selection at the supermarket. But should market principles trump human needs and more global approaches? Should there be a separate line for the "huddled masses" or no line at all?

Either way, the romantic "golden door" allusion offered by Emma Lazarus seems to be a relic. More prosaic immigration analysts are apt to invoke various other entrance metaphors. Front doors are reserved for settlers who stand in line and enter legally under quota systems. Temporary foreign workers enter through side doors, and generally are expected to exit after a set period of time. And then there are the massive back doors used by migrants who either cross borders illegally or who overstay visas.

But none of those broad descriptions does justice to more finely tuned methods of admission, control, and selection being debated in the United States and in vogue in other industrial nations. Increasingly, policymakers are addressing questions about how to make sure the doormen and bouncers at political boundaries differentiate between the right people and the riffraff.

Even during the most restrictive periods of U.S. immigration policy, business interests worked to make sure America's gatekeepers were sufficiently discriminating. The Chinese Exclusion Act of 1882, intended to keep out Chinese laborers, led in 1905 to a flood of letters of protest from chambers of commerce and other business groups intent on making sure Chinese businesspeople and officials were not also barred. President Theodore Roosevelt issued a 1905 order making clear that the exclusion law did not apply to "higher-class Orientals," as the *New York Times* put it.

"[A]ll Chinese of the coolie or laboring class—that is, all Chinese laborers, skilled or unskilled—are absolutely prohibited from coming to the United States," directed Roosevelt. "[B]ut the purpose of the Government of the United States is to show the widest and heartiest courtesy toward all merchants, teachers, students, and travelers who may come to the United States, as well as toward all Chinese officials or representatives in any capacity of the Chinese government."

Subsequent immigration measures also exempted numerous categories of workers from restrictions. The 1921 quota law made special allowances for "professional actors, artists, lecturers, singers, nurses, ministers of any religious denomination, professors for colleges or seminaries, aliens belonging to any recognized learned profession, or aliens employed as domestic servants."

The bracero program, enacted during World War II, opened the side door to temporary farm workers, while the 1952 Immigration and Nationality Act, among many other provisions, gave a quota preference to skilled foreign workers whose services were deemed to be urgently needed.

The 1990 Immigration Act, which pretty much governs current policy, set an annual cap of permanent (front-door) immigrants. The limit of 675,000 is flexible, since it does not apply to immediate family members or refugees. Excluding those categories of immigrants, a maximum of 480,000 "green cards," making the recipients legal permanent residents, are family-sponsored, and 140,000 are employment-based. The law also set a limit that is now 65,000 a year for temporary (side-door) migrants with special skills under the H-1B program.

Complex formulas and numerical ceilings determine how many people from each part of the world may migrate to the United States. Many people issued green cards have already arrived in the country as tourists or workers. Employers wanting to import workers have to petition the U.S. Department of Labor, which certifies that there is a shortage of workers in the occupational category before they can be admitted. "Priority workers" with "extraordinary ability" can obtain green cards without job offers as long as they work in the area of their expertise. The lines can be long and take years. Each month, the government issues a bulletin updating the extent of the backlog. In April 2009, the State Department was processing applications for skilled workers and professionals, including nurses, that had been filed six years previously. By the next month, it had stopped processing work visas for the year, since the quota was filled.

The U.S. government's immigration priority of family reunification is reflected in the statistics. Of the 3.4 million green cards handed out between 2005 and 2007, some 62 percent went to family-sponsored immigrants.

But there has been pressure to change the system to one more attuned to America's economic needs. The unsuccessful immigration legislation considered by the Senate in 2007 did just that. It contained provisions to grant preferences to migrants who were skilled and highly educated—workers whose occupations were in high demand.

By mapping out a strategy to carefully determine the makeup of American migrants, the proposal departed from the long-standing policy of giving priority to divided families. But the social engineering model of migration control is not an untried method. In contrast to the United States, in a number of countries in the developed world, policymakers are attempting to take a much more nuanced and discriminatory approach to controlling the migration turnstiles, deciding whom to admit and whom to exclude on the basis of trade arrangements as well as perceived economic and business requirements.

An increasingly unified Europe is more carefully policing its frontiers, creating buffer zones around the continent, setting the stage for a process to try to carefully manage who gets in and who doesn't. In the United Kingdom, officials have adopted a "managed migration" policy, attempting to finely tune the system on the basis of preferred national origin and occupation.

The United Kingdom's history as a colonial power, and more recently as a member of the European Union, has led to an evolving series of policies that has alternately expanded and inhibited the rights of different racial groups and nationalities. As a result, Britain has adopted migration rules with their own unique logic and rationale.

Like America, England has grappled with rapidly changing demographics. Within the span of a generation, the nation has witnessed a profound transition, moving from a basically all-white to a multiracial society. The changes are particularly apparent to an occasional visitor like me. Although I was born there, my visits have been infrequent. So in 2008, when I visited my boyhood home in a northwestern London suburb, I was surprised to see how much the old neighborhood (or, I should say, "neighbourhood") had changed. The local shops included an "International Food Centre" offering halal meat (slaughtered according to Islamic law). Signs in Arabic and Chinese advertised merchandise; restaurants featured Indonesian and Sri Lankan food. My old elementary school comprised large numbers of students whose parents had come from India and Bangladesh.

The old semidetached Victorian homes remain, but on the cul-de-sac where I lived, the thirty-one houses that only decades ago were inhabited by whites constituted a mini–United Nations that, according to the current inhabitant of my former home, included natives of Iran, Poland, India, China, Pakistan, Africa, France, and Scotland as well as England.

"I came from Italy," Maria Dello told me, explaining that she had migrated in 1958 without knowing a word of English. She invited me in for coffee, and we sat and talked at a table in the kitchen, which looked a lot different from the way I remembered it. She and her late husband had completely remodeled it.

They had moved from southern Europe for the same reason my family left England. "There was no job, no working, so we came here to work," she explained. Her husband worked in a restaurant; she got a job first doing domestic work, and later she also went to work in a restaurant. Now she was retired and proud to show me her family pictures and tell me how much she enjoyed the house where she had lived since 1974.

"Very nice neighbors I got. All nice people. All get on well," she said, smiling broadly.

But Mrs. Dello's apparent tolerance toward the influx of fellow migrants is apparently not shared by most Brits. A 2009 public opinion survey showed that 66 percent of British respondents saw the United Kingdom's immigration levels as more of a problem than an opportunity, and tough, new government policies reflect those attitudes.

"We're putting together the biggest shake-up of our system in forty-five years," Lin Homer, the chief executive of the U.K. Border Agency, told me when I met her at the Home Office, the British equivalent of the U.S. Department of Homeland Security.

"Put at its simplest, we think we need to establish strong borders. We need to have an approach to selective migration where we bring into the country the people that the country needs, where we signal very clearly that we expect people to play by the rules, and we'll enforce our laws when they don't. But at the end of that, we want our systems to be firm and fair."

Homer oversees a staff of twenty-five thousand charged with carrying out a two-pronged approach to management, one that tries to select for admission people with the right skills while at the same time rooting out and deporting migrant scofflaws.

In recent decades, the rules have altered, mirroring the nation's history as a faded colonial power, and, since 1973, as a member of the European Union. Within a relatively short time, changing preferences over who's "in" and who's "out" have come to resemble a children's playground of classmates whose popularity ebbs and flows according to status and perceived advantage. As an imperial ruler, Britain was the leader of its own club, dictating terms of entry to members of its far-flung empire. The decline of the Commonwealth and the rise of Europe as a political entity led to an evolving series of policies that alternately expanded and reduced the rights of different racial groups and nationalities. Shifting international alliances, allegiances, and priorities led to situational migration policies governed by the politics of the times.

In half a century, the size of Britain's foreign-born population more than doubled, rising from 4.2 percent of the country in 1951 to nearly 10 percent of the nation in 2005.

After World War II, until 1962, the law made no distinction between natives of former British colonies and those born in the United Kingdom. But as the influx of migrants—notably from India, Pakistan, Jamaica, and other Caribbean nations—changed the complexion of the populace, British antipathy toward nonwhites grew. The legal upshot was the 1962 Commonwealth Immigrants Act, which required migrants from Commonwealth countries to have job vouchers or skills needed in the United Kingdom. The law had unintended consequences. It ended up encouraging immigration, particularly from South Asia. One reason was that in anticipation of its passage, migrants entered the country to get in under the wire, before the law took effect. After it passed, the legislation stimulated even further migration because it allowed settlers to bring over members of their immediate family.

Rising unemployment, racism, and the formation of immigrant neighborhoods led to social tensions and race riots. In 1968, the Conservative Party politician Enoch Powell inflamed passions with his infamous "Rivers of Blood" speech.

"We must be mad, literally mad, as a nation to be permitting the annual inflow of some fifty thousand dependents, who are for the most part the material of the future growth of the immigrant-descended population," he ranted. "It is like watching a nation busily engaged in heaping up its own funeral pyre."

(This provocative rhetoric remained posted for historical value on the Internet site of the conservative *Daily Telegraph* newspaper. In 2009, the same Web page that carried Powell's warning about the "preventable evils" of immigration featured an adjacent ad that seemed to taunt him across the decades. Serving as testament to a dramatically altered and multicultural Britain, a notice for Muslima.com, a matrimonial and dating site for single Muslims, offered its services.)

Influenced by the U.S. civil rights movement, the United Kingdom enacted legislation to curb discrimination and racism. But at the same time, beginning in 1968, it passed immigration laws which, because they favored migrants of British ancestry, had the effect of encouraging white and European immigration. That trend persisted after Britain joined the European Union. Now the "in" group is explicitly European, since Europeans are free to enter and stay in the United Kingdom. Among the "outs" are residents of the former colonial and largely nonwhite outposts in the West Indies, South Asia, and Africa.

The more recent adoption by the United Kingdom of a "managed migration" policy continues the country's inclination to favor Europeans over migrants from elsewhere. Britain is one of four countries to have embraced a so-called points-based system that gives preferential treatment to migrants possessing the skills needed by the admitting countries. (The others are Canada, Australia, and New Zealand.)

Under the British system, employers may import workers from outside Europe only if the employees qualify under a setup that awards points according to needed skills. The government appointed the Migration Advisory Committee, composed of economists and government officials, to study the jobs situation and publish reports listing occupational shortages. The first one, issued in September 2008, recorded a need for managers of construction projects, civil and mechanical engineers, various doctors, scientists, nurses, teachers of math and science, highly paid chefs, and, curiously, skilled ballet dancers and sheep shearers.

"The important thing for business is that the managed migration system allows them to hire people from outside the United Kingdom when they can't get the right people with the right skills in the U.K. labor market as it is," explained Neil Carberry, an official with the 240,000-member Confederation of British Industry. The influential CBI pushed for the system before the government adopted it in 2008. "So the system has to be flexible and demand-led and responsive to the economy. But our members understand that you've also got to balance that off against the social costs, for instance on health, education and local services, and local integration costs, and that's why a managed system works well."

But how well the British approach does work, and for whom, is a matter of dispute.

On the enforcement end, teams of agents conduct surprise raids on workplaces to hunt down and root out illegal immigrants.

"We're looking for people who are from outside the European Union that are either here unlawfully or don't have permission to work in the United Kingdom," Len Nembhard told me as he prepared to lead a multiracial squad of immigration agents on raids of London-area fast-food restaurants. The agency's efforts are targeted at low-skilled workers, Nembhard explained. "For the most part it's restaurants, cleaning companies, a lot of the service industries," he said.

A crew of about a dozen drove in unmarked vans from the center of London to Ilford, a suburb with a large concentration of South Asians. Dressed in black uniforms and protective vests, the agents made for an imposing sight, marching down the high street and entering a fast-food restaurant.

"Come outside!" they yelled to cooks back in the kitchen of the fried chicken joint, ordering employees to sit at customer tables and produce their identification. It was the same routine at the three restaurants they raided on the day I accompanied them. Round up workers. Inspect their papers. Interrogate the foreigners. Call in to verify visas.

Employers are required to check documents such as passports and work visas and to keep copies. They can pay fines of up to $15,000 for each illegal worker.

At the first two places, they found nothing unusual. "Everyone's immigration status checks out," said agent Shane Healy. "So obviously no arrests have been made and we're now leaving the premises," he explained on the way out.

But their next target, another fast-food eatery, offered better prospects. They had arrested people there previously.

As they questioned employees and ran checks, they pulled apart holes in their stories. A fellow restaurant worker translated for a Pakistani cook. The man said he had been in the country for four years and had been planning to apply for asylum. But he had been scared. The explanation angered agent Vikki Lacey.

"We're not in Pakistan!" she yelled at the interpreter. "We're in England! Why now? Why not four years ago? If he was that scared for his life, he would have done it when he got here. Clearly, he's taking the mick [putting one over]!"

Another Pakistani's story also fell apart under scrutiny. He told the agents he had a valid marriage visa, allowing him to stay in the country as long as he lived with a British wife. But when an agent called the woman from a mobile phone, she said they had broken up.

"Okay, thank you very much," said the agent, hitting the "off" button with a sense of triumph. He turned to the worker, who had stood passively, wearing a baseball cap and a sweatshirt, listening to the agent's end of the incriminating conversation. "You're busted, mate! Your wife said to me you're living here illegally. Right?" Then came the zinger. "She separated with you in 2005."

Agents patted down the two men, relieved them of the possessions in their pockets, then fingerprinted and handcuffed them.

"Anything that you do or say may be given in evidence. You're coming with me," said Lacey, before she and the other agents led their quarry across the high street into a waiting van and off to jail for deportation proceedings.

At the time of my visit, UK immigration officials were boasting that they were kicking out of the country, on average, one person every eight minutes, the highest deportation level since 2002. I wondered about procedures and civil rights. The agents I accompanied had entered businesses and questioned workers without search warrants or judges' orders.

"It's basically a fishing trip," agent Shane Healy acknowledged. "Obviously we know that these sorts of premises do employ a lot of illegal workers. It's very much part-time work, part-time worker, cash in hand, so we've got a good idea really."

But the Border Agency's enforcement practices have drawn fire from civil rights groups and minority business leaders. In particular, owners of Britain's twelve thousand Bangladeshi and Indian "curry houses" complain that they have been unfairly targeted.

"We believe the way people are treated in this country by immigration, totally a racist treatment we got," said Nur-Ur Rahman Khandaker, sitting at a table in the Gandhi Tandoori Restaurant, his family-owned eatery southeast of London, in Kent. "Sometimes we feel we are the second-class citizens of this country."

Khandaker, the secretary-general of the Bangladesh Caterers Association, said his own restaurant had been raided twice by immigration agents. Once they arrested four workers and then released them. The second time they accused Khandaker of hiring an illegal migrant, but the restaurant owner contested the charge, saying the man was there for a job interview. Khandaker complained that Britain's managed migration policy would not allow him to bring in needed workers from outside Europe.

"We're trying to make them understand that the curry houses are suffering from staff shortages for the last ten years," he said, explaining that the industry couldn't find qualified chefs. "And my son or my daughter is not interested to work in my premises," he said.

Khandaker recounted how an immigration official had suggested he hire Polish migrants. It was a plan that failed miserably. He laughed as he told what happened.

"So I bring them in," he said. "They say, 'Oh, stinky curry. I can smell it.'" Within a few days, they left. "And I can't blame him, 'cause the poor fellow, he's not used to this sort of experience."

The policy of giving preferential treatment to Europeans is insidious, suggested M. Habib Rahman, chief executive of the Joint Council for the Welfare of Immigrants (JCWI), an advocacy group established in 1967.

The JCWI had urged the government not to adopt the points-based system. It argued that the policy would replicate "the racial injustice which is a feature of our socially unjust planet with its huge gaps in international wealth and development."

"When you are talking about workers coming from developing countries and coming from the European Union, there should be a level playing field for that," Rahman, a native of Bangladesh, told me.

"In the interest of Britain's economy, if the job needs to be done here, and we invite people to come and do the work, we want people from non-E.U. countries and E.U. countries to be given the same opportunity to come and fulfill those vacancies. Because that's treating people of the world in the same way, and there is no discrimination to people from developing worlds . . . mainly they're black and Asian people."

I asked Lin Homer at the UK Border Agency to explain the justification for the policy. I told her about the raid I'd witnessed and the Pakistanis who had been arrested.

"Had they been Poles, or had they been from Spain, they'd still be working," I pointed out. "Why do you make the distinction between certain people?"

"Put at its simplest, we are saying if you are going to be in this country, you play by our laws," she replied. "And I think this is the same as you would find in most countries, including your own. So if you're Spanish, so if you are Polish, or British, you have a right not only to be in the country, but to work, and of course, we would respect those rights. If you come here as an illegal, and you don't have a right to be here, we will take action against you."

To me, that was more a *description* of the current policy, not a reasonable explanation for it. I pressed the point.

"I understand that, but why pick one country over another? Why say, 'He's Pakistani, he's got to go. He's Polish, he can stay'?"

"We don't take those decisions based on ethnicity at all," Homer replied. "We take them based on the legal status of the individual. So— 'He's European; he has a freedom of movement in Europe, and a right to work. He is not European or British, and does not have legal status.'"

I tried again. "And the principle behind that is what?"

"The principle behind that is legality," Homer answered firmly.

The policy has dire consequences for non-Europeans working in Britain without permission. An estimated five hundred thousand illegal immigrants live in the United Kingdom, most of them in the London area. Among them is Alfonso Camiwet, who came to the United Kingdom on a tourist visa from the Philippines in 2002. I met him in the tony London suburb of Rickmansworth, caring for a man who had suffered a stroke. Camiwet was living in the man's house, earning the equivalent of about $7.50 an hour, but he also had worked as a janitor, cleaning offices. Camiwet said he was living a shadow existence.

"Underground economy, secretly," he explained. The agencies that farm out workers as caregivers and cleaners look the other way and "will sort out things."

In exchange for the work, he said, illegal migrants take jobs at low wages.

"Instead of being given the minimum, instead of six or seven pounds, they will receive only five," he said. "They'll work because they have families to feed, and they have bills to pay."

The careful migration management cordon that the UK is trying to erect is gradually being replicated by Europe as whole. Members of the European Union are introducing a "blue card" system that would allow a process of admissions for highly skilled workers. Europeans see themselves in competition with the United States.

Italian foreign minister and former European Commission vice president Franco Frattini, a supporter of the blue card, proposed tackling Europe's looming demographic crisis by attracting some twenty million extra workers from abroad. "The challenge is to attract the workers needed to fill specific gaps," he said.

European politicians are trying to pull in more skilled employees, and at the same time, they are constructing barriers to contain the movement of unskilled labor.

In East London, Vaughan Jones, the chief executive of Praxis, a social services agency for migrants, told me the trends both in the European Union and Europe as a whole are clear and disturbing.

"The general thrust is 'Fortress Europe,'" he said. "The general thrust is to keep a wall around the continent . . . because they want to allow free movement of labor within the economic union."

At the edges of Europe and beyond, budgets for migrant detention camps, border posts, patrols, and guards are increasing. I visited Europe's so-called green border, the name given to much of the eight-hundred-mile frontier between Poland to the west and the former Soviet republics of Ukraine and Belarus to the east.

"The border between Poland and the Ukraine is a line you must imagine," Polish Border Guard major Jerzy Ostrowski explained as we stood on a verdant hill overlooking farmlands in both countries. The border strip along the Bieszczady Mountains resembles a fire road, even though in places, leftover structures from the Soviet Union, which took borders seriously, remain.

Ostrowski, a burly and affable Border Guard veteran dressed in green camouflage fatigues, pointed out a double fence. "It is called *sistema*," he said. "It's an old Russian or Ukrainian word. It means 'fence, electrical one,' not high-voltage. However, if you cut the wire, it makes the alarm at the closest post. It was created at the Soviet Union time but nowadays it can work."

Polish authorities are doing their part in the construction of a new version of an iron curtain around the European economic zone. The European Union's distinctive flag—a circle of gold stars on a blue background—has been planted on the Polish Border Guard's migrant detention centers and patrol vehicles, as well as on aircraft and helicopters with surveillance systems that carry high-powered cameras and infrared gear.

Unable to effectively patrol the mountainous green border on the ground, crews in six-seat helicopters fly along the frontier, using heat detection devices, onboard TV cameras, and monitors to spot possible intruders. If they see people who seem suspicious, the aerial spotters then call in their locations by radio to patrol agents. With roads and villages close to the border, speed is of the essence. "If you don't catch them immediately, you lose them," said Ostrowski.

Poland became a part of a more or less borderless Europe in December 2007, when the so-called Schengen zone expanded to include the other new European Union members—Estonia, Hungary, Latvia, Lithuania, Malta, the Czech Republic, Slovakia, and Slovenia. As European officials lifted internal border controls, they also allocated more than $5 billion to a five-year program with the umbrella title of Solidarity and Management of Migration Flows. A good chunk of the funding (about 38 percent) was allotted to programs concerned with refugees, asylum cases, and integration, but the lion's share went to controlling Europe's more than fifty-six thousand miles of land and sea borders, hiring and training new guards, building crossing points, and installing surveillance systems.

The Europeans also have integrated a continent-wide computer database that is used to check passport information. At Poland's

Medya border crossing point on the border with Ukraine, newly up-graded with European funds at a cost of more than $4 million, I watched as recently hired Polish guards methodically approached each vehicle, collected passports, brought the documents inside to their booths, and scanned each one on two computer networks—one linked to a Polish system headquartered in Warsaw, the other to a Europe-wide network. Outside, customs officials and dogs checked automobiles and trucks. The thorough inspections resulted in waiting times of up to twenty-five hours.

Ostrowski explained that Poland is often a transit country for migrants trying to make it to other European nations. Because of that, he said, Polish border guards have a broad responsibility.

"We work for all Europe," he said. "Poland is a member of the European Union, so our work must be at an acceptable level for all countries of Europe. We are the guards of the external border of Europe."

Between 2004 and 2006, Polish border authorities received more than $400 million from the European Union.

Ostrowski took me to see another European-financed contribution to Poland's new status as sentinel, a $3.5 million migrant detention center in a former military headquarters in Przemysl, a town on Poland's southeastern border. The Przemysl migrant prison is one of an estimated 224 migrant camps spread across the European Union.

Poland has thirteen prisons for foreign nationals, four of them along the nation's eastern border. With separate rooms for men, women, and children, the Przemysl center can house 173 people. At the time of my visit, most of the detainees were Russians. But there were almost as many Vietnamese. Border Guard major Marek Osetek, who was in charge of the prison, said they were waiting for a flight chartered by the European Union to deport the Vietnamese detainees.

Many of the Vietnamese the Poles deport had been smuggled into Poland, explained Osetek. "The smugglers are organized in Vietnam," he said. "They arrange for the Vietnamese to fly to Moscow and stay in housing. From there, some go by train, others by car through Ukraine to the Polish border. . . . There is one person in Vietnam, another in Moscow, then guides who pick them up in Ukraine and take them in," he said.

"These are organizations that span thousands of kilometers," he said, sounding somewhat in awe. "It's more profitable than smuggling drugs. If you get caught with cocaine, you lose your product, but if you get caught with illegals, it's not your problem anymore."

An estimated forty thousand to fifty thousand Vietnamese live in Poland, many illegally. A good number arrived in the early 1990s — a legacy of exchange programs and other networks established by Vietnam with Poland when the Eastern European country was Communist-run.

Tran Van Minh seemed in fairly decent spirits, considering he was facing deportation. Maybe it was that he was engrossed in reading a Vietnamese translation of Dale Carnegie's *How to Win Friends and Influence People* when I met him, sitting on his bed in a six-man cell he shared with other Vietnamese migrants. Carnegie's teachings were unlikely to do him much good, at least as far as the Polish authorities were concerned. The forty-year-old shopkeeper had lived in Krakow, running a clothing stall in a bazaar. After immigration police questioned him, he decided to move to Sweden and was in transit when he was arrested. His wife and two Polish-born children had already returned to Vietnam.

"You know how it is," he said, speaking in Polish. "You've got to go abroad to make money. There's no way to make money in Vietnam."

European efforts to manage migration extend beyond Europe's own borders. Europeans are creating buffer zones and outposts. By equipping and financing non-European nations, they are essentially deputizing them to carry out satellite operations.

One program is the E.U. Border Assistance Mission to Moldova and Ukraine (EUBAM), launched in 2005 to reinforce the 760-mile border between those two nations. By the end of 2007, the European Union had poured more than $26 million into the program, had posted 122 experts from twenty-two European Union countries, and had pledged an additional $35 million in assistance.

Although ostensibly started as a result of requests from the presidents of both Moldova and Ukraine, both countries need foreign assistance and have eventual designs on European Union membership. So it is not surprising that analysts use blunt language to describe what they see as payoffs. "It is often the financial aspect that motivates countries like Ukraine and Moldova to give up sovereignty over their borders," wrote commentators in the leftist *Monthly Review*. "Many other states on the European periphery are vulnerable to this kind of interstate bribery."

Europe also is trying to control migration from Africa. The results have been mixed. Income disparities between Africa and Europe, combined with the intractable problems of poverty, famine, and war, continue to make for a powerful lure. So rather than stopping migration, the most significant consequence of stepped-up border enforcement and control has been to change the routes used by migrants who have resorted to increasingly longer and hazardous journeys.

In the 1990s, growing numbers of sub-Saharan Africans bound for Europe traveled through Morocco, Africa's northwesternmost nation, and tried to enter one of two Spanish enclaves, Melilla or Ceuta on the Mediterranean. Even though the cities are nestled in Morocco, because they are owned by Spain, once migrants get to the enclaves, they have technically made it to Europe. Spain detains them, but since many lack documents and can't be deported, Spain eventually releases them on the Spanish mainland. In 2005, thousands of desperate African migrants hoisted ladders and tried to storm over the fences into the Spanish cities. Spain deployed troops to stop them, as did Morocco. Five migrants were killed and scores were injured.

At Spain's request, Moroccan authorities built higher fences, dug ditches, and set up military camps adjacent to Ceuta and Melilla in efforts to prevent migration. Moroccan security forces patrolled nearby forests and towns, hoping to catch African migrants hiding out.

When I visited in 2006, the new fences reminded me of ones I had seen along the U.S.–Mexico border in San Diego. Activist Boubker Khamlichi, coordinator of a human rights association known as Shabaka ("the Web" in Arabic), complained that by cracking down on migrants, Morocco was doing Europe's dirty work.

"It is horrible what Morocco did, even though it's an African country," he said. "It shouldn't go against the Africans, but there has been pressure from the European Union. For many years, Morocco didn't buckle under, but for the last two or three years, it agreed to be the gendarme of Europe because Europe is very strong and it pressured the regime."

Human rights groups criticized Morocco for using excessive force. The humanitarian organization Médecins sans Frontières (Doctors without Borders) accused the country of dumping hundreds of migrants in the desert without food or water.

"We have recognized that we made mistakes. I mean nobody's perfect," said Khalid Zerouali when I interviewed him at the Ministry of the Interior in the capital of Rabat. Zerouali had recently been appointed by the Moroccan king, Mohammed VI, to head the country's Migration and Border Surveillance Directorate.

Zerouali attributed the "mistakes" to inadequate training. He denied that Morocco was under any pressure from Europe to crack down on illegal migrants, and estimated that in 2005 the nation had spent the equivalent of about $74 million on migration-related security and deportations. The nation was negotiating with Europeans for financial assistance to help shoulder the costs, but, sensitive to any suggestion of a quid pro quo, he emphasized that Morocco had taken the initiative.

"We are doing this because Morocco is a country that assumes its regional and international responsibilities," he said. "So far, Morocco has not, as of today, received one dime from anyone."

In actuality, Morocco had received billions of dollars worth of aid, though not specifically tied to the issue of securing its borders with Melilla and Ceuta. With Morocco eager for closer ties with Europe, Moroccan and European officials had a series of meetings that culminated in a 2008 decision by the European Union to grant Morocco "advanced status" relations, giving the African nation greater access to European markets and participation in E.U. agencies. Under the deal, the European Union agreed to provide Morocco with assistance amounting to $893 million for a four-year period. For its part, Morocco accepted an "action plan" acknowledging that "[I]n relations with the European Union member states the issue of illegal migration is one of the principal sources of concern." Morocco pledged increased cooperation with Europe but remained opposed to forcible deportations of migrants from Europe.

•   •   •

One effect of Morocco's tightened border security was to trap migrants who had trekked, often for weeks and months, from sub-Saharan regions expecting to get across the Mediterranean into Europe.

Scattered through a warren of alleyways in Takadoum, a Rabat slum, were buildings crammed with sub-Saharan migrants. In one apartment, thirty men shared three rooms, a makeshift kitchen, and a hole in the floor that served as their bathroom. They were afraid to leave, terrified they would encounter authorities. Some watched TV all day; others prayed constantly.

"There is nothing to do, so we pray all the time," said one man. I asked him what he prayed for. "We pray for better conditions," he replied.

In addition to cornering people who were unable or unwilling to return to their homes, the border security measures also had the effect of redirecting migrants away from Morocco. Thousands instead headed to Mauritania, south of Morocco, to find vessels that would transport them to the Spanish-owned Canary Islands. It was a dangerous gambit. Week after week, flimsy wooden boats were lost in the Atlantic. Migrants often traveled for days crowded together without food or water. In 2006, Spanish authorities reported that thirty-one thousand migrants had successfully reached the shores of the islands, more than six times as many as in the previous year. But those numbers were only part of the tragic story. Each day, on average, two bodies washed up on the beaches of West Africa and the Canaries. Authorities estimated that six thousand were killed trying to get across.

To try to stem the exodus, the Europeans called out a relatively new multinational organization, the European Agency for the Management of Operational Cooperation at External Borders (Frontex). The growing importance of the Warsaw-headquartered agency is reflected in its budget, which ballooned from €6.2 million when it was started in 2005, to €83.3 million ($122 million) in 2009. Much of the work of Frontex is in running training exercises and conducting joint operations among migration law enforcement agencies within Europe and on the borders of the continent. But the unprecedented scope of the migration flow to the Canary Islands brought Frontex to West Africa.

The Frontex operation involved European personnel, predominantly from Spain, but also from France, Germany, Italy, Portugal,

Luxembourg, the Netherlands, Norway, and the United Kingdom. Boats and aircraft conducted patrols around the Canary Islands and also along the coast of West Africa, intercepting boats and turning them back. The European-led operation required the cooperation of Morocco, Cape Verde, Gambia, Guinea, and Nigeria. It also included the active participation of Senegal and Mauritania, which signed bilateral agreements with Spain and provided personnel for the operations.

In a major way, and for all practical purposes, Europe had extended its borders to Africa.

"We don't like to be identified as part of this 'Fortress Europe,'" explained Gil Arias Fernández, a veteran Spanish police official who in December 2005 was appointed Frontex's deputy executive director. "The aim is not to build a wall in between Europe and the African or Asian countries. It is just to have a gate where you know who is coming and what are the [intentions] of these people coming," he told me during an interview in his Warsaw office.

"If we do it closer to the European coast, then the only thing that can be done is search and rescue operations. . . . So what we try is to patrol more closer to the points of departure in order to prevent these people to depart from the coast."

But as the U.S. immigration experience has shown, when border enforcement tightens in one area, illegal migrants cross at another, just as a balloon squeezed in the middle bulges at the ends. In Africa, as border patrols interdicted migrants trying to make it to the Canary Islands, the traffic across the Mediterranean from Africa to southern Italy, Malta, Cyprus, and Greece increased. According to the UN Refugee Agency, in 2008 more than thirty-six thousand African "boat people" arrived in Italy, an 80 percent rise from the previous year.

Europe's migration control regime boosted its Mediterranean presence, while continuing efforts to hold the line in West Africa. South of Mauritania, the former French colony of Senegal, Africa's westernmost country, with a population of 11 million people, has assigned its police and military to assist European border management.

Over the centuries, Senegal's capital port city of Dakar has been an important crossroads for trade, as well as a center for migration, with a history of tragic consequences.

Heading out from the harbor on a Senegalese Navy migrant patrol boat, Lieutenant Omar Sagna pointed out the island of Gorée as we sped by. For some three hundred years, Gorée was a shipping point for the transatlantic slave trade, the most massive migration in human history. These days, Senegalese try to prevent Africans from leaving. The Canary Islands are about nine hundred perilous miles away. Dressed in a blue jumpsuit, Sagna, the vessel's commanding officer, picked up binoculars to look for signs of boats attempting the crossing.

"We have seen many people, but as time goes, they have reduced their travel to Europe and we don't see many anymore," he said. The Senegalese Navy vessels are often joined by European counterparts. As we headed out of port, we passed patrol boats operated by Spain's military police force, the Guardia Civil.

Along the shore, Senegal's gendarmes run beach patrols on foot and on motorized three-wheel bikes. They are shows of force in areas police believe have been departure points for migrants and human smugglers.

Sagna said it is an intense and ongoing struggle. "We have the policemen on land and at sea. We have the air force; we have the foreign ships like Spanish and Italians. And the Portuguese they have been here in a frigate," he said. "Oh, and Luxembourg," he added. "They have patrol aircraft which have been here."

Outside the harbor, Sagna spotted a boat that he decided merited investigation. "It's a big boat, and we're going to cross it and investigate it and see what it's going to do."

Sagna said he looked for boats with a number of people. This one had eleven. Plenty of food, provisions, and fuel for a several-day trip might also be a giveaway. The navy lieutenant waved them down and had what seemed like a friendly conversation in Wolof, the common Senegalese language.

"They're fishermen," he concluded as the wooden boat slowly motored away. They were looking for a decent catch, not a way out of Africa.

Much of the equipment used by Senegal was donated by Spain. In December 2006, the nation's socialist prime minister, José Luis Rodríguez Zapatero, came to Dakar to formalize a deal that included a gift of two coastal patrol boats, five all-terrain vehicles, and communications gear. He also pledged the equivalent of $27 million in development aid.

I wondered what, outside the realm of bilateral governmental relations, Senegalese foot soldiers felt about their role in Europe's migration battles. So I put the question to the police agent Bienvenu Agboton, who directs the migration patrols. To him it was a matter of pride and safety.

"The Senegalese are very concerned about this situation mainly because young Senegalese are leaving the country under very dangerous circumstances and risking their lives," he said. "It was a matter of dignity. In order to preserve our dignity, we felt we had to be involved in this fight."

The Europeans also are aware that the demands they make of African nations need to be politically palatable to the leaders they want to accept them. "Experiences have demonstrated that to broker a deal the European Union needs to offer something in return," European Commission officials announced in a November 2006 policy declaration. The document made it clear that those governments that were not part of the club would have to earn the right for their residents to travel to Europe for work: "Once certain conditions have been met, such as cooperation on illegal migration and effective mechanisms for readmission, the objective could be to agree [sic] Mobility Packages with a number of interested third countries which would enable their citizens to have better access to the E.U."

Translation: If poor governments agreed to take back illegal migrants who had been deported, Europe would use legal migrants in temporary worker programs. From the European point of view, this would enable member nations to better regulate migration and have access to cheap foreign labor.

"We need the immigration, but what we need is to have it in a channeled way," explained the Frontex official Arias. "Then also to make it fit with the needs of Europe."

"The aim," he continued, is to attract young migrants. "Because in Europe, the average age in the European population is getting older, so this is not good. So we need somehow fresh blood from the immigrants. They are the only ones that can do this, that can refresh the European blood."

Visions of Count Dracula aside, the most common argument in developed countries for managed migration is the one Arias put in a nutshell—the need to import workers because of aging labor forces and populations. It may be a predatory and self-serving justification, but it's one that has strong advocates on both continents.

"The American people want their government to be serious about protecting the public, enforcing the rule of law, and creating a rational system of legal immigration that will proactively fit our needs rather than reactively responding to future waves of illegal immigration," declared Senator Charles Schumer of New York, chairman of the Senate Immigration Subcommittee in summer 2009, trying to set the tone for a renewed immigration debate in Washington.

Bringing order out of chaos by controlling migration with laws that "fit our needs" has become an immigration mantra of the developed world's politicians.

The political calculation is that a statute adopted by a representative democracy would be seen as inherently just, particularly if it established clear categories with rules that could be universally understood by various constituencies.

"People who enter the United States without our permission are illegal aliens, and illegal aliens should not be treated the same as people who entered the United States legally," said Schumer. The message was identical to one that Janet Napolitano, the secretary of the Department of Homeland Security, had delivered only a few days earlier in a speech that repeated the phrase "the rule of law" five times.

"We begin with immigration with the concept that it is an embodiment of the rule of law and that the rule of law will be fully and fairly and effectively applied across the spectrum," she said.

It also was the same point that UK official Lin Homer had made to me about that country's immigration laws: "[W]e expect people to play by the rules, and we'll enforce our laws when they don't. But at the end of that, we want our systems to be firm and fair."

The "firm and fair" enforcement of rules is, of course, a bit of a smoke screen. Rules may be fairly enforced, but if the regulations themselves are unfair or inconsistent, implementing them isn't much of a salve. By its nature, legislation is political and situational, reflecting the dispositions of its authors. U.S. laws once condoned the importation of slaves and the exclusion of Asians. As a character in an Anatole France novel observed, "the majestic quality of the law . . . prohibits the wealthy as well as the poor from sleeping under the bridges, from begging in the streets, and from stealing bread."

The use of laws by wealthier economies to better adjust migration—to try to ensure that the admission, care, and feeding of migrants best suits our own purposes—presupposes that our needs and desires are paramount. The approach is not new. It does nothing to address the root causes of migration, nor does it make either sending or receiving countries more sustainable. It's just a twenty-first-century iteration of a golden rule: he who has the gold makes the rules.

CHAPTER 13

"Torn Apart for the Need to Survive"

On Monday, January 5, 2009, with the economic downturn in full bore, President-elect Barack Obama, just two weeks short of his swearing in, went to Capitol Hill and held a series of New Year meetings with congressional leaders. Afterward, he remarked on the obvious, stating that the national economy was "bad and getting worse." As the first full trading day drew to a close, his observation was reflected in the stock market results. The Dow Jones, NASDAQ, and Standard & Poor's indexes all fell. The bond market weakened. Among the bad news rumors circulating on the Internet at the time was that Microsoft Corporation would be announcing massive job cuts.

That day, as anonymous Microsoft "sources" tried to dampen speculation about possible plans to trim the workforce, company officials also were looking down the road. The corporate colossus sent a very public "Microsoft Word" to the incoming administration that one company program the United States really needed to adopt was a plan to relax restrictions on the importing of migrant workers.

The policy proposal came in the form of a posting from Microsoft's legal and corporate affairs department on the Web site of President-elect Obama's transition team. Citing the need to attract and retain "the brightest, most talented people from around the world," the computer giant called on the Obama White House to "remove caps that bar entry into the U.S. by high-skilled immigrants" not only on a temporary basis, but for good. "Rather than pretend that we want these highly skilled, well-trained innovators to remain for only a temporary period, we should accept and indeed embrace the fact that we want them to become permanent U.S. residents, so that they can drive innovation and economic growth alongside America's native-born talent."

Microsoft's long-term plan for more migrant employees to spur economic growth stood in sharp contrast to the firm's immediate financial reality. With declining revenue, Microsoft needed to control costs. As one arm of the company pushed to be allowed to import more foreign workers, another was preparing dismissal notices. Two and half weeks after making its case to import "people from around the world," the company announced that it would be eliminating fourteen hundred jobs right away, and might lay off up to twenty-six hundred additional employees over the next eighteen months.

To the Microsofts of the world, the globe is a mighty chessboard with pieces that need to be moved around in accordance with long-term goals, grand strategies, challenges from other major players, and the circumstances of play. Mobility is key, and if the rules of play inhibit movement, then the players seek to change them. Generally missing from the calculation is a sense of the common good. It's a global system that I earlier referred to as "coyote capitalism," one whose skewed priorities place the welfare of migrants at the bottom of the list. Properly addressing migration requires not only a commitment to address its causes, but a reexamination of values, a better understanding of enforcement regimes and vested interests, and the realization that an international issue entails a global approach.

Even though the demand for migrant workers rises and dips over time and with economic fluctuations, the overall appetite in the developed world for the brains and brawn of foreign labor seems unrelenting. Like addicts, we need the next fix. We are hooked.

The cravings come from all sectors of the economy.

"There are only so many brains available," the president of a U.S. high-tech market research firm told *Investor's Business Daily*. "And either they're going to get them or we are."

California landscape contractors made a similar case for their need to import low-skilled workers: "Any employer of immigrants, Mexican and other nationalities, will tell you that immigrant workers are some of their best, hardest-working employees and, in many cases, the business could not survive without them."

Policymakers and advocates on both sides of the Atlantic present identical justifications for moving millions of workers across borders.

"We have an aging workforce and declining workforce participation, and job growth will continue in both higher-skilled and lower-skilled jobs," contend U.S. business leaders.

"Europe is facing a demographic time-bomb which could go off as early as 2010 when the EU labour force is expected to decrease significantly due to a deadly combination of an aging and declining population," wrote Graham Watson, a European Parliament member from England and the leader of the Parliament's Alliance of Liberals and Democrats. "[O]ur economy is set to lose 20 million workers (and their tax payments) in the next twenty years if we do not actively increase migration flows or take radical action to encourage European women to have more children."

Watson did not elaborate on exactly what "radical action" might persuade women to pump out offspring in numbers sufficient to adequately populate the workforce. But common assumptions on both continents see migrants not only as indispensable to the economic machinery but also as replacement parts to be shipped in and used when old ones slow down, wear out, or are otherwise unavailable.

The inexorable desires of companies to hire migrant workers and of migrants to cross borders have combined with the often complex dynamics of parochial and national politics and competing interests to produce a global fog of contradictory and inconsistent immigration policies and attitudes. No international bodies regulate migration, nor is there consensus about "best practices." National policies fluctuate with economic needs and fickle public opinion.

The industrialized and undeveloped countries of the world tend to look through the immigration telescope from opposite ends. As a result, they inevitably wind up with seemingly irreconcilable perspectives.

Wealthy nations debate the costs and benefits of new arrivals, often blaming migrants for depressing wages, for crime and social problems. Foreigners may be recognized for their economic and cultural contributions, but the often lurking undercurrents are concerns about assimilation, race, cultural change, and ethnic identity.

On the other hand, in the sending nations of the developing world, leaving home and going abroad for work is about balancing expectations of opportunity and betterment with the difficulties of separation. Even if family members and policymakers understand the benefits of remittances sent home by migrants, they also have varying degrees of apprehension about the "brain drain," the effects of talented professionals leaving, and about fractured families.

Migration permits countries on both ends of the pipeline to avoid and defer problems. Where sending nations should be addressing such urgent needs as developing their economies and finding ways to keep families and communities together, instead, outflows of migrants let them off the hook. By the same token, in destination countries, migration reduces the incentive to create sustainable economies that are able and willing to tap their own resources.

Having ready access to migrant labor has bred the love-hate relationship that has stoked the raging immigration debates in the word's wealthier countries. On the one hand, they contribute to our economic bounties; on the other, the arrival and presence of migrants can be unsettling. I remember the calamitous tones used by the news media to describe Mexican migration in the early eighties.

"Invasion from Mexico; It Just Keeps Growing," harrumphed a *U.S. News & World Report* issue in 1983, as Mexicans, responding to the deepening economic crisis in their own country, moved across the porous border in record numbers. To describe the influx, in addition to the use of military "invasion" metaphors, journalists trotted out watery, cataclysmic ones—"tidal waves," "floods," "torrents," and "surges."

A nation under assault must defend itself, so the focus of the immigration issue shifted to the alleged harm being done by the invaders and to appropriate methods of defense. Residents, witnessing change and unprepared or unwilling to adapt, often voiced their discomfort.

In 1984, producing a public television documentary about the rapidly changing demographics of Los Angeles, I interviewed one very candid former resident of a San Fernando Valley neighborhood. The all-white area where she had lived had seen an influx of Latinos and a marked exodus of longtime residents. I asked her why she had joined the "white flight" flock.

"It sounds like a terrible thing to say, but I'm going to say it anyway," said Cynthia Horacek, explaining her discomfort. "I was really tired of going to the market and not hearing much English spoken. It was really starting to bother me. And I started feeling like when the billboards are going up in Spanish, it's time to move. And it sounds like white flight, but because of the kids, and because of the schools, and because of the percentage of the homes in our neighborhood that weren't taken care of, it was just, it was time to leave."

I've heard echoes of that attitude expressed elsewhere. In Sweden, Åje Carlborn, a researcher and social anthropologist at Malmö University, explained how he felt it necessary to move his family in 1998 when migrants from the Middle East and Africa moved into his neighborhood.

"The main reason was really that our son was about to start school and it wouldn't have been good for him to go in the school in the neighborhood," Carlborn explained. "Not because of any criminal activities, but because of language problems. Many children born and raised in the neighborhood, they don't know a word of Swedish when they start school."

In Poland, Border Guard major Marek Osetek, the warden of a migrant prison, told me his concern about the country's Vietnamese population, estimated at thirty thousand to fifty thousand. "It's just an impenetrable social group," he said, as Vietnamese prisoners awaiting deportation looked on, peering at us standing in the courtyard through the windows of their dormitory-type cells. "They work with each other only. They break the laws. It's standard procedure for them. And when we meet people who have been living in Poland for four to five years, and they don't speak any Polish, it means they've been cut off from the rest of society."

Those, of course, are among the tamer reactions to migration. As we've seen, economic downturns have exacerbated intolerance and spawned restrictive legislation. Lethal brews of racism and xenophobia have produced race riots and nationalist hate movements. In Russia, neo-Nazi thugs have attacked migrants from Central Asia, lured to the country in recent years by relative prosperity. A human rights group recorded 122 murders of foreigners in 2008, up from 25 in 2005. One Tajik man was beheaded. A communiqué from a militant group threatened to kill officials who refused to "evict the blacks."

In Italy, in February 2009, the interior minister, reacting to reported crimes by migrants, announced his support for an emergency decree authorizing local vigilante patrols to hunt out and report on any "illegal activities" perpetrated by immigrants.

And in England at about the same time, construction workers went on strike at a power station, demonstrating against the employment of foreign contractors. After the UK government released 2008 figures showing that British citizens had lost jobs as foreign workers gained them, the bishop of Manchester reportedly warned of a "serious risk of disturbances" with the possibility that racist groups would "try to win support by blaming migrants."

Visceral reactions to the strangers among us can be explained by fear or prejudice. Well-meaning intermediaries try to bridge gaps through dialogue or appeals to our better instincts. But, particularly in a climate of economic difficulties, enforcement measures tend to overshadow efforts aimed at mutual understanding and accommodation.

Laws and regulations governing migrants vary from one industrial nation to the next. In the United States, migrant workers, regardless of their legal status, rightly have the same labor rights as any other employees. Working with state agencies as well as with consulates from Central America and Mexico, the U.S. Department of Labor set up a program in 2004 called the Employment Education and Outreach partnership (EMPLEO), to assist Spanish-speakers on work issues. (The acronym EMPLEO also spells out the Spanish word for employment.) In the first three years of operation, the program collected more than $5.5 million in back wages and overtime.

"We don't ask the person who's calling about their legal status," explained Priscilla Garcia, a U.S. Department of Labor official in Los Angeles. "The law does not distinguish if the employee is here legally or not legally," she said. "Our laws are enforced to protect employees that work in the United States."

So under the U.S. system, theoretically, while one federal department could be representing ripped-off illegal migrant workers, another agency, the Immigration and Customs Enforcement (ICE) office of the Department of Homeland Security, could be arresting and deporting them.

Illegal immigrants also face different levels of enforcement from one local jurisdiction to another. The city of Los Angeles, for example, specifically prohibits police from using immigration law to go after accused criminals, a policy that the former chief of police Bill Bratton enthusiastically endorsed at the time he ran the department.

"The fact of their immigration status is of no concern to me. It isn't. I'm interested in the acts that they're committing, if they're committing crimes: rapes, robberies, dope dealing, I'll address that. I have no interest because I don't have the capacity to deal with the immigration laws of the United States. It's that simple," he told me, explaining that the regulation allows migrants to cooperate with police without facing deportation.

"[The policy] was also intended to try to encourage people who might be here illegally to come forward if they're victims of crime or come forward and assist us as witnesses to a crime without fear that . . . the police would, in fact, then turn them in to the federal government," Bratton said.

But an illegal migrant in Maricopa County, Arizona, might have an altogether different experience if he or she were to encounter a deputy sheriff in the Phoenix area.

"It's a three-pronged attack, the 'Triple I,' which means 'Illegal Immigration Interdiction,'" said Joseph M. Arpaio, the county's tough-talking sheriff. As nearly seventy state and local law enforcement agencies around the country have done, Arpaio signed a partnership agreement with ICE that allows his deputies to enforce immigration laws once they've received special training.

"I am allowing our deputy sheriffs, in the course of their duties, when they come across a criminal violation, whether it be speeding or what have you, and they find out that there's some illegals involved, or in the car, they will put their ICE hat on and investigate those suspects," Arpaio explained.

"For example, in a traffic violation, there's five others; they're not all driving the car, but we investigate them if we think they're illegal. Then we process them, we have computers, ICE computers. We do the investigation . . . and arrest them, process them, and take them to jail. Then they will take the ICE hat off and go back to their regular deputy sheriff duties."

Not surprisingly, the American Civil Liberties Union, along with Latino rights groups, stepped forward to challenge the strategy in federal court. Representing people who said they had been targeted during "crime suppression sweeps," the lawsuit accused Arpaio of adopting "an unlawful, racially biased policy of stopping, detaining, questioning, and/or searching persons in vehicles in Maricopa County who are or appear to be Latino to interrogate them about their perceived immigration status based on nothing more than their race, color, and/or ethnicity."

In response to complaints, the federal government started taking action against Arpaio. In March 2009, the civil rights division of the U.S. Justice Department opened an investigation into the Maricopa County Sheriff's Office, focusing on "patterns or practices of discriminatory police practices and unconstitutional searches and seizures." Seven months later, the Department of Homeland Security cut back on the authority of his deputies to enforce federal immigration laws. Nonetheless, Arpaio continued his sweeps. "It doesn't bother me, because we are going to do the same thing," Arpaio told reporters. "I am the elected sheriff. I don't take orders from the federal government." It was a stance that seemed to meet with the approval of a good portion of his constituents. As the sweeps continued, 61 percent of Maricopa County voters told pollsters that they approved or strongly approved of the sheriff's job performance.

Similar migration law enforcement issues have played out in the United Kingdom. There, the U.K. Border Agency drew fire in late 2008 when it announced that newly formed "local immigration teams" up and down the country "will work shoulder-to-shoulder with police, Her Majesty's Revenue and Customs, and local partner agencies, in a new series of partnerships."

In reaction, an advocacy group, the Migrant Rights Network, said the new policy would foster anti-immigrant sentiment. "As well as criminalising undocumented migrants, the pressure on these institutions from the Government to monitor migrants is likely to encourage suspicion of all foreigners, damaging race relations more widely."

Another U.K. rights group, Positive Action for Refugees and Asylum Seekers (PARAS), summarized what it suspected was the underlying government intent: "On the one hand the concerted energy spent on 'shutting down illegal working' aims to ensure that a flexible market has the cheap, disposable workers that it requires; on the other those who are designated as 'irregular migrants' are to be criminalised and where possible removed."

The PARAS description of the policy was just a slightly sharpened version of what Lin Homer, the head of the U.K. Border Agency, had told me at the Home Office: "We need to have an approach to selective migration where we bring into the country the people that the country needs."

But enforcing rules that give preferential treatment to Europeans and discriminate against South Asians and Africans makes a mockery of any reasonable claims to fairness. A policy of pulling up the drawbridge and denying entry to non-Europeans smells a lot like America's nineteenth-century Chinese Exclusion Act.

The British system of selective or managed migration throws into sharp relief a fundamental divide in the migration debate—not only in the United Kingdom but also in the United States and globally. The division is between those who place the economic needs of businesses and countries above all other factors, and others whose paramount consideration is the welfare of the migrants.

In London's East End, a longtime hub for migrants—from Huguenots of the seventeenth and eighteenth centuries, to Eastern European Jews (my relatives among them) who arrived in the last part of the nineteenth, to South Asians who started coming in the middle twentieth century—Praxis, founded in 1973, provides support and counseling for migrants and refugees, regardless of legal status. The center describes itself as "the place for the displaced."

In a room of the church building where the group is headquartered, a language instructor taught a tableful of women from Eastern Europe and South Asia the complex fundamentals of English verb tenses. In the kitchen, a cook prepared low-cost meals. Elsewhere, counselors met with clients from Africa and the Philippines, and worked the phones trying to straighten out bureaucratic snafus by government agencies.

Upstairs, in an airy office, Praxis's chief executive, Vaughan Jones, a soft-spoken minister of the United Reformed Church, ticked off some of the criteria for what he considers to be the prerequisites of a decent migration policy: "The right to a decent wage. The right to come and go and not be trapped. The right to a family life and to bring family here. All of those important issues."

Jones described his frustration with the British immigration system. "The managed migration program fails to take into account the human stories," he said. "The bureaucracy just cannot deal with the fact that people come and decide to stay. They come to work for a short period of time and then fall in love. The system doesn't deal with romantic migration, for example."

I was struck by the contrast between his and his government's priorities. "It's a completely different approach than looking at migration in terms of economic needs," I observed.

"Yes it is," he agreed. "Politicians feel that the public needs to see a government which is being tough on immigration, and it helps them in the sense that they try to manage the migration processes, so that they have the right person in the right place at the right time. But what they forget is that they're dealing with human beings, that human beings . . . make choices about whether to leave their country or not, very often because of impossible difficult circumstances in which they find themselves."

Being "tough on immigration" doesn't have to mean being tough on immigrants. Managing or controlling migration sensibly shouldn't be a one-way street. A host of players need to be called to account, from the world's employers of migrants to the nurse recruiters and Indian "body shops" to the exporting nations that use migration as a substitute for development.

On the international scene, debates about migration have been dominated by wealthy nations intent on preserving their own economic interests and setting global priorities. In 1990, the UN General Assembly adopted the "International Convention on the Protection of the Rights of All Migrant Workers and Members of Their Families." The purpose of the agreement was to guarantee to migrants human rights and humane conditions. It takes a middle ground, upholding the rights of sovereign nations to determine who can and who cannot enter and to deport illegal migrants. It seeks to prevent exploitation and trafficking, outlaws indentured servitude, and discourages the employment of undocumented or irregular workers. At the same time, it upholds standards of treatment and human rights of all migrants, regardless of legal status.

It might appear to be noncontroversial, but it's not. By the summer of 2009, of the United Nations' 192 member states, just 41 had ratified it. Just about all of the signatory states (including Mexico and the Philippines) send out more migrants than they take in. Not one of the world's migrant-dependent industrialized countries (including the United States) had signed the agreement.

There may be other ways to regulate migration. In 2003, experts, most prominently then UN secretary-general Kofi Annan and economist Jagdish Bhagwati, called for a global agency to regulate immigration policies and put forward best practices. Bhagwati proposed a World Migration Organization (WMO), similar to the World Trade Organization (WTO).

"Up to now, rich countries have been far too comfortable with a policy framework that allows them to benefit from immigrant labor, while denying immigrants the dignity and rights of a legal status," said Annan.

The proposal for an agency that might rein in rich countries troubled U.S. officials. "The United States is skeptical about the ability of the United Nations to address the migration issue effectively at the global level and is concerned about efforts to develop a rights-based migration regime," said Arthur E. Dewey, assistant secretary of state for population, refugees, and migration in 2005. "The United States would not support the creation of any UN agency on international migration," he added. "The United States continues to believe that the International Organization for Migration's Council Session is the appropriate forum to discuss general international migration issues."

The Geneva-based International Organization for Migration (IOM) operates independently of the United Nations. With offices in some 100 countries and a membership of 125 states, the IOM correctly describes itself as "the world's leading intergovernmental organization in the field of migration." The organization's goals are far-reaching: "[The IOM] is committed to the principle that humane and orderly migration benefits migrants and society and is instrumental in helping to meet the operational challenges of migration, to advance understanding of migration issues, to encourage social and economic development through migration, and to work toward effective respect for the human rights and well-being of migrants."

The IOM spends much of its resources working with refugees and on health issues, providing disaster and emergency relief, as well as combating human trafficking. Nonetheless, its "primary goal is to facilitate the orderly and humane management of international migration." Just over 40 percent of its 2009 operating budget of $631 million was provided by the United States.

At least a third of its budget goes to controlling migration for the benefit of its richest members, detecting migration routes, advising governments, training border guards, operating detention camps, and deporting migrants. It also "facilitates" migration, funding and working on temporary migrant worker programs, according to the labor requirements of the destination countries.

In her threadbare office in the Senegalese capital of Dakar, Awa Fall, an official with the Department of Youth and Sports, flipped through a notebook and showed me computer records of young men who had applied to go to Spain as temporary workers. She runs an IOM-funded program to regulate migration.

"About nineteen thousand people have registered," she said. Of that number, seven hundred people actually made it to Spain, most of them to work in strawberry fields.

During Spain's more prosperous years, before the recession hit, Spanish farm workers were leaving the fields for better jobs in construction. Spain needed workers in the fields, and at the same time wanted to prevent so many people from Senegal making runs on the Canary Islands.

So as part of its mission to manage migration, the IOM helped in both respects. It coordinated the training of Senegalese border guards to slow the illegal migration, and it funded the temporary worker program to attempt to manage the legal entry of farmhands into Spain. The temporary worker program needed to be arranged between government ministries in Spain and Senegal. The IOM brokered the deal.

"There is a need for setting up a system," the IOM's Laurent de Boeck told me as we talked in his office in a converted beach hotel up the coast from Dakar. "It's complicated. When you need a migrant, you need a worker that you want to take from another country; you need to set up a proper system for informing the population, to register and for the selection. That needs to be done by a structure recognized by the other country that is recruiting."

I asked de Boeck about the long-term benefit of the program. He said the workers sent to Spain would return with new skills. But, he said, more importantly, the IOM was trying to offer alternatives.

"We're not in favor of providing legal migration to everybody, or half of Africa would go somewhere else," said. "So what we want to ensure is that there are youth staying in the country, investing in the country, learning and applying their skills in a country. So what we have done is set up a mechanism to support national institutions, providing business training, how to set up a business, to manage a business to find appropriate partners, study their business plans and provide them with technical and financial support."

To me, that sounds like a good idea. Funding development seems a better alternative to border patrols and fences. De Boeck told me that in 2008, the IOM had provided funding for fifty-seven projects in Senegal.

I went to visit one, a school for garment manufacturing set up in an old apartment building. Women were learning how to design, cut, and sew clothes. Boubacar Diehiou, a director of the center, connected the dots.

"If we did not have this center that provides good training and at the same time provides them with work right after the training, for sure these girls may have thought about immigrating," he said. "This is really a solution for them."

Maybe. But for the IOM, such projects are not its highest priorities. The office in Senegal spent just 10 percent of its budget on development plans. It spent twice as much supplying Spain with farm workers, and four times as much providing assistance for border controls and deportation efforts.

Even as wealthy nations devote ever-increasing resources to border enforcement and efforts to manage migration, the number of migrants, both legal and illegal, has increased, leading experts in both the United States and Europe to question the effectiveness of strict enforcement and the allocation of resources.

"Despite massive increases in border enforcement and congressional actions undertaken to discourage legal immigration, the number of legal and illegal entries from Mexico has continued to grow, implying the waste of billions of dollars (not to mention hundreds of lives) in the futile effort to prevent the movement of labor within a rapidly integrating North American economy," wrote Douglas S. Massey of Princeton University in 2005.

In Europe the following year, Stephen Castles from the International Migration Institute at Oxford University reached a similar conclusion: "Building walls (between the USA and Mexico) and increasing naval patrols (between the EU and Africa) increases the death rate and the smugglers' profits, but does not solve the problem."

One other effect of the buildup of borders has been the creation of gargantuan immigration bureaucracies with vested interests and stakes in self-perpetuation, not only in the public sphere. Much of the immigration bureaucracy has been outsourced to the private sector.

Aerospace and defense companies such as Boeing, Raytheon, Lockheed Martin, and Northrop Grumman are now part of what might be called the migration-industrial complex. In the United States, corporate immigration work runs the gamut from processing visa and passport applications, to handling call centers, to operating the E-Verify system that checks the immigration status of workers, to guarding deportees. In fiscal year 2008 (October 1, 2007, to September 30, 2008), more than a third of the $5.6 billion budget of the Bureau of U.S. Immigration and Customs Enforcement (ICE) went to private contractors. The number one recipient ($158.8 million) of ICE contracts was the San Diego–based computer giant Science Applications International Corporation (SAIC), which runs cyber security systems for ICE.

From sophisticated biometrics, to aerial surveillance, to the raw stopping power of metal fences, walls, and weapons, controlling and monitoring the movement of people is very much in the hands of a global network of private global companies. One leader is the Bermuda-based Accenture, once known as Andersen Consulting, which runs border management systems on five continents. Along

Europe's frontier in eastern Poland, Zeiss and Motorola outfitted new border watchtowers with state-of-the-art electronic and optical devices. The German firm Carl Zeiss AG (whose motto is "We Make It Visible") has installed four hundred border surveillance systems in more than ten countries. The Polish installations were equipped by a team involving Alcatel-Lucent and Elbit Systems, a major Israeli defense company. A Swedish firm, Precise Biometics, is a global leader in the development of national identity card systems. Its customers include Portugal, Thailand, and Qatar.

The increased criminalization of unauthorized border crossers has also led to a construction boom in migrant detention facilities in both the United States and Europe.

With some 43 percent of the ICE budget allotted to "detention and removal operations," security firms and private prisons have become big winners of federal efforts to jail and deport illegal migrants. In 2008, nearly $1 billion went to companies providing guard services. Among them, AKAL Security is itself an immigrant success story. Founded by a Pakistan-born guru who immigrated to the United States in 1968, AKAL, a subsidiary of the New Mexico–based Sikh Dharma religious group, runs five migrant prisons, in addition to being the largest contractor in the federal court security program. In 2008 it received ICE contracts worth more than $132 million.

The removal aspect of immigration enforcement also has proved to be profitable for the private sector. A New Mexico air charter company, CSI Aviation Services, Inc., received $55.6 million in 2008 for flying illegal migrants out of the country.

A growing population of deportees has helped make the private prison industry virtually recession proof. Detention firms have reported glowingly optimistic news to shareholders. Cornell Companies, Inc., suggested it was prepared to take advantage of a bullish market: "[H]eightened attention has been placed on border patrol and immigration enforcement. We believe that our adult secure service line is well positioned to respond to these marketplace conditions."

Executives from the Florida-headquartered GEO Group (known as Wackenhut Corrections Corporation until 2003) offered a similar analysis. "My personal view is that the U.S. border security and the detention that is necessary to detain illegal aliens will increasingly be seen as a national imperative to protect U.S. workers and their jobs," company chairman and CEO George Zoley told analysts. In 2009 the firm housed ten thousand illegal immigrants in its U.S. prisons. Zoley expected that number to grow, offering a financial outlook for his firm "which reflects the continued growth of our company in a tough economic environment."

Many private prison firms have global reaches: They cross frontiers to build and manage prisons to incarcerate people for often doing what they themselves do — cross borders to find work. GEO's international operations generated $128.7 million in 2008 (12.3 percent of its revenue). Besides managing a "migrant operations center" housing largely Haitians and Dominicans at Guantánamo Bay, the GEO Group also runs two UK migrant prisons — one in Oxfordshire, the other next to Heathrow International Airport, outside London. In fact, of Britain's eleven "immigration removal centres," eight are run by private firms. In June 2009, Serco, one of the British prison management companies, expanded its operations in the Pacific, signing a five-year contract, worth approximately $300 million in U.S. currency, to operate seven immigrant prisons in Australia.

Perhaps all that money could be better spent. I asked Vaughan Jones at the Praxis project in London what a more reasonable migration policy might look like.

"It should first of all begin to tackle the causes of migration," he said. "So where migration is forced, where displacement happens as a result of conflict, deal with the conflict. Where it comes as a result of underdevelopment, deal with the underdevelopment. Where it results from changes in the climate, then have some sensible adaptation policies in relationship to climate change. So first of all, deal with what the real problem is."

It's an approach that makes sense, but one that would require a fundamental attitude shift, especially by nations that import workers. Countries preoccupied by their own needs and economies would have to consider others'. Just as the corporate sector takes an increasingly international perspective, importers and exporters of people would have to think globally.

Oxford University's Stephen Castles has portrayed the current system of global labor migration as one that "allows rich countries to plunder the scarce human capital of poor countries." It is perhaps another way of describing "coyote capitalism."

A workable and fair alternative, Castles suggests, is a multilateral approach aimed at protecting worker rights, combating abuse and exploitation, and getting "migrant labour importing countries to work together with the governments of sending countries to achieve mutually beneficial economic outcomes."

It's an ambitious plan, but one that would help to correct the current system of labor migration, which is tilted in favor of wealthier nations. Economies that have come to depend on migrant labor need to more fully pay for that privilege. Businesses and governments in nations that rely on migrants not only need to make sure they have decent wages, protections, and working conditions, they also need to reach across international boundaries to help construct strategies for development, sustainable economies, and poverty reduction.

Our conversations and debates about migration are too often based on our own selfish needs. Since the older population of Americans and Europeans is growing, many see younger migrants as one solution to questions about who will take care of *us*. That formulation is problematic. Not only does it view migration as if it were the solution to the demographic shifts of wealthier countries by seeing the developing world as a host for incubation factories and a breeding ground for labor, a dubious moral equation, but it also ignores the obvious. When our migrant caregivers themselves age, who will take care of *them*? Or do we just send them home and order up replacements? We don't say, or we don't ask.

We certainly could import ever-increasing numbers of migrants to look after us, but what about building economies capable of sustaining themselves? In destination countries, instead of wholesale import programs, might incentives—better compensation, working conditions, and training—get more people to take work so fundamental to our existence as food production and health care?

In Southern California, where I live, we're trying to cut down on imports—of the liquid variety. Because of its desert ecology, Los Angeles imports most of its water from the north, hundreds of miles away. But in a drought, with even less to go around, communities are finding ways to conserve and cut back on imports. The city of Los

Angeles pays homeowners to rip out thirsty lawns, and, to the south, Orange County recycles water. By the same token, successive presidents have advocated weaning ourselves off imported oil. If shaking our foreign petroleum habit and cutting back on imported water are desirable goals, why can't the same be said for breaking our addiction to migrant workers?

At the same time, labor-importing nations need to help alleviate conditions that prompt people to leave their families, communities, and countries. It's a matter not only of developing policies that are sustainable and fair but also of give-and-take. Companies and countries that take migrants for their labor should be prepared to give back. But doing it right would require internationally agreed-upon rules and priorities, as well as a regulatory framework, perhaps along the lines of the World Migration Organization (WMO) idea endorsed by the former UN secretary-general Kofi Annan.

There are ample precedents for planning rewards and disincentives to encourage good behavior. For example, serious building projects require environmental impact assessments. Should there be migration impact assessments? Should trade deals and treaties contain reports of their likely effects on migration? What about the massive subsidies governments dole out to agricultural concerns? In the wealthy countries of the world, price supports account for about a quarter of farmers' gross receipts. Short of eliminating or drastically reducing them, might legislation such as farm bills that authorize them also provide estimates of the number of people who are likely to move because they've been put at a competitive disadvantage?

American companies that move abroad are required to provide trade adjustment assistance (TAA) to U.S. workers who lose jobs as a result. Should migratory corporations be required to bear the burden not only for lost U.S. jobs, but also for other costs of migration attributable to their moves? What about businesses that use foreign workers? If they import goods, they often have to pay excise taxes. Should they be able to bring in migrants duty-free? Do they bear any responsibility for the "brain drain" or for the toll on communities or families left behind? Should they have to pay some form of compensation?

Perhaps a migration tax on recruiters and employers of migrants is called for. Filipino researchers have proposed hospital-to-hospital partnerships between wealthy and developing countries. They suggested that health care companies that recruit nurses from abroad should pay fees to the hospitals where the employees worked, so they can train replacement nurses to join their staff.

If limiting migration is a desirable goal, for the have-nots to stop banging on the doors to the developed world, they'll need good reasons to stay put—economies that work, opportunities to prosper. This might be "pie in the sky," but the alternatives are even bigger prisons, more police, and higher walls—because like it or not, widening economic differences between countries give impetus to the ongoing global march. Migrants who move from lower- to higher-income economies are often able to earn twenty or thirty times more than they can by staying at home. So unless massive income disparities are eliminated or reduced, if migrants believe the potential rewards of leaving home outweigh any risks of migrating, people naturally will up and leave.

In November 2005, outside a small village in Guatemala, reporting on the effects of a recent hurricane, I met a family hard at work. The rural area, impoverished even before the storm ravaged the place, had been devastated. António García, along with his wife, kids, and cousins, were working together along a riverbed. Using crude hand tools, they made gravel for a living. They smashed boulders into little rocks, then hammered away to crush the stones into material they could sell to the local construction company. They, like some billion other workers around the world, made no more than about $3 a day. Given the opportunities, why wouldn't that family want to migrate? And who could really blame them if they did?

In Hazleton, Pennsylvania, Amilcar Arroyo, the newspaper publisher from Peru, questioned the effectiveness of the relentless focus on enforcement. "Build a fence, you won't stop people coming," he said. "It may be less, but when you have to support a family, and you know that crossing a line, just crossing a line, you can find a job, you can work for $5 an hour instead of $5 a day, always there will also be people crossing that border. The only solution to me," he said, "is help these countries. Make the economies of these countries better so these people won't have reason to come to the United States."

At the central bus station in Monterrey, Mexico, Rubén Bugarín sat in the waiting room with other farm workers. Soon they'd be on a bus, on their way to the Tennessee tobacco farm that had recruited them under the H-2A temporary worker program. He was a large man with skin parched from his years in the fields. He looked tough. On a table next to him was his cowboy hat. He told me he was making his eighth work trip to the United States, leaving home for ten-month stretches.

I asked him about his family, and he said he had a wife and three children. He became quiet and looked away. His eyes were tearing as he turned back.

"*Es doloroso* [It's painful]," he said.

In a Manila apartment, forty-year-old Eddie Gaborni was getting ready to ship out to Saudi Arabia. He'd been there before, in the late nineties, and stayed almost three and a half years living in a labor camp working in construction. He was reluctant to return because he'd been underpaid.

"I'm afraid the same thing will happen, but we have no choice," he said. "I have to provide for the children." He had tried to find work in the Philippines as a general contractor but had had only one small job in a year. He and his wife, Gina, decided he needed to go abroad to earn money to support their family. They had six children.

Going away was a long-practiced custom in the household. "We are the family of the OFWs [Overseas Filipino Workers]," Eddie joked. His brothers and sisters had all worked abroad, as had Gina's three sisters, brother, and cousins.

Eddie's seventy-two-year-old mother, Rosie, came into the room. She said she had worked as a maid in Kuwait, and while she was away, her husband, who had remained in the Philippines, lived with another woman.

"That's the human face of migration," said Gina.

I asked their three youngest children, Lucky, Eddie Jr., and Jason, ages seven through eleven, what they expected to do when they grew up. Jason wanted to be a cop. Lucky and Eddie Jr. both said they'd probably go abroad to work. They said they were not looking forward to their father's departure the following week, remembering that when he had been away previously, they had cried when he phoned.

"Even me," added Eddie Sr. "Every time I call, I cry."

Gina, a slender, animated woman, was a political activist who had just been elected the deputy secretary-general of Migrante International, which advocates for Filipino migrants.

As we all headed over to the Migrante office and continued our conversation, I was curious to hear the perspective of a couple whose lives had been so bound up with migration. I was interested to find out what they saw as the problem. I'd been used to viewing the issue through American eyes, seeing it framed from the point of view of a country on the receiving end. The debates in the United States are generally about the costs and benefits of migration, about whether border enforcement is sufficient, or whether we are getting the right kinds of migrants with the needed skills. Do migrants bring disease? Do they cause crime? Do they pay more or less in taxes than they consume in services?

None of those matters were issues for Gina and Eddie Gaborni. We walked through a courtyard and upstairs to the modest second-story office of Migrante. Leaflets were stacked on a table. Poster boards used in their political demonstrations were at the ready. But a T-shirt caught my eye. On it was a colorful illustration and a one-sentence slogan that expressed a sentiment about migration rarely heard in debates in the United States. Black-and-white cut-out figures linked hands circling a blue-and-green globe. White lettering said simply, "We dream of a society that will never be torn apart just for the need to survive." It seemed elegant. Just a simple declaration of family values.

We've built a global society in which goods, money, and ideas can move virtually unfettered, but people cannot. In an ideal world, a person would have as much freedom of movement as a sack of rice destined for the world market. While the utopian vision of open borders is appealing, there is not much chance of a meaningful debate on the issue. Besides, as migration expert Castles has written, while open borders may be a desirable aim for the long term, "in the current global context, it could lead to an anarchic situation in which the weakest—in both sending and receiving countries—would be even more disadvantaged."

In the United States, there is little support for either open borders or the status quo, and general agreement that the immigration system, such as it is, is the result of a messed-up political standoff. If these were family dynamics, they would be labeled dysfunctional. How else to describe a situation in which upward of twelve million people, most of them essential to the U.S. economy, live in the shadows, often fearing raids and deportations, cut off from certain benefits, knowing that if they are able to remain below the radar, there is neither the political will nor the capacity to round up, imprison, and deport all of them?

In the final analysis, how we respond to migration and how we treat the strangers among us are reflections of our connections to humanity. Politicians arguing over who is deserving of human rights need look no further than their own family trees for insight. More fundamentally, despite the wishes of migration restrictionists, ancient impulses to escape hardships or to go in search of greener pastures are not going to come to a halt just because political lines have been drawn and laws passed. Our quests for betterment have the same basic drives as those of our primordial ancestors who migrated out of bogs looking for sources of food. Build walls, and people will go over, around, or under them. Hire border guards, and smugglers will bribe them. Step up patrols, and migrants will find alternate routes. Provide better-paying jobs, and workers will get to them. Migration will not be stopped. But in the best of all possible worlds, nations should strive to ensure that migrants cross borders because they want to, not because they have to.

NOTES

Introduction

2 *My father was a jeweler, a craftsman* Harry Kaye, "My Life" (Los Angeles, unpublished, 1999).

2 *Humans are a migratory species* Patrick Manning, *Migration in World History* (New York: Routledge, 2005), 87–88; Stephen Oppenheimer, "The First Exodus," www.geographical.co.uk (July 2002).

2 *The world is experiencing an exodus* Thomas Friedman, *The World Is Flat* (New York: Farrar, Straus, & Giroux, 2007), 10.

2 *While a large proportion of migrants* "Trends in Total Migrant Stock: The 2005 Revision," Department of Economic and Social Affairs, Population Division, United Nations (February 2006), 1; "About Migration," International Organization for Migration, 2007. http://www.iom.int/jahia/Jahia/pid/3 (accessed June 11, 2009).

3 *Despite the fact that in raw numbers the United States* "Trends in Total Migrant Stock: The 2005 Revision," Department of Economic and Social Affairs, Population Division, United Nations (February 2006), 1.

4 *While people obviously migrate for many reasons* "Facts on Labour Migration," International Labour Office, United Nations (June 2006); *International Migration Outlook 2009* (Paris: Organisation for Economic Development and Cooperation, 2009).

4 *Such indignation on the basis of supposedly unblemished family trees* Lawrence Downes, "America the Generous: A Lost Story of Citizenship," *New York Times*, May 27, 2007.

4 *The notion that U.S. immigration policy has a long and consistent legal record* Mae M. Ngai, *Impossible Subjects: Illegal Aliens and the Making of Modern America* (Princeton, N.J.: Princeton University Press, 2004), 4.

5 *It is a global system that may be called "coyote capitalism"* Gilbert G. Gonzalez and Raul A. Fernandez, *A Century of Chicano History: Empire, Nations, and Migration* (New York: Routledge, 2003), 109.

6 *In the face of such forces, efforts to fashion rational* Benjamin Johnson, "Examining the Need for Comprehensive Immigration Reform, Part II," U.S. Congress, Senate Judiciary Committee hearing, July 12, 2006.

8   *When Ted Turner owned CNN, he banned*   Jacqueline Trescott, "CNN's Ted Turner, Front and Center," *Washington Post,* July 18, 1988.

8   *The nouns "immigrants" and "migrants"*   immigrant. Dictionary.com. *Dictionary.com Unabridged (v 1.1).* Random House, Inc., http://dictionary.reference.com/browse/immigrant (accessed June 11, 2009).

8   *The various adjectives are fraught with political undertones*   Ngai, *Impossible Subjects,* 5.

11   *I don't know which version of the story*   Michael Bloomberg, U.S. Senate Judiciary Committee field hearing on federal immigration legislation, New York, July 5, 2006.

1. Lures and Blinders

13   *The influx of Latinos*   Richard Fry, *Latino Settlement in the New Century* (Washington, D.C.: Pew Hispanic Center, 2008), 35.

15   *The landmark*   Markle Building home page, http://www.marklebuilding.com/intro.htm (accessed January 13, 2009).

16   *In 2001, a fatal shooting*   Terrie Morgan-Besecker, "Drug Murder Case Plea Accepted," *Wilkes-Barre Times Leader,* January 4, 2005.

16   *So on July 13, 2006*   Mark Scolforo, "Small Pennsylvania Town Council Passes Ordinance against Illegal Immigrants," Associated Press Worldstream, July 14, 2006.

16   *The new law put Hazleton*   Peter Schrag, "Immigration Hardliners Try to Unhinge "America," *Alternet, the Nation,* December" 29, 2007.

16   *"Illegal aliens are a drain on our resources"*   Julie Bykowicz, "Pa. Town Center of Immigration Reform Debate," *Centre Daily Times,* July 13, 2006.

16   *And while crime definitely increased*   Michael Rubinkam, "Mayor Takes Stand in Hazleton Illegal Immigrant Trial," Associated Press state and local wire, March 15, 2007.

18   *"Perhaps the most obvious result of the racial mixture"*   William Paul Dillingham, "Reports of the Immigration Commission," U.S. Immigration Commission (1907–1910), vol. 16 (Washington, D.C.: U.S. Government Printing Office, 1911), 678.

18   *"Among the Italians, violence is more the result of quick temper"*   Immigration Commission, 674.

18   *"The fact is there are some respected citizens in all the races"*   Immigration Commission, 697.

18   *"The large number of Germans in Hazleton in 1880"*   Harold Aurand, *Population Change and Social Continuity: Ten Years in a Coal Town* (Selinsgrove, Pa.: Susquehanna University Press, 1986), 48.

19   *Northeastern Pennsylvania had the world's largest deposits of anthracite*   Randall M. Miller and William Pencak, *Pennsylvania: A History of the Commonwealth* (University Park: Pennsylvania State University Press, 2002).

19   *By the mid-nineteenth century*   Thomas Dublin and Walter Licht, *The Face of Decline: The Pennsylvania Anthracite Region in the Twentieth Century* (Ithaca, N.Y.: Cornell University Press, 2005), 14.

19   *Industrialization, the demands of the Civil War*   U.S. Immigration Commission (1907–1910), *Immigrants in Industries,* Part 1: *General Survey of the Anthracite Coal Mining Industry* (Washington, D.C.: U.S. Government Printing Office, 1911), 587.

19   *But around 1875, the composition of the workforce*   Sister M. Accursia Bern, "Polish Miners in Luzerne County, Pennsylvania," *Polish Roots,* February 15, 2008,

http://www.polishroots.org/paha/luzerne_penn.htm; also Emily Greene Balch, *Our Slavic Fellow Citizens* (New York: Charities Publication Committee, 1910), 238–239.

20 *The newest arrivals were typically at the lowest rungs on the job ladder*   U.S. Immigration Commission, 61st Cong., *Immigrants in Industries*, Part 19: *Anthracite Coal Mining* (Washington, D.C.: U.S. Government Printing Office, 1911), 656.

20 *With jobs as the magnet*   Frank Julian Warne, "Some Industrial Effects of Slav Immigration," *Charities* 13, no. 1 (1904): 58, 223–224.

20 *Social and ethnic conflicts flared*   "The Progress of the World," *American Monthly*, October 1897, 388.

20 *It turns out that the present-day depiction of old-time Hazleton*   Aurand, *Population Change and Social Continuity*, 28.

21 *In the latter part of the nineteenth century*   Ibid., 73.

21 *Divisions and resentments among migrant communities*   Mine Safety and Health Administration, U.S. Department of Labor, History of Anthracite Coal Mining, January 14, 2009, http://www.msha.gov/district/dist_01/history/history.htm

22 *The nation was at the end of the "Long Depression"*   Steven Patrick Schroeder, "The Elementary School of the Army: The Pennsylvania National Guard, 1877–1917" (Ph.D. diss., University of Pittsburgh, 2006), 215–217.

23 *For miners, the problems were piling up*   Michael Novak, *The Guns of Lattimer: The True Story of a Massacre and a Trial, August 1897–March 1898* (New York: Basic Books, 1978), 18; also William C. Kashatus, "Shot at Like Dogs," *Wilkes-Barre Citizens Voice*, March 3, 2008.

24 *Despairing about the preponderance of German*   Benjamin Franklin, "The Support of the Poor," *The Writings of Benjamin Franklin: Philadelphia, 1726–1727*, May 9, 1753. The History Carper http://www.historycarper.com/resources/twobf2/letter18.htm (accessed July 9, 2009).

25 *But legal avenues to attack the "problem"*   William M. McKinney, Greene McKinney, and H. Noyes, eds., *Annotated Cases American and English* (Northport, N.Y.: Edward Thompson, 1917), 287.

25 *As for Hazleton's 2006 Illegal Immigration Relief Act Ordinance,*   *Lozano v. City of Hazleton,* No. 3:06-cv-01586-JMM, pp. 188–189, U.S. District Court, Middle District of Pennsylvania, July 26, 2007.

26 *Still standing in Hazleton law*   Official English ordinance, 2006.

26 *Score one for Barletta*   Kent Jackson, "Barletta Looks toward Future as Hazleton's Mayor," *The Hazleton Standard-Speaker*, November 6, 2008.

26 *On July 26, 2006, two weeks after Hazleton enacted its immigration policy*   Jennifer Moroz, "A New Jersey Town, a Brazilian Deluge, Diverging Hopes," *Philadelphia Inquirer*, October 19, 2005; also Illegal Immigration Relief Act Ordinance 2006–16, Riverside Township, 2006.

27 *The immediate consequences were, in part, predictable*   Samantha Henry, "Town Sued Over Crackdown on Illegals; Suit Challenges Local Ordinance," (*Passaic County, N.J.*) *Herald News*, August 16, 2006; also verified complaint, *Riverside Coalition of Business Persons and Landlords et al. v. Township of Riverside*, Superior Court of New Jersey, Burlington County Law Division, October 18, 2006.

27 *But as the lawsuits proceeded*   Brian Donohue, "Small Town Grapples with Tough Law on Immigrants," Newhouse News Service, September 29, 2006; also "N.J. Town Rescinds Anti-Immigrant Law," Associated Press Online, September 18, 2007; also David Holthouse, "How Illegal Immigration Is Dividing a Town's

Business Owners," *Fortune Small Business*, April 18, 2008; also Ken Belson and Jill P. Capuzzo, "Towns Rethink Laws Against Illegal Immigrants," *New York Times*, September 26, 2007.

28   *The complex and interconnected*   Rubén Hernández-León, *Metropolitan Migrants: The Migration of Urban Mexicans to the United States* (Berkeley: University of California Press, 2008).

2. Growing People for Export

30   *I had come to Tondo to learn*   Annie Gorman, "Unbalanced Care: Nurse Migration in the Philippines," *Heinz School Review* 4 (2007).

31   *In 2008, the top-ranking destination countries*   Dilip Ratha, "Remittance Flows to Developing Countries Are Estimated to Exceed $300 Billion in 2008," *People Move* 18 (2009), World Bank, http://peoplemove.worldbank.org/en/content/remittance-flows-to-developing-countries (accessed March 14, 2009).

31   *Remittances accounted for nearly 11 percent of the GDP*   International Monetary Fund, *World Economic Outlook Database*, April 2009; also Mikka Pineda, "How Far Will Remittances to the Philippines Fall in 2009?," *RGE Monitor* (March 2, 2009).

32   *But the glaringly obvious could not be ignored*   Office of the President, Republic of the Philippines, Administrative Order No. 247 (December 4, 2008).

32   *The tradition of Filipino labor migration*   Victoria P. Garchitorena, Ayala Foundation, *Diaspora Philanthropy: The Philippine Experience* (Cambridge, Mass.: Harvard University, Philanthropic Initiative, and Global Equity Initiative, 2007), 1.

33   *In America, the Philippines has long been*   "The Registered Nurse Population," Health Resources and Services Administration, U.S. Department of Health and Human Services (June 2006); Rebecca Ray, "A Proud Nursing Heritage," *NurseWeek* (April 11, 2005); Barbara Marquand, "Philippine Nurses in the U.S.— Yesterday and Today," Minoritynurse.com (Spring 2006), http://www.minoritynurse.com/features/other/06-06-06-5.html (accessed January 24, 2009).

34   *Disturbing reports suggested*   Fely Marilyn E. Lorenzo et al., "Nurse Migration from a Source Country Perspective: Philippine Country Case Study," *Health Services Research* 42, no. 3 (2007): S1406 (13).

35   *The average pay for doctors*   Blaine Harden, "In Rural Philippines, a Dearth of Doctors: Thousands of Physicians, Retrained as Nurses, Take Jobs Abroad," *Washington Post*, September 20, 2008, A13.

39   *In May 2009, the Philippine congressman Roilo S. Golez*   "Bill Promotes Overseas Labor, Corrects Policy," Public Relations and Information Department, House of Representatives, Congress of the Philippines (May 6, 2009).

39   *"Instead of getting down to business*   D'Jay Lazaro, "Group 'Outraged' over Passage of Labor Export Bill," *GMANews.TV*, May 17, 2009.

40   *Forty percent of the population lives*   Pineda, "How Far Will Remittances to the Philippines Fall in 2009?"; "Philippines: Critical Development Constraints," Economics and Research Department, Asian Development Bank (December 2007); Virginia A. Miralao, "Globalization, Democracy, and Development: Some Asian Patterns and the Philippines' Experience," in *Globalization and the Washington Consensus: Its Influence on Democracy and Development in the South*, ed. Gladys Lechini (Buenos Aires: CLACSO, Consejo Latinoamericano de Ciencias Sociales, 2008), 147–160; Dharel Placido, "Quality of Life Worst in 7 Mindanao Provinces," *Newsbreak*, May 20, 2009,

Newsbreakhttp://newsbreak.com.ph/index.php?option=com_content&task=view& id=6159&Itemid=88889066 (accessed May 21, 2009).

40   *While the dependence on the income*   Jared Ferrie, "Drop in Remittances Threatens Unrest in Philippines," *National*, March 26, 2009.

41   *In May 2009, Bangladesh's Expatriates Welfare*   Rashidul Hasan, "Manpower Export Shrinks Alarmingly: JS Body Recommends Urgent Steps," *Dhaka Daily Star*, May 14, 2009.

41   *"Going back to Bangladesh now would be a problem for me"*   Beh Lih Yi, "Bad to Worse for Migrant Workers in Asia as Crisis Bites," *Agence France Presse*, July 2, 2009.

3. Migrants in the Global Marketplace

43   *In 2008, remittances they sent home*   The World Bank, *Remittances Data* 2008, February 11, 2009, http://siteresources.worldbank.org/INTPROSPECTS/Resources/ 334934-1110315015165/RemittancesData_Nov08(Release).xls

45   *But the catch is getting increasingly meager*   ActionAid, *SelFISH Europe: How the Economic Partnership Agreements Would Further Contribute to the Decline of Fish Stocks and Exacerbate the Food Crisis in Senegal*, ActionAid (August 11, 2008), 6.

46   *Industrial-size trawlers from Europe, Japan, the United States*   Michaela Schiessl, "Africa's Unfair Battle—The West's Poverty Subsidies," *Spiegel Online*, May 14, 2007, http://www.spiegel.de/international/world/0,1518,482209,00.html (accessed February 11, 2009); ActionAid, *SelFISH Europe*, page 3; Sharon Lafraniere, "Europe Takes Africa's Fish, and Boatloads of Migrants Follow," *New York Times*, January 14, 2008.

47   *Between 2006 and 2008, rice farmers in higher-income economies*   "Agricultural Policies in OECD Countries: Monitoring and Evaluation 2009." (Paris, France: OECD Publishing, 2009, https://www.oecd.org/secure/pdfDocument/0,2834, en_21571361_33622309_43249837_1_1_1_1,00.pdf. (accessed July 10, 2009).

47   *Senegal's president, Abdoulaye Wade*   "Scrap 'wasteful' FAO says Senegal." *Gulf Daily News*. June 11, 2008.

47   *A 2008 investigation by Laurie Garrett*   Laurie A. Garrett, *Food Failures and Futures*, Council on Foreign Relations (Council on Foreign Relations, 2008), 7.

48   *To put those amounts into perspective*   The World Bank, *Remittances Data*.

49   *Corn cultivation originated in Mexico*   Monica Campbell and Tyche Hendricks, "Mexico's Corn Farmers See Their Livelihoods Wither Away. Cheap U.S. Produce Pushes Down Prices under Free-Trade Pact," *San Francisco Chronicle* (Atlacomulco, Mexico), July 31, 2006.

49   *U.S. corn producers saw the deal*   Alejandro Nadal, "Corn and Nafta: An Unhappy Alliance," *Seedling* (June 2000); Steven Zahniser and William Coyle, "U.S.–Mexico Corn Trade During the NAFTA Era: New Twists to an Old Story" (Washington, D.C.: U.S. Department of Agriculture, FDS-04D-01, May 2004).

49   *Not surprisingly, Mexican farmers were little match*   Office of the United States Trade Representative, "NAFTA Good for Farmers, Good for America" (June 1, 2001); "Mexico: NAFTA, Corn," *Migration News* 6, no. 4 (2000), http://migration .ucdavis.edu/mn/; John J. Audley et al., *NAFTA's Promise and Reality* (Washington, D.C.: Carnegie Endowment for International Peace, 2004), 51.

49   *Just after Christmas of 1994, Alan Greenspan*   Robert Rubin and Jacob Weisberg, *In an Uncertain World* (New York: Random House, 2003).

50   *The effects of the deal were staggering*   Alan Greenspan, *The Age of Turbulence: Adventures in a New World* (New York: Penguin, 2007).

51   *The repayment plan coupled with the conditions*   Peter Cervantes-Gautschi, *Wall Street and Immigration: Financial Services Giants Have Profited from the Beginning* (Washington, D.C.: Americas Program, Center for International Policy [CIP], 2007), 6; *Senado de la Republica*, LX Legislatura, *Evaluación de la Política Económica de México durante el Periodio 1996–2007 y Sus Repercusiones en la Banca Mexicana, la Deuda Publica, y el Bajo Desarrollo del País*, Comision Especial para Determinar las Causas del Bajo Financiamiento para el Desarrollo y del Elevado Monto de la Deuda Pública y sus Instrumentos, Precisar Responsabilidades y Proponer Acciones Correctivas, con Objeto de Alentar el Crecimiento del Mercado Interno y Promover el Desarrollo del País (Report 2008).

51   *Beginning in 1991, the Mexican government*   Timothy A. Wise, "Fields of Free Trade," *Dollars & Sense* (November 2003–December 2003); Luis Hernández Navarro, "The New Tortilla War," *Americas Program Special Report* (May 7, 2007), Center for International Policy, http://americas.irc-online.org/am/4205 (accessed February 8, 2009); Antonio Yunez-Naude, "The Dismantling of CONASUPO, a Mexican State Trader in Agriculture," *World Economy* 26, (January 2003): 97–122.

52   *As transnational companies rely on migrants to overcome*   Thomas L. Friedman, "The Dawn of E2K in India," *New York Times*, November 7, 2007.

52   *As a report for Manpower, Inc,*   Laveesh Bhandari and Payal Malik, *India's Borderless Workforce* (Haryana, India: Manpower India, 2008), 13.

52   *With increasing numbers of firms operating globally*   Charles B. Keely, "Globalization Transforms Trade-Migration Equation," *Migration Policy Institute* (December 1, 2002).

53   *Human migration reflects the larger picture*   United Nations Conference on Trade and Development, United Nations, *World Investment Report 2008: Transnational Corporations and the Infrastructure Challenge* (2008), xvii.

53   *In 2007, of the world's hundred largest economic entities*   United Nations, *World Investment Report 2008: Transnational Corporations and the Infrastructure Challenge*, 220; International Monetary Fund, *Report for Selected Countries and Subjects.* 2008 http://www.imf.org/external/pubs/ft/weo/2008/02/weodata/weorept .aspx?; Sarah Anderson and John Cavanagh, "Of the World's 100 Largest Economic Entities, 51 Are Now Corporations and 49 Are Countries (2000)," (January 3, 2002), http://www.corporations.org/system/top100.html (accessed April 11, 2009).

53   *A poster child for the nexus*   Peter Stalker, *Workers without Frontiers: The Impact of Globalization on International Migration* (Geneva, Switzerland: International Labour Organization, 2000), 45.

54   *In the past thirty years, China's growing economy*   Simon Rabinovitch, "China's Great Migration Wrenched Back by Crisis," *Reuters* (CHENGDU, China) (December 30, 2008).

54   *In the Socialist Republic of Vietnam,*   Vietnam News Agency, "Textile, Garment Sector Sets \$9.5b Export Target," *Vietnam News Agency* (July 9, 2008), http://vietnam news.vnagency.com.vn/showarticle.php?num=03BUS090708 (accessed February 12, 2009).

55   *According to one estimate, by 2008*   Ian Coxhead, Diep Phan, and Erin Collins, "Income Growth and Internal Migration in Vietnam: Trends and Projections," *Globalization, Poverty, and the Environment in Vietnam—Project Papers* (May 9,

2008), abstract of Research in Progress. http://www.aae.wisc.edu/gpe-vn (accessed February 12, 2009).

56 *Meager wages amid an inflation rate of nearly 23 percent* Communist Party of Vietnam (CPV) Online Newspaper, "New Salary Levels Benefit Employees," *Communist Party of Vietnam (CPV) Online Newspaper,* October 21, 2008, http://www.cpv.org.vn/cpv/Modules/News_English/News_Detail_E.aspx?CN_ID=253616&CO_ID=30113 (accessed February 12, 2009).

57 *Hanesbrands has put in place* Hanesbrands, Inc. *Preliminary Info Statement,* Hanesbrands, Inc. (August 10, 2006).

57 *As it expanded in Southeast Asia* Hanesbrands, Inc., "Hanesbrands, Inc., Advances Planned Consolidation and Globalization Strategy to Further Improve Cost Competitiveness," press release (June 27, 2007); Richard Craver, "Hanesbrands to Close Nine Plants, Cut 8,100 Jobs Worldwide," *Winston-Salem Journal,* September 24, 2008.

59 *The veteran CEO has been well rewarded* Forbes.com, "Richard A. Noll Profile –Forbes.com." http://people.forbes.com/profile/richard-a-noll/39218 (accessed July 10, 2009).

60 *The organization was founded in 1983* Alan Howard, "The Women of Monclova," *ZMagazine* (February 2004).

4. Switching Course

62 *"The quays are crowded every day"* Freeman, "Emigration," *Cork Examiner,* April 5, 1847.

62 *"Each day brings with it its own horrors"* John O. Rourke, *The History of the Great Irish Famine of 1847* (Dublin and London: M'Glashan & Gill; James Duffy, Sons, & Co., 1875), 366.

62 *The immediate cause of the horror* Kerby Miller, *Emigrants and Exiles* (Oxford, U.K.: Oxford University Press, 1985), 286.

64 *For most of the 1980s, unemployment* Index Mundi, "Ireland Unemployment Rate," http://www.indexmundi.com/ireland/unemployment_rate.html (May 16, 2008) (accessed February 8, 2009).

64 *However, the tide was turning* United Nations Conference on Trade and Development, "UNCTAD WID Country Profile: IRELAND," in *FDI Country Profiles,* United Nations Conference on Trade and Development; Sean Dorgan, "How Ireland Became the Celtic Tiger," www.heritage.org/Research/Worldwidefreedom/Bg1945 .Cfm (June 23, 2006). *The Economic Freedom Project,* The Heritage Foundation (accessed February 8, 2009); Benjamin Powell, "Markets Created a Pot of Gold in Ireland," April 15, 2003, http://www.cato.org/pub_display.php?pub_id=3070 (accessed February 8, 2009).

65 *Over the next few years, Irish prosperity* "Tiger Economy Returns with a Celtic Panther," *Irish Times,* February 11, 2004.

66 *As Irish expatriates returned home* Central Statistics Office, *Census 2006* (March 2007), 24.

68 *Fewer and fewer migrants* "Huge Decline in Migrants Seeking Work Permits," *Irish Examiner,* December 16, 2008.

68 *But Carroll's own employment* "Downturn Forces Sisk Group to Lay Off 300 Workers," Dublin, *Herald.ie,* August 27, 2008.

70   *In a January 2009 press statement*   Dell, Inc., *Dell to Migrate Manufacturing Operations from Ireland to Poland and Partners by Early 2010* (press release, January 8, 2009).

70   *As the lateral journeys of Irish and Poles illustrate*   International Organization for Migration, World Migration 2008), 2008. *International Organization for Migration (IOM)*; UN General Assembly, *International Migration and Development: Report of the Secretary-General* (May 18, 2006), http://www.unhcr.org/refworld/docid/44ca2d934.html (accessed May 23, 2009).

70   *In the case of Ireland, as fortunes there*   Dell Computer, "Dell Opens Second European Plant to Meet Growing Customer Demand" (press release. January 28, 2008), http://www.dell.com/content/topics/global.aspx/corp/pressoffice/en/2008/2008_01_23_rr_000?c=us&l=en&s=corp (accessed February 10, 2009).

71   *Exact numbers are impossible to come by*   Damian Whitworth, "The Polish Dream," *Times* of London), June 16, 2007; Jonathan Petre, "Anglicans: England Is Not a Catholic Nation," www.telegraph.co.uk (April 19, 2008).

73   *Encouraging the growth were generous corporate tax breaks*   Poland in Numbers, Polish Information and Foreign Investment Agency, http://www.paiz.gov.pl/index/?id=a5e308070bd6dd3cc56283f2313522de (accessed February 10, 2009).

74   *Between 2005 and 2008, foreign investors*   Polish Information and Foreign Investment Agency, http://www.paiz.gov.pl/index/?id=a5e308070bd6dd3cc56283f2313522de; Central Statistical Office (http://www.stat.gov.pl./gus/45_5749_ENG_HTML.htm, 2009).

75   *The Polish resurgence made the country*   Jerome Taylor, "Poland Launches Campaign to Lure Back Migrant Workers," *Independent*, April 24, 2008.

75   *The Internet site, titled in Polish*   Polish Ministry of Labor and Social Policy, http://www.powroty.gov.pl/home (accessed April 11, 2009).

76   *Sweden has not adopted that policy*   Joellen Perry, "The Czech Republic Pays for Immigrants to Go Home," *Wall Street Journal*, April 28, 2009.

5. Recruitment Agencies and Body Shops

79   *With as many as fifteen thousand firms*   Manpower, Inc., *Form 10K, Annual Report* (2009).

80   *In 2007, Sri Lanka had 691 licensed agencies*   Sri Lanka Bureau of Foreign Employment, *Number of Licensed Agencies in Year 1985–2007*.http://www.slbfe.lk/feb/statistics/pdf/statis10.pdf (accessed May 24, 2009); Bangladesh Association of International Recruiting Agencies, *History & Background*. http://www.hrexport-baira.org/history_background.htm (accessed May 24, 2009); Ministry of Overseas Indian Affairs, http://moia.gov.in/showinfo1.asp?linkid=447; *Bureau of Emigration and Overseas Employment*, Bureau of Emigration and Overseas Employment, http://www.beoe.gov.pk/index.asp (accessed February 4, 2009).

80   *In the Philippines, competition*   Philippine Overseas Employment Administration, *2007 Annual Report* (2008), 17.

80   *The recruitment industry is notorious*   Cynthia Balana, "Twenty-nine Thousand Warrants out for Illegal Recruiters." *Philippine Daily Inquirer*, May 18, 2009.

81   *John Lawson Burnett of Alabama may have been short in stature*   U.S. Congress, House of Representatives, "John L. Burnett Memorial Addresses," 66th Cong., 3rd sess. (1920); Relative to the further restriction of immigration: Hearings before the

Committee on Immigration and Naturalization, House of Representatives, 62nd Cong., 2nd sess. (Washington, D.C.: U.S. Government Printing Office (1912).

81 *The padrone system was a corrupt pratice* Kitty Calavita, "U.S. Immigration and Policy Responses: The Limits of Legislation," in *Controlling Immigration: A Global Perspective*, ed. Wayne A. Cornelius, Philip L. Martin, and James F. Hollifiel (Palo Alto, Calif.: Stanford University Press, 2004), 57.

82 *In 1890, a congressional investigator* "The Padrone System: Slave Labor in New York and How It Is Monopolized by Sharks," *Waterloo (Iowa) Courier*, July 2, 1890; Thomas Sewall Adams and Helen Laura Sumner, *Labor Problems: A Text Book* (New York: Macmillan, 1921); "Poor Sons of Sunny Italy: How They Are Swindled at Home and Abroad," *New York Times*, July 27, 1888; John Koren, "The Padrone System and Padrone Banks," in *Bulletin of the Department of Labor* no. 9, ed. Carroll D. Wright and Oren W. Weaver (Washington, D.C.: U.S. Government Printing Office, 1897), 113–129; Prescott F. Hall, *Immigration and Its Effects upon the United States* (New York: Henry Holt, 1906), 131–133.

82 *The padrone system was not confined to Italians* Thomas Sowell, *Ethnic America: A History* (New York: Basic Books, 1983), 114.

82 *While the padrone arrangement was a particularly odious practice* Paul Bernstein, *American Work Values: Their Origin and Development* (Albany: State University of New York Press, 1997), 118; Joshua L. Rosenbloom, *Looking for Work, Searching for Workers: American Labor Markets During Industrialization* (New York: Cambridge University Press, 2002), 27.

83 *At the end of the century, U.S. railway companies* Lawrence A. Cardoso, *Mexican Emigration to the United States, 1897–1931 Socioeconomic Patterns* (Tucson: University of Arizona Press, 1980), 34–35.

83 *Recruitment of migrant workers during the nineteenth century* Bruce Goldstein and Catherine K. Ruckelshaus, *Lessons for Reforming 21st Century Labor Subcontracting: How 19th Century Reformers Attacked "The Sweating System"* http://nelp.3cdn.net/541b69ad88a3a26317_7cm6bx6g4.pdf (accessed October 11, 2009); Farmworker Justice Fund and National Employment Law Project, 2001); Peter Stalker, *The Work of Strangers: Survey of International Labor Migration* (Geneva: International Labor Office, 1994), 11.

83 *Over the past century, various U.S. government programs* Philip Martin, "Guest Workers: Past and Present," Vol. 3, *Factors That Influence Migration*, in *Migration between Mexico and the United States: Binational Study* (Washington, D.C.: U.S. Commission on Immigration Reform, 1997), 877–897; Susan Ferris, Immigrant Labor: Document Requirements Frustrate Some; Monday's Last Day for Bracero Wage Claim," *Sacramento Bee*, January 3, 2009; Joe Rodriguez, "Faces of Our Fathers: The Braceros' Legacy of Labor, a Cry for Justice," *San Jose Mercury News*, November 29, 2008.

84 *In 1952, the Immigration and Nationality Act* Table XVI(B), Nonimmigrant Visas Issued by Classification, U.S. Department of State, http://www.travel.state.gov/pdf/ FY08-AR-TableXVI(B).pdf (accessed May 26, 2009).

84 *All of the programs have come in for criticism* Ron Hira, "Outsourcing America's Technology and Knowledge Jobs" (Washington, D.C.: Economic Policy Institute, March 28, 2007).

84 *For employers of H-1B workers, the bar is low* Philip Martin, "The H-1B Program and PERM: Implications for Engineering Workers," in *Attestation and PERM: The H-1B*

Program and Labor Certification (University of California at Davis: Sloan West Coast Program on Science and Engineering Workers, January 16, 2008).

84 *Companies need only* attest *that* U.S. Department of Labor, "Strategic Plan for Fiscal Years 2006–2011," September 29, 2006, http://www.dol.gov/_sec/stratplan/strat_plan_2006-2011.pdf. 35 (accessed May 26, 2009).

84 *When the U.S. Government Accountability Office* Sigurd R. Nilsen, *H-1B Visa Program: More Oversight by Labor Can Improve Compliance with Program Requirements* (Washington, D.C.: U.S. Government Accountability Office, June 22, 2006).

85 *"When any American company needs programmers* 60 *Minutes* (CBS News, 1993).

85 *Work and workers were going* Marianne Kolbasuk McGee and Chris Murphy, "Feds Cast Wary Eye on Indian Outsourcers' Use of H-1B," *InformationWeek*, May 21, 2007, 32.

85 *At the same time, recruitment firms* William Branigin, "White-Collar Visas: Importing Needed Skills or Cheap Labor?," *Washington Post*, October 21, 1995.

86 *At any given time, as many as five hundred thousand people* Moira Herbst, "Are H-1B Workers Getting Bilked?; Overseas Companies Are Accused of Underpaying Foreigners on Work Visas—and Hurting U.S. Wages," *Business Week*, February 11, 2008; U.S. Citizenship and Immigration Services, Department of Homeland Security, *Fact Sheet: Changes to the FY2009 H-1B Program* (2008); U.S. Citizenship and Immigration Services, U.S. Department of Homeland Security, *USCIS Continues to Accept FY 2010 H-1B Petitions* (2009).

88 *In 2000, the* Baltimore *Sun* Gary Cohn and Walter F. Roche Jr., "Indentured Servants for High-Tech Trade; Labor: For a Rich Fee, Companies Called "Body Shops" Supply Waves of Unwitting Immigrants to the Nation's Computer Industry," *Baltimore Sun*, February 21, 2000.

88 *In 2007, Patni Computer Systems* U.S. Department of Labor, "Cambridge, Mass.-Based International IT Company Agrees to Pay $2.4 Million to Underpaid H-1B Non-immigrant Workers Following U.S. Labor Department Investigation," press release; Herbst, "Are H-1B Workers Getting Bilked?"

88 *A number of high-profile cases* Daniela Perdomo, "Two Lawyers Punished in Worker Visa Case," *Los Angeles Times*, March 12, 2008.

88 *In July 2008, authorities arrested* Peter J. Sampson, "Ringwood Man Pleads Guilty to Visa Fraud," (*Passaic County, N.J.*) *Herald News*, February 20, 2009; Steve Hamm and Moira Herbst, "America's High Tech Sweatshops," *BusinessWeek*, October 1, 2009; *United States of America v. Dasondi et al.*, U.S. District Ct., District of New Jersey, June 16, 2008, "Amended Criminal Complaint," 2:08-mj-07091-ES; Robert E. Kessler, "7 Arrested in Immigration Scam," New York *Newsday*, June 11, 2008.

89 *Even more damning than the criminal cases* U.S. Citizenship and Immigration Services, *H-1B Benefit Fraud and Compliance Assessment*, Office of Fraud Detection and National Security (September 2008), 15.

89 *The economic downturn made the extensive use of H-1B visas* FLC Disclosure Data, FY2008, The Foreign Labor Certification Data Center. http://www.flcdatacenter.com/CaseData.aspx (accessed February 5, 2009).

89 *The ironic juxtaposition of foreign worker recruitment* "Questions and Answers: Employ American Workers Act and Its Effect on H-1B Petitions," States News Service, March 20, 2009; "Durbin, Grassley Introduce Legislation to Reform H-1B Visa Program," press release, April 23, 2009, http://durbin.senate.gov/showRelease

.cfm?releaseId=311910 (accessed July 10, 2009); "Government's Brief in Support of Resistance to Defendant's Motion to Dismiss Counts Two and Three and Strike Portions of Count One," *United States of America v. Vision Systems Group, Inc.,* U.S. District Court for the Southern District of Iowa, no. 4:09-CR-004, April 13, 2009, 7; "Defendant's Reply in Support of Motion to Dismiss Counts 2 through 9 and to Strike Portions of Counts 1 and 10 of the Indictment," *United States of America v. Vision Systems Group, Inc.,* U.S. District Court for the Southern District of Iowa, no. 4:09-CR-004, April 30, 2009, 3.

90   *The high-tech industry is not the only one to witness*   Health Resources and Services Administration, "The Registered Nurse Population," U.S. Department of Health and Human Services (June 2006), PGA-46.

91   *Most of the larger recruiters*   Patricia Pittman et al., *U.S.-Based International Nurse Recruitment: Structure and Practices of a Burgeoning Industry,* AcademyHealth (November 2007), 41.

93   *But the story didn't end there*   Maureen Shawn Kennedy, "In the News: An American Dream Gone Wrong," *American Journal of Nursing* 107, no. 8 (2007): 17-18; Frank Eltman, "NY Appeals Court Clears Nurses of Neglect Rap," Associated Press, January 16, 2009; Ridgely Ochs, "Attorney: Smithtown Nurses May Still Face Civil Suits," *Newsday,* January 21, 2009; *In the Matter of Felix Vinluan,* Opinion and Judgment, Supreme Court of the State of New York, Appellate Division: Second Judicial Department, 2008-02568, January 13, 2009; Joseph Berger, "Filipino Nurses, Healers in Trouble," *New York Times,* January 27, 2008; Michael Amon and Ridgely Ochs, "How a Long Island Nursing Home Empire Got Its Way," *Newsday,* September 24, 2007; "POEA Dismisses Case Filed by 26 Nurses against Sentosa Care Agency," *Manila Times,* September 13, 2007.

94   *Human rights groups, unions, and prosecutors*   Southern Poverty Law Center, *Close to Slavery: Guestworker Programs in the United States* (March 12, 2007), 1–2.

94   *In 2002, an employment agency*   Teresa Watanabe, "Human Trafficking Case Ends for 48 Thai Welders: A Firm Settles Claims of Immigrants Who Arrived on Work Visas and Were Forced into Near-Slavery," *Los Angeles Times,* December 8, 2006, 1.

95   *In March 2008, about a hundred walked off*   Julia Preston, "Workers on Hunger Strike Say They Were Misled on Visas," *New York Times,* June 7, 2008.

95   *By 2009, as a labor supplier*   *Welcome to ACI H2 Program!* http://www.acih2program .com (accessed April 4, 2009).

97   *The contention that importing migrants is a salvation*   Beth Shulman, "Rewarding 'Unskilled' Workers," *Washington Post,* September 6, 2004.

97   *Determined to right such wrongs*   FY 2010 Detailed Budget Documentation, 2009, U.S. Department of Labor. http://www.dol.gov/dol/budget/ (accessed May 25, 2009); U.S. Congress. House of Representatives. Labor, Health and Human Services, Education, and Related Agencies Subcommittee of the House Appropriations Committee, *The Department of Labor* (accessed May 12, 2009).

6. Smugglers as Migration Service Providers

100   *The fortunes of the smuggling business are tied*   Pia M. Orrenius, "Illegal Immigration and Enforcement along the Southwest Border" (Federal Reserve Bank of Dallas, June 2001).

100   *In other words, as border controls tighten*   Wayne A. Cornelius, Scott Borger, Adam Sawyer, David Keyes, Clare Appleby, Kristen Parks, Gabriel Lozada, and Jonathan Hicken, "Controlling Unauthorized Immigration from Mexico: The Failure of 'Prevention through Deterrence' and the Need for Comprehensive Reform" (Center for Comparative Immigration Studies, Immigration Policy Center, University of California at San Diego, June 10, 2008).

100   *("Coyote" is an old term*   Guido Gómez de Silva, "Diccionario Breve de Mexicanismos," 2 Academia Mexicana de la Lengua, A.C. (2001), http://www .academia.org.mx/dicmex.php (accessed August 17, 2008).

101   *Though many were deterred*   Brady McCombs, Andrew Satter, and Michael Marizco, "Death on the Border," *Arizona Daily Star*.http://regulus.azstarnet.com/ borderdeaths (accessed May 26, 2009).

102   *Mexico was mired in an economic depression*   Julie Brossy, "The 'Brain Flight' from Tijuana: Educated Workers Drawn to U.S," *San Diego Union-Tribune*, July 13, 1989.

103   *It is a common business model*   Jezmín Fuentes and Olivia García, "Coyotaje: The Structure and Functioning of the People-Smuggling Industry," in *Four Generations of Norteños: New Research from the Cradle of Mexican Migration*, ed. Wayne A. Cornelius, David Fitzgerald, and Scott Borger (Boulder, Colo.: Lynne Rienner, 2008).

104   *In the 1890s, Chinese migrants entered*   Erika Lee, "Enforcing the Borders: Chinese Exclusion along the U.S. Borders with Canada and Mexico, 1882–1924," *Journal of American History* 89, no. 1 (June 2002): 54–67; "Big Smuggling Game Revealed by Chance," *San Antonio Light and Gazette*, June 6, 1909; Lawrence H. Officer and Samuel H. Williamson, "Purchasing Power of Money in the United States from 1774 to 2008," MeasuringWorth, 2009. http://www.measuringworth .com/ppowerus/ (accessed May 26, 2009).

104   *U.S. newspapers carried story after story about Chinese*   NEA Services, "Aliens and Illicit Liquor Flow in through Uncle Sam's "Back Door,' " *Portsmouth (N.H.) Daily News*, May 22, 1924, 12; "Charged with Smuggling," *Los Angeles Times*, November 14, 1907.

104   *Between 1907 and 1909, U.S. officials*   Lee, "Enforcing the Borders"; "Big Smuggling Game Revealed by Chance."

105   *Smugglers provided Chinese immigrants*   NEA Services, "Aliens and Illicit Liquor Flow in through Uncle Sam's 'Back Door.'"

105   *One enterprising immigration business*   "Smuggling of Chinese," *Los Angeles Times*, June 13, 1904; Marie Rose Wong, *Sweet Cakes, Long Journey* (Seattle: University of Washington Press, 2004), 132.; Grace Peña Delgado, "At Exclusion's Southern Gate: Changing Categories of Race and Class among Chinese *Fronterizos*, 1882– 1904," in *Continental Crossroads: Remapping the History of the U.S.-Mexico Border*, ed. Samuel J. Truett and Elliot Young (Durham, N.C.: Duke University Press, 2004), 199.

106   *The new immigration law required migrants*   Bureau of Immigration, U.S. Department of Labor, *Reports of the Department of Labor, 1918. Report of the Secretary of Labor and Reports of Bureaus*, 551–552.

106   *Despite "the vigilance of"*   U.S. Department of Labor, *Reports of the Department of Labor, 1918*.

106   *But in the meantime, if government officials worried*   Mark Reisler, *By the Sweat of Their Brow: Mexican Immigrant Labor in the United States, 1900–1940* (Westport, Conn.: Greenwood Press, 1976), 30.

106   *Secretary of Labor William B. Wilson*   Ibid., 33.

107   *"The origin of illegal immigration is to be found in the farmers*   Manuel Gamio, *Mexican Immigration to the United States: A Study of Human Migration and Adjustment* (Chicago: University of Chicago Press, 1930), 11.

108   *Getting a handle on the size*   Dennis Wagner, "New Twist on Wire Transfers; Arizona Battling Latest Strategy Used by Human Smugglers to Launder Money," *Arizona Republic*, October 13, 2006; Alex Kotlowitz, "The Smugglers' Due," *New York Times Magazine*, June 11, 2006.

109   *What is clear is that the industry generates*   David Spener, "Mexican Migration to the United States, 1882–1992: A Long Twentieth Century of Coyotaje," in *Research Seminar Series*, ed. Center for Comparative Immigration Studies, San Diego, 2005, 47–48.

109   *The corporate structure of the coyotaje industry is both fractured*   Fuentes and García, "Coyotaje."

110   *The tanking economy and the bursting housing bubble*   Sean Holstege, "Foreclosed Homes Are Drop House Favorites," *Arizona Republic*, August 31, 2008.

110   *The full extent of bribery and corruption at checkpoints*   U.K. House of Commons, Home Affairs, Fifth Report, "Immigration Decisions Taken in the UK," July 23, 2006,   http://www.publications.parliament.uk/pa/cm200506/cmselect/cmhaff/775/77508.htm (accessed May 26, 2009).

111   *Along Europe's eastern borders*   Ani Horvath, "Illegal Immigrants Mass at Europe's New Eastern Border," *Sunday Tribune* (Ireland), December 23, 2007.

111   *On both sides of the U.S.–Mexico border, drug and migrant traffickers*   Ralph Vartabedian, Richard A. Serrano, and Richard Marosi, "The Long, Crooked Line," *Los Angeles Times*, October 23, 2006; Randal C. Archibold and Andrew Becker, "Border Agents, Lured by the Other Side," *New York Times*, May 27, 2008.

111   *Senior U.S. Border Patrol agents Mario Alvarez and Samuel McClaren*   News release, office of the U.S. attorney, Southern District of California, San Diego, October 31, 2006; Vartabedian, Serrano, and Marosi, "The Long, Crooked Line."

111   *The take can be rewarding*   "Eight-Count Indictment Charging Border Patrol Agents with Conspiracy," office of the inspector general, U.S. Department of Homeland Security, *US Fed News*, March 9, 2006; news release, office of the U.S. attorney, Southern District of California, San Diego, March 26, 2007.

114   *Similar heartrending stories about smugglers*   Niki Kitsantonis, "Greece Struggles to Curb Influx of Illegal Immigrants," *International Herald Tribune*, October 4, 2007; Caroline Brothers, "Waves of Migrants Increase Pressure on Greece," *International Herald Tribune*, December 27, 2007.

7.   "We Rely Heavily on Immigrant Labor"

117   *Lindsay, California, a dusty speck of a town*   "Lindsay City, California—Population Finder—American FactFinder," U.S. Census Bureau, http://factfinder.census.gov/servlet/SAFFPopulation?_event=ChangeGeoContext&geo_id=16000US0641712&_geoContext=&_street=&_county=lindsay&_cityTown=lindsay&_state=&_zip=&_lang=en&_sse=on&ActiveGeoDiv=&_useEV=&pctxt=fph&pgsl=010&_submenuId=population_0&ds_name=null&_ci_nbr=null&qr_name=null&reg=null%3Anull&_keyword=&_industry= (accessed July 15, 2009).

119   *Lindsay is a perfect example*   University of California Agricultural Issues Center, "Agriculture's Role in the Economy," in *The Measure of California Agriculture*,

2006 (Davis: University of California Agricultural Issues Center, 2006), 6; Economic Research Service, "Background Information and Statistics: California's Citrus Industry," January 19, 2007, http://www.ers.usda.gov/News/CAcitrus.htm (accessed January 24, 2009).

121   *Of all the migrant-dependent industries*   Fred W. Friendly, Edward R. Murrow, and David Lowe, "Harvest of Shame" (CBS News, 1960).

121   *The treatment of migrant farm workers*   Thoraya Ahmed Obaid, *State of World Population 2007: Unleashing the Potential of Urban Growth* (United Nations Population Fund, 2007), 1; International Labour Office, "Promotion of Rural Employment for Poverty Reduction," in *International Labour Conference, 97th Session* (Geneva, 2008), 8; Anne Renaut, "Migrants in European Agriculture: Open Season for Exploitation," *Trade Union World Briefing* (December 2003).

121   *Even according to the official reports*   Office of the assistant secretary for the Policy, Employment, and Training Administration, U.S. Department of Labor, *The National Agricultural Workers Survey (2001–2002)* (March 2005).

122   *Not surprisingly, immigrants are overrepresented*   U.S. Department of Labor, "Foreign-Born Workers: Labor Force Characteristics in 2008," Bureau of Labor Statistics (March 26, 2009) http://www.bls.gov/news.release/pdf/forbrn.pdf (accessed December 8, 2009); Bureau of Labor Statistics, "The Employment Situation— October 2009," http://www.bls.gov/news.release/archives/empsit_11062009.htm (accessed December 10, 2009), U.S. Census Bureau, "Foreign-Born Population of the United States Current Population Survey—March 2008, Table 3.7, Occupation of Employed Foreign-Born Civilian Workers 16 Years and Over by Sex and World Region of Birth: 2008," http://www.census.gov/population/socdemo/foreign/cps2008 /tab3-7.xls (accessed December 8, 2009); U.S. Census Bureau, "Foreign-Born Population of the United States Current Population Survey—March 2008, Table 3.8, Industry Status of Employed Civilian Foreign-Born Workers 16 Years and Over by Sex and World Region of Birth: 2008," http://www.census.gov/population/ socdemo/foreign/cps2008/tab3-8.xls (accessed December 8, 2009).

123   *"In Texas, we rely heavily on immigrant labor"*   Sterling Construction Company, Inc., Form 10-K, Annual Report (March 17, 2008), http://idea.sec.gov/Archives/edgar/data/ 874238/000114036108006929/form10k.htm#sig (accessed January 22, 2009).

123   *Infosys Technologies, which imports high-tech workers*   Infosys Technologies Ltd., Form 6-K, Report of Foreign Private Issuer (January 22, 2009), http://www.sec .gov/Archives/edgar/data/1067491/000106749109000006/index.htm (accessed January 22, 2009).

123   *And a garment manufacturer in Los Angeles*   American Apparel, Inc., Form 10-K, Annual Report (March 17, 2008), http://www.sec.gov/Archives/edgar/data/1 336545/000119312508059085/d10k.htm (accessed January 22, 2009); "American Apparel Announces Developments Regarding Inspection by U.S. Immigration and Customs Enforcement" (July 1, 2009), http://www.sec.gov/Archives/edgar/ data/1336545/000134100409001484/ex99-1.htm (accessed July 15, 2009); Tim Rutten, "Obama's Pink Slips for Garment Workers," *Los Angeles Times*, October 3, 2009; Julia Preston, "Immigration Crackdown With Firings, Not Raids," *New York Times*, September 30, 2009.

124   *One visible symbol of America's reliance*   Abel Valenzuela Jr. et al., *On the Corner: Day Labor in the United States* (Los Angeles: UCLA Center for the Study of Urban Poverty, 2006), i.

124 *Disregard for such niceties*   Joan Vennochi, "Nominees and Double Standards," *Boston Globe*, January 18, 2009.

125 *One of Chertoff's top deputies, Lorraine Henderson*   Katie Zezima, "Official Accused of Hiring Illegal Immigrants," *New York Times*, December 6, 2008.

125 *President Obama's Treasury secretary, Michael Geithner*   U.S. Senate Committee on Finance, *Documents Regarding Treasury Nominee Geithner* (2009), 4.

125 *Even Tom Tancredo, the bombastic former Colorado congressman*   Holly Bailey, "A Border War," *Newsweek*, April 3, 2006, 22; Michael Riley, "Illegal Labor Aided Tancredo Workers Say They Redid Basement for Immigration Critic," *Denver Post*, September 19, 2002.

125 *Then there was the case that epitomized irony*   U.S. Immigration and Customs Enforcement, U.S. Department of Homeland Security, "Company Executives Sentenced for Hiring Illegal Alien Workers," press release, March 28, 2007.

126 *Not to be outdone, across the pond*   James Tapsfield, "Immigration Control Body Employed Illegal Worker," Press Association Newsfile, July 21, 2008.

126 *"Immigrants are a critical part of the U.S. workforce*   "Immigration's Economic Impact," White House Council of Economic Advisers, Executive Office of the President, June 20, 2007.

126 *"The Treasury estimates that migration contributed*   "Managing Global Migration: A Strategy to Build Stronger International Alliances to Manage Migration," Foreign and Commonwealth Office, U.K. Home Office, June 2007, 4.

126 *For the early European colonizers of the New World*   Benjamin Balak and Jonathan Lave, "The Dismal Science of Punishment: The Legal-Economy of Convict Transportation to the American Colonies," *Journal of Law and Politics, University of Virginia* 18, no. 4 (2003), 3; A. M. Simons, *Social Forces in American History* (New York: Macmillan, 1918), 19.

127 *Colonial development was*   William Dudley, *American Slavery* (San Diego: Greenhaven Press, 2000), 22.

127 *The new American nation saw little other recorded migration*   Douglas S. Massey, "Patterns and Processes of International Migration in the 21st Century," paper presented at the Conference on African Migration in Comparative Perspective, June 4–7, 2003, 2.

127 *The scale of emigration from Europe*   Peter Stalker, *Workers without Frontiers: The Impact of Globalization on International Migration* (Boulder, Colorado: International Labour Organization, 2000), 13.

128 *At the same time, political changes in Mexico*   Douglas Massey et al., *Return to Aztlan: The Social Process of International Migration from Western Mexico* (Berkeley: University of California Press, 1987), 41; Lawrence A. Cardoso, *Mexican Emigration to the United States, 1897–1931: Socioeconomic Patterns* (Tucson: University of Arizona Press, 1980), 13–14; Dan La Botz, "Migration of Workers to the United States in Historical Perspective" (April 2006), http://www.floc.com/documents/IRHistory.pdf (accessed January 26, 2009).

128 *The U.S. reliance on Mexican labor*   Jeffrey Kaye, "Ties That Bind," *The MacNeil/Lehrer NewsHour*, PBS-TV, May 18, 1993.

129 *(The custom has had dramatic consequences*   "Mexican Immigrants in the United States, 2008," Pew Research Center, Washington, D.C. (April 15, 2009), http://pewhispanic.org/files/factsheets/47.pdf (accessed June 7, 2009).

129 *In the United States, the number of immigrants*   U.S. Bureau of the Census, "Table 1, Nativity of the Population and Place of Birth of the Native Population: 1850 to

1990" (March 9, 1999), http://www.census.gov/population/www/documentation/twps0029/tab01.html (accessed April 8, 2009); U.S. Census Bureau, "Foreign-Born Population of the United States Current Population Survey—March 2008, Table 1.1, Population by Sex, Age, Nativity, and U.S. Citizenship Status: 2008," http://www.census.gov/population/socdemo/foreign/cps2008/tab1-1.xls (accessed December 8, 2009); "Transatlantic Trends, Immigration Topline Data 2009," German Marshall Fund of the United States (December 3, 2009), http://www.gmfus.org/trends/immigration/doc/TTI_2009_Top.pdf (accessed December 12, 2009).

130   *"The absence of the estimated 1.4 million*   Texas Comptroller of Public Accounts, *Undocumented Immigrants in Texas: A Financial Analysis of the Impact to the State Budget and Economy*, ed. Carole Keeton Strayhorn (2006).

130   A *think tank at Rutgers*   Ira N. Gang and Anne Morrison Piehl. "Destination, New Jersey: How Immigrants Benefit the State Economy," Eagleton Institute of Politics (Camden: Rutgers, the State University of New Jersey, 2008).

130   *Similarly, in New York in 2007, the Fiscal Policy Institute*   Fiscal Policy Institute, "Working for a Better Life," in *Working for a Better Life: A Profile of Immigrants in the New York State Economy* (New York City: Fiscal Policy Institute, 2007).

131   *In the monument's shadows*   National Park Service, *Ellis Island—History*, http://www.ellisisland.org/genealogy/ellis_island_history.asp (accessed May 26, 2009).

131   *Many modern-day conservative idolizers*   Otis Graham, "Ronald Reagan's Big Mistake," *American Conservative* (January 27, 2003).

8. Servitude and Cash Flows

132   *The UAE is more than simply a study in indulgence and excess*   "Expat Growth Widens UAE Demographic Gap; UAE—the Official Web Site—News," September 25, 2008, http://www.uaeinteract.com/docs/Expat_growth_widens_UAE_demographic_gap__/32128.htm (accessed July 16, 2009); "Labor Rights in the UAE," UAE Embassy in Washington, D.C. (June 16, 2009), http://www.uae-embassy.org/uae/human-rights/labor-rights (accessed July 16, 2009); "Defence, Remittances Bear Down on UAE Surplus," *Agence France Presse*, January 6, 2007; Rachna Uppal, "Remittances from UAE second highest in GCC," *Gulf News*, June 3, 2009.

133   *In 2008, Filipino workers in the UAE sent home more than $584 million*   Rachna Uppal, "Remittances from UAE Second Highest in GCC," *Gulf News*, June 3, 2009.

134   *The Palms are a series of artificial islands*   Johann Hari, "Beneath the Gold and Glory," *Sunday Independent (South Africa)*, April 19, 2009; *Burj Al Arab Suites*, May 27, 2009, http://www.jumeirah.com/en/Hotels-and-Resorts/Destinations/Dubai/Burj-Al-Arab/Suites/ (accessed May 27, 2009).

137   *To me, the workers seemed*   Human Rights Watch, *Building Towers, Cheating Workers: Exploitation of Migrant Construction Workers in the United Arab Emirates*, Human Rights Watch (November 2006); International Covenant on Civil and Political Rights, Article 12(b) (United Nations entered into force March 23, 1976).

139   *In 2003, asked about oversight of the conditions*   Duraid Al Baik, "Ministry of Labor Focuses on Strengthening Inspection Department," Gulfnews.com, July 6, 2003.

139   *But three years later, in 2006*   Jim Krane, "Report: Workforce Abused in Emirates," Associated Press, November 12, 2006.

139   *In May 2009, Human Rights Watch acknowledged*   Human Rights Watch, "The Island of Happiness: Exploitation of Migrant Workers on Saadiyat Island, Abu Dhabi" (May 2009); "Labor Rights in the UAE," UAE Embassy in Washington, D.C., June 16, 2009, http://www.uae-embassy.org/uae/human-rights/labor-rights (accessed July 16, 2009).

139   *"Respecting workers' rights"*   UAE Rebuffs Human Rights Watch Report on Saadiyat Island," Gulfnews.com, May 19, 2009.

140   *The Philippine government has set a wage minimum*   Wafa Issa, "Maids Work in UAE for Lower Salaries," *Gulf News*, August 4, 2008.

140   *The problem is not confined to the UAE*   Philippine Overseas Employment Administration, *2007 Annual Report* (2008), 21.

142   *Hyperbole aside, unquestionably many migrants*   Matthew Brown, "UAE's Drive for Emirati-Run Economy Is Thwarted by Handouts," *Bloomberg*, October 4, 2007; Mohammad Masad, "Dubai: What Cosmopolitan City?, *ISIM Review* 2 (Autumn 2008).

142   *Families and economies around the world are dependent*   Dilip Ratha, Sanket Mohapatra, and Ani Silwal, Migration and Remittances Team, Development Project Group, World Bank, "Migration and Development Brief 11; Migration and Remittance Trends 2009; A Better-Than-Expected Outcome so Far, but Significant Risks Ahead," World Bank (November 3, 2009); Dilip Ratha, "Sending Money Home: Trends in Migrant Remittances," International Monetary Fund (December 2005).

143   *In 2009, as the economy worsened*   Marc Lacey, "Money Trickles North as Mexicans Help Relatives," *New York Times*, November 15, 2009; Samantha Henry, "Strapped Immigrants Seek 'Reverse Remittances,'" Associated Press, July 1, 2009; Dilip Ratha, Sanket Mohapatra, and Ani Silwal, Migration and Remittances Team, World Bank, "Migration and Development Brief 10; Migration and Remittance Flows 2009–2011: Remittances Expected To Fall By 7–10 Percent In 2009," World Bank (July 13, 2009); Dilip Ratha, "Migration and Remittance Trends 2009: A Better-Than-Expected Outcome so Far, but Significant Risks Ahead," People Move, World Bank, November 3, 2009, https://blogs.worldbank.org/peoplemove/migration-and-remittance-trends-2009-a-better-than-expected-outcome-so-far-but-significant-risks (accessed December 9, 2009).

144   *In Senegal, remittances in 2007*   Dilip Ratha, "Remittance Flows to Developing Countries Are Estimated to Exceed $300 Billion in 2008," *People Move*, February 18, 2009, World Bank, http://peoplemove.worldbank.org/en/content/remittance-flows-to-developing-countries (accessed March 14, 2009).

144   *To put the scope of global remittances into perspective*   Organization for Economic Cooperation and Development, "United States Gross Bilateral ODA," http://www.oecd.org/dataoecd/42/30/41732048.jpg (accessed May 27, 2009); Organization for Economic Cooperation and Development, "Aid Targets Slipping out of Reach?," (November 24, 2008).

144   *Migration experts and scholars*   Devesh Kapur, "Remittances: The New Development Mantra?," paper presented at the G-24 Technical Group meeting (Harvard University and Center for Global Development, August 25, 2003); Jason DeParle, "World Banker and His Cash Return Home," *New York Times*, March 17, 2008; Tasneem Siddiqui and Chowdhury R. Abrar, "Migrant Worker Remittances and Micro-Finance in Bangladesh," Social Finance Program, International Labor Office (September 2003).

145 *Migrants transfer remittances using a number of methods* Adam Higazi, "Ghana Country Study" (Oxford, U.K.: ESRC Centre on Migration, Policy, and Society [COMPAS], January 15, 2005), 10.

145 *Money transfer companies make their money two ways* Lauren Pollock, "MoneyGram Names New Chairman, CEO after Recapitalization," Dow Jones Newswires, January 21, 2009.

146 *In March 2009, a Western Union official* Nadim Kawach, "UAE Foreign Remittances to Rise: IMF," *Emirates Business* 24, no. 7 (2009).

146 *Western Union has long stood at the intersection* Western Union Co. http://corporate.westernunion.com/history.html; Western Union Co., Annual Report, Form 10-K, U.S. Securities and Exchange Commission (February 19, 2009), 38; "Q4 2008 Western Union Co. Earnings Conference Call—Final," FD (Fair Disclosure) Wire, February 5, 2009.

146 *Western Union is facing increasing competition* Send Money to India, Money Remittance to India, Remit2India, http://www.timesofmoney.com/remittance/jsp/home.jsp (accessed March 15, 2009).

146 *Credit and debit card companies* iKobo—Money Transfer Services—Send Money Online, https://www.ikobo.com/ (accessed March 15, 2009).

146 *Banks also have been jumping on the migrant money train* Bank of America, SafeSend, http://www.bankofamerica.com/safesend/index.cfm?&context=en (accessed March 15, 2009); Wells Fargo International Money Transfers, Wells Fargo ExpressSend Service, https://www.wellsfargo.com/per/intl_remittance/ (accessed March 15, 2009).

147 *Banks in India and the Philippines* Muzaffar Chishti, "The Rise in Remittances to India: A Closer Look," Migration Policy Institute (February 1, 2007); Nkechi Carroll, "Record High Remittances to the Philippines Lead to Increased Competition among Philippine Banks," Asia Focus, Federal Reserve Bank of San Francisco (January 2008).

147 *The latest entry in the global remittance industry* "Mobile Money Transfer— GSM World," http://www.gsmworld.com/our-work/programmes-and-initiatives/mobile-money/mobile-money-transfer/index.htm (accessed March 15, 2009).

147 *In Kenya, Safaricom teamed with Vodafone and the Commercial Bank of Africa* Giles Turnbull, "Technology: Inside IT: Cash Faces Its Final Call: Kenya's M-Pesa Service Proves That Transferring Money by Mobile Works—Will It Catch on in the UK?" *Guardian* (London), February 19, 2009; *Safaricom: M-PESA Services*, Safaricom Limited, http://www.safaricom.co.ke/index.php?id=747 (accessed March 15, 2009).

148 *South Africa and the Philippines have similar systems in place* Stephen Timewell, "Mobiles Begin Calling Shots on Banking and Payments," *Banker*, February 1, 2007; Romilly Gregory, "Dialing Change," *World Today*, October 2008, 22; Globe GCAS, http://www.g-cash.com.ph/subsectionpagearticle.aspx?secid=25&ssid=42&id=82 (accessed March 15, 2009).

148 *At the other end of the technological spectrum* "Global Profiteers aboard Booming Piracy Racket," *New Zealand Herald*, December 12, 2008; "Majority of Expats Still Using Hundi for Remittances; Says PEW Report," Pakistan Newswire (Islamabad), December 26, 2008.

148 *Other comparatively low-tech money transfer systems* Rubén Hernández-León, *Metropolitan Migrants: The Migration of Urban Mexicans to the United States* (Berkeley: University of California Press, 2008).

149   *Such grievances are common*   Dilip Ratha et al., Development Prospects Group, Migration and Remittances Team, "Migration and Development Brief 3" (World Bank, November 29, 2007), 1; *Boycott Western Union!*, http://www.boycottwestern-union.net/En/index.html (accessed January 29, 2009). Western Union Co., Annual Report, Form 10-K, 38.

149   *The massive sums moved by the remittance industry*   Cerstin Sander, Bannock Consulting, "Migrant Remittances to Developing Countries," prepared for the U.K. Department of International Development (June 2003), 8; Tasneem Siddiqui and C. R. Abrar, "Contributions of Returnees: An Analytical Survey of Postreturn Experience." International Organization for Migration (IOM), Regional Office for South Asia, Dhaka (November 2002). "Migrant Remittances from the United States to Latin America to Reach $45 Billion in 2006, Says IDB—Inter-American Development Bank" (October 18, 2006), http://www.iadb.org/NEWS/detail.cfm?artid=3348&language=En&id=3348&CFID=708962&CFTOKEN=27594862 (accessed July 10, 2009).

9. "Help Wanted" or "No Trespassing"

150   *To environmentalists, the steep canyon*   Rasa Gustaitis, "Threat to Tijuana Reserve: Mexico Border Fence Worries Neighbors," *Coast & Ocean Magazine*, Summer 1998.

150   *"Smuggler's Gulch is an area"*   Congressional Record, U.S. House of Representatives, February 10, 2005, H556.

150   *Over the protests of the Sierra Club, the Audubon Society*   Leslie Berestein, "Border Gulch Fill-in Faces the Wet Test," *San Diego Union-Tribune*, November 27, 2008; Thomas Watkins, "San Diego Officials Mark Completion of Border Berm," Associated Press, July 6, 2009.

151   *"Look at the policy decisions being made"*   Dan Stein, "Cheap Labor Uber Alles," *Federation for American Immigration Reform*, September 15, 2003, http://www.fairus.org/site/PageServer?pagename=media_media29a9 (accessed February 14, 2009).

151   *In that respect, advocates of tougher border enforcement*   Jeffrey S. Passel and D'Vera Cohn, "A Portrait of Unauthorized Immigrants in the United States," Pew Research Center, Washington, D.C., April 14, 2009.

152   *During the medieval ages in Western Europe*   James Harvey Robinson, *Medieval and Modern Times: An Introduction to the History of Western Europe from the Dissolution of the Roman Empire to the Opening of the Great War of 1914* (Lexington, Mass.: Ginn, 1916), 100; Peter Kolchin, *Unfree Labor* (Cambridge, Mass.: Harvard University Press, Belknap Press, 1987), 4–8.

152   *King George III's lame effort*   David Brion Davis and Steven Mintz, *The Boisterous Sea of Liberty* (New York: Oxford University Press, 2000), 146; King George III, October 7, 1763, Yale Law School Library, http://avalon.law.yale.edu/18th_century/proc1763.asp (accessed February 14, 2008).

152   *In nineteenth-century Europe, the spread of industrial capitalism*   Jean-Louis Robert, Antoine Prost, and Chris Wrigley, *The Emergence of European Trade Unionism*. Ashgate, 208; "Law on Freedom of Movement, November 1, 1867," http://germanhistorydocs.ghi-dc.org/sub_document.cfm?document_id=1827. Deutsches Historisches Institut, Deutsche Geschichte in Dokumenten und Bildern (accessed June 17, 2009); Hajo Holborn, *A History of Modern Germany* (Princeton, N.J.: Princeton University Press, 1969), 201; Theodore Hamerow, *Restoration,*

Revolution, Reaction (Princeton, N.J.: Princeton University Press, 1958), 253; Eli Nathans, *The Politics of Citizenship in Germany* (Oxford, U.K.: Berg, 2004), 78–81; Jonathan Wagner, *A History of Migration from Germany to Canada, 1850–1939* (Vancouver, B.C.: University of British Columbia Press, 2006), 23; Klaus Bade, *Migration in European History* (Cambridge, U.K.: Blackwell, 2003), 47–48; George Steinmetz, "The Myth of an Autonomous State: Industrialists, Junkers, and Social Policy in Imperial Germany," in *Society, Culture, and the State in Germany, 1870–1930,* ed. Geoff Eley (Ann Arbor: University of Michigan Press, 1997), 277–283; Perry Anderson, *Lineages of the Absolutist State* (London: Verso Editions, 1979), 207–276. John C. Torpey, *The Invention of the Passport: Surveillance, Citizenship, and the State* (Cambridge, U.K.: Cambridge University Press, 2000), 78.

153   *The freedom to travel came as new*   Aristide R. Zolberg, "The Age of Border Control," *Politik* (2004). http://www.tidsskriftetpolitik.dk/index.php?id=74 (accessed February 15, 2009).

154   *The Border Patrol had been very specific*   Customs and Border Protection, Procurement Directorate, Department of Homeland Security, 2008; Allied Tube & Conduit Corp., *Selector Guide,* 2008, http://www.alliedtube.com/perimeter-security/barbed-tape/supermaze-nato-barrier.asp (accessed June 6, 2009).

154   *The federal foray into migration management came*   Kitty Calavita, "U.S. Immigration and Policy Responses: The Limits of Legislation," in *Controlling Immigration: A Global Perspective,* ed. Wayne A. Cornelius, Philip L. Martin, and James F. Hollifield (Palo Alto, Calif.: Stanford University Press, 2004), 57; "A Singular Letter from Mayor Gunther," *New York Times,* September 15, 1864.

155   *In the late nineteenth century*   Leonard Dinnerstein and David Reimers, *Ethnic Americans* (New York: Columbia University Press, 1999), 29.

155   *The captains of enterprise found migration*   Andrew Carnegie, *Triumphant Democracy* (New York: Charles Scribner's Sons, 1887), 35.

155   *During the 1860s and 1870s*   "California Immigration Association," *New York Times,* August 10, 1868; John Higham, *Strangers in the Land* (Piscataway, N.J.: Rutgers University Press, 2002), 16–17.

155   *Between 1880 and 1914, some 22.3 million people arrived*   Ellis Island Ship Database, Statue of Liberty–Ellis Island Foundation, http://www.ellisisland.org/search/ship_passengers.asp?letter=n&half=1&sname=Nieuw*Amsterdam&year=1907&sdate=04/17/1907&port=Rotterdam,*Holland&page=1 (accessed June 6, 2009); B. Colin Hamblin, "Ellis Island," http://sydaby.eget.net/swe/ellis_island.htm (accessed June 6, 2009); "Ellis Island Congested," *New York Times,* April 19, 1907, 18; U.S. Immigration and Naturalization Service, *Statistical Yearbook of the Immigration and Naturalization Service,* 1999, 19–20; Isaac Aaronovich Hourwich, *Immigration and Labor: The Economic Aspects of European Immigration to the United States,* (New York: G. P. Putnam's Sons, 1912), 87.

156   *In the southwestern states*   Mark Reisler, *By the Sweat of Their Brow: Mexican Immigrant Labor in the United States 1900–1940* (Westport, Conn.: Greenwood Press, 1976), 17.

156   *Loose controls accommodated industry's needs*   Mario T. Garcia, "Mexico Immigration in U.S.-Mexico History: Myths and Reality," in *Myths, Misdeeds, and Misunderstandings: The Roots of Conflict in U.S.-Mexican Relations,* ed. Jaime E. Rodríguez and Kathryn Vincent (Lanham, Md.: Rowman & Littlefield, 1997), 202.

156 *Unregulated migration served both countries* Manuel Gamio, *Mexican Immigration to the United States: A Study of Human Migration and Adjustment* (Chicago: University of Chicago Press, 1930), 30.

156 *A 1910 U.S. congressional commission reported* U.S. Immigration Commission (1907–1910), *Immigrants in Industries. Part 1: General Survey of the Anthracite Coal Mining Industry* (1911); Reisler, *By the Sweat of Their Brow*, 129.

157 *Mexico wasn't the only source of cheap labor in the West* U.S. Business Cycle Expansions and Contractions," National Bureau of Economic Research, http://www.nber.org/cycles/cyclesmain.html (accessed February 17, 2009).

157 *Mobs attacked Chinese businesses and homes in San Francisco* "Mass Meeting," *Los Angeles Times*, March 5, 1882, 3.

158 *Comparatively little attention was focused on Mexicans* Ian F. Haney Lopez, *White by Law: The Legal Construction of Race* (New York: New York University Press, 1996, 31; Mae M. Ngai, "The Architecture of Race in American Immigration Law: A Reexamination of the Immigration Act of 1924," *Journal of American History* 86, no. 1 (June 1999): 88.

158 *The vitriol that spewed forth against migrants* Henry Cabot Lodge, "The Restriction of Immigration," *North American Review* 152, no. 410 (1891): 27–37, http://cdl.library.cornell.edu/cgi-bin/moa/moa-cgi?notisid=ABQ7578-0152&byte=107128306 (accessed June 6, 2009).

159 *By 1907, immigrants from southern and eastern Europe* Jeremiah W. Jenks and W. Jett Lauck, *The Immigration Problem* (New York: Funk & Wagnalls, 1911).

159 *Nativists found support from prominent academics* Madison Grant, *The Passing of the Great Race: or, the Racial Basis of European History* (New York: Charles Scribner's Sons, 1921), 90–91.

160 *Even following the establishment of the Border Patrol* U.S. Department of Homeland Security, "Border Patrol History—CBP.Gov," July 15, 2003, U.S. Customs and Border Protection, http://www.cbp.gov/xp/cgov/border_security/border_patrol/border_patrol_ohs/history.xml (accessed February 15, 2009); Robert Van Giezen and Albert E. Schwenk, "Compensation from before World War I through the Great Depression," January 30, 2003, U.S. Department of Labor, Bureau of Labor Statistics, http://www.bls.gov/opub/cwc/cm20030124ar03p1.htm (accessed February 15, 2009).

160 *Industries competed for Mexican laborers* Reisler, *By the Sweat of Their Brow*, 58.

160 *But with the onset of the Great Depression* Francisco Balderrama and Raymond Rodríguez, *Decade of Betrayal* (Albuquerque: University of New Mexico Press, 2006).

161 *During the 1940s and 1950s, U.S. immigration policies* David Spener, "Mexican Migration to the United States, 1882–1992, A Long Twentieth Century of Coyotaje," in *Research Seminar Series*, ed. Center for Comparative Immigration Studies, San Diego (2005), 33.

162 *With the end of the Korean War* John Dillin, "How Eisenhower Solved Illegal Border Crossings from Mexico," *Christian Science Monitor*, July 6, 2006; Joanna Griffin, *Mexico and the United States*, ed. Lee Stacy (London: Marshall Cavendish, 2003), 609; Philip L. Martin, *Promise Unfulfilled: Unions, Immigration, and the Farm Workers* (Ithaca, N.Y.: Cornell University Press, 2003), 47–49.

162 *The rise of the civil rights movement* "Remarks at the Signing of the Immigration Bill," (Liberty Island, New York, October 3, 1965). *Public Papers of the Presidents of the United States: Lyndon B. Johnson, 1965*, vol. II, entry 546, pp. 1037–1040. Washington, D.C.: U.S. Government Printing Office, 1966.

163   *There were three main reasons for the increase in the number*   Michael Barone, "The Newest Americans," *Wall Street Journal*, April 11, 2006, A16; Department of Homeland Security, *Yearbook of Immigration Statistics*, Office of Immigration Statistics, table 6 (2007).

163   *"We're facing a vast army"*   Lou Cannon, "Struggling up the Ladder," *Washington Post*, March 27, 1978.

163   *The United States had come through a period of high inflation*   James F. Hollifield, Valerie F. Hunt, and Daniel J. Tichenor, "Immigrants, Markets, and Rights: The United States as an Emerging Migration State," *Washington University Journal of Law and Policy* 27 (2008): 24.

163   *In the White House, members of the National Security Council*   Robert Hormats, "The Mexican Float—Many Unanswered Questions, in National Security Council," memorandum, September 14, 1976, http://www.gwu.edu/~nsarchiv/NSAEBB/NSAEBB115/doc7.pdf (accessed July 15, 2009).

164   *It's an ironic but obvious fact*   Información Sobre el Flujo Migratorio Internacional de México," Sistema Nacional de Información Estadística y Geográfica, June 5, 2009, http://www.inegi.org.mx/inegi/contenidos/espanol/prensa/comunicados/flujomigratorio.asp (accessed June 5, 2009); Julia Preston, "Mexican Data Show Migration to U.S. in Decline," *New York Times*, May 14, 2009.

164   *As migration from Mexico increased*   Richard L. Strout, "Illegal Mexican Aliens: Who's Counting?" *Christian Science Monitor*, January 4, 1980, 23.

164   *"Invited and uninvited, rich and poor"*   James Kelly, D. L. Coutu, and Eileen Shields, "Closing the Golden Door: As the Immigrant Tide Rises, So Does the Search for Ways to Stem It," *Time*, May 18, 1981, 24.

164   *"This country has lost control of its borders"*   Leon Daniel, "America's Borders Are Out of Control: Congress Tackles Illegal Immigration," November 27, 1983.

164   *With proposals for federal immigration legislation stymied*   Jeffrey Kaye, "Border Clashes," *MacNeil/Lehrer NewsHour*, July 8, 1985.

165   *But employers had managed to*   Immigration Control and Reform Act of 1986; Pia M. Orrenius, Federal Reserve Bank of Dallas, *Do Amnesty Programs Encourage Illegal Immigration? Evidence from IRCA* (2001); U.S. House of Representatives. Committee on the Judiciary. Subcommittee on Immigration, Citizenship, Refugees, Border Security, and International Law (2007).

166   *However, stepped-up border enforcement was hardly a partisan issue*   Douglas S. Massey, "Backfire at the Border," Cato Institute's Center for Trade Policy Studies, June 13, 2007.

166   *Congress's focus on deterrence continued*   U.S. Department of Homeland Security, *Budget-in-Brief* (2008).

166   *But the effects of border enforcement*   Mark Stevenson, "Mexico: Exodus of Migrants Falls by More Than Half," Associated Press, February 19, 2009.

167   *In addition to policing at the border, the Bush administration*   U.S. Immigration and Customs Enforcement, "Worksite Enforcement," December 4, 2008, http://www.ice.gov/pi/news/factsheets/worksite.htm (accessed February 20, 2009); Perryman Group, "An Essential Resource: An Analysis of the Economic Impact of Undocumented Workers on Business Activity in the US with Estimated Effects by State and by Industry" (Waco, Tex.: Perryman Group, April 2008), http://www.ilw.com/Articles/2008,1008-perryman.pdf (accessed June 2, 2009); Elizabeth Benton, "City Reports Increase in Nonviolent Crime in '08," *New Haven (Conn.) Register*, January 3, 2009.

167   *By contrast, the Obama administration embarked* "Prepared Remarks by Secretary Napolitano on Immigration Reform at the Center for American Progress," November 13, 2009, http://www.dhs.gov/ynews/speeches/sp_1258123461050.shtm (accessed December 10, 2009); "ICE Assistant Secretary John Morton Announces 1,000 New Workplace Audits to Hold Employers Accountable for Their Hiring Practices," November 19, 2009, http://www.ice.gov/pi/nr/0911/091119washingtondc2.htm (accessed December 10, 2009). "The Agenda: Immigration," White House, http://www.whitehouse.gov/agenda/immigration/ (accessed June 5, 2009); "Secure Border Initiative: Technology Deployment Delays Persist and the Impact of Border Fencing Has Not Been Assessed" (U.S. Government Accountability Office, September 17, 2009).

168   *The Obama administration also continued the buildup* "Secure Border Initiative: Technology Deployment Delays Persist and the Impact of Border Fencing Has Not Been Assessed" (U.S. Government Accountability Office, September 9, 2009).

168   *As the administration's top official responsible* Mel Melendez, "Napolitano Answers Student Queries; Phoenix College Forum Also Aims to Raise Young Voter Participation," *Arizona Republic*, March 8, 2006.

169   *By promising to get tougher* "Fact Sheet, ICE Fiscal Year 2010 Enacted Budget," U.S. Department of Homeland Security, Office of Public Affairs, November 5, 2009, http://www.ice.gov/doclib/pi/news/factsheets/2010budgetfactsheet.doc (accessed December 10, 2009); "Budget-in-Brief, Fiscal Year 2010," U.S. Department of Homeland Security, May 12, 2009, www.dhs.gov/xlibrary/assets/budget_bib_fy2010.pdf (accessed December 10, 2009).

169   *In the end, for all the words, money, and passion* "New York City, New York—Population Finder—American FactFinder," U.S. Census Bureau, http://factfinder.census.gov/servlet/SAFFPopulation?_event=ChangeGeoContext&geo_id=16000US3651000&_geoContext=&_street=&_county=new+york&_cityTown=new+york&_state=04000US36&_zip=&_lang=en&_sse=on&ActiveGeoDiv=&_useEV=&pctxt=fph&pgsl=010&_submenuId=population_0&ds_name=null&_ci_nbr=null&qr_name=null&reg=null%3Anull&_keyword=&_industry= (accessed July 20, 2009); "Overstay Tracking: A Key Component of Homeland Security and a Layered Defense" (U.S. General Accounting Office, May 2004); Passel and Cohn, "A Portrait of Unauthorized Immigrants in the United States."

10. Politics, Influence, and Alliances

171   *Nonetheless, the voice of the L.A. business community* Los Angeles Area Chamber of Commerce, "LA Area Chamber Statement on Immigration Reform," *Los Angeles Area Chamber of Commerce*, May 1, 2008; Rick Orlov and Kerry Cavanaugh, "End to Raids Sought by Villaraigosa; Immigration: Feds' Focus on LA Businesses Said to Hurt Economy," *Daily News of Los Angeles*, May 2, 2008.

172   *One organization, the National Immigration Forum* "National Immigration Forum—About the Forum." National Immigration Forum, 2009, http://www.immigrationforum.org/about/board (accessed April 7, 2009).

172   *In 2007, the U.S. Department of Homeland Security* "National Council of La Raza: Policies," 2007, http://www.nclr.org/content/policy/detail/48220/ (accessed April 7, 2009).

173   *The odd political groupings also have*   "Brief of Amici Curiae," *Lozano et al v. City of Hazleton*, no. 07-3531. U,S, Court of Appeals for the Third Circuit, April 17, 2008.

173   *In 2006, when the United States was preoccupied with terrorist threats*   Bill Ong Hing, "Guest Workers Program with a Path to Legalization," American Immigration Law Foundation, April 11, 2006, http://web.archive.org/web/20060614065507/www .ailf.org/ipc/2006_april_perspective.shtml (accessed June 17, 2009).

173   *Three years later, the Immigration Policy Center*   "The Economics of Immigration Reform: Legalizing Undocumented Immigrants a Key to U.S. Economic Recovery," Immigration Policy Center 2 (March 2009).

173   *A business-backed national lobbying group, ImmigrationWorks USA*   Immigration Works USA, "Action Alert—Support the H2B Fly-in Today," February 25, 2009.

174   *With the economy in the doldrums*   "Talking Points for Congressional Visits," ImmigrationWorks USA, January 9, 2009, http://www.immigrationworksusa .org/uploaded/file/IW%20congressional%20talking%20pts.pdf (accessed July 18, 2009).

174   *ImmigrationWorks USA was founded in 2008*   ImmigrationWorks USA, "IW Talking Points—Why We Need Migrants Even in a Recession," April 8, 2009; Tamar Jacoby and Cesar V. Conda, "Immigration Realism," *National Review Online,* August 2, 2006, http://article.nationalreview.com/?q= NmU5NDg4M TNmMzdiMzUzOGYxODQ4MGY3ZjU3ZjdhZDI= (accessed February 25, 2009); ImmigrationWorks USA, *ImmigrationWorks USA—Principles,* http://www .immigrationworksusa.org/index.php?p=50 (accessed February 25, 2009).

175   *In 1917, with the approach of the summer harvest season*   "Prompt Action Needed. Ranchers Blamed in Part for Acute Labor Shortage," *Los Angeles Times,* May 27, 1917; "Loss of Immigrants," *Los Angeles Times,* May 24, 1918.

175   *American industrialists voiced similar complaints*   Gordon S. Watkins, *Labor Problems and Labor Administration in the United States during the World War* (Champaign: University of Illinois Press, 1919), 55.

175   *The drumbeat from the "employing class" about worker shortages*   "Report of the Proceedings of the Annual Convention of the American Federation of Labor," American Federation of Labor, 1917, 210–445.

176   *A subsequent union report on the labor shortage*   United Mine Workers of America, "Proceedings of the 26th Consecutive and Third Biennial Convention," United Mine Workers of America, January 15, 1918, 70.

176   *Nearly a century later, American business owners*   John Quiñones, "Worker Shortage; Spoils of Labor," *ABC World News with Charles Gibson,* November 24, 2006; also Tom Bearden, "Farmers in Colorado Struggle with Labor Shortage," *NewsHour with Jim Lehrer* (PBS-TV), August 20, 2007.

176   *Across the country, an apple farmer in upstate New York*   Diana Louise Carter, "Immigration Rules Hit Farmers Hard," *Rochester (N.Y.) Democrat and Chronicle,* August 19, 2007.

176   *The flurry of apocalyptic-sounding news reports*   Philip Martin, "Farm Labor Shortages: How Real? What Response?" (Washington, D.C.: Center for Immigration Studies, November 2007).

177   *Farmers were not the only employer group*   Michael W. Horrigan, "Employment Projections to 2012: Concepts and Context," *Monthly Labor Review, Bureau of Labor Statistics* 127, no. 2 (February 2004); Moira Herbst, "Labor Shortages: Myth and Reality," *Business Week,* August 21, 2007.

177   *The common wisdom that Americans just won't do*   Anastasiya Bolton, "Farming Jobs Being Picked Clean by U.S. Residents," KUSA-TV, June 22, 2009, http://www.9news .com/news/article.aspx?storyid=118219 (accessed June 25, 2009); Emily Bazar, "Unemployed U.S.-Born Workers Seek Day-Labor Jobs," *USA Today*, December 1, 2009.

177   *The list of business groups advocating looser immigration laws*   "U.S. Chamber of Commerce—Immigration Issues." http://www.uschamber.com/issues/index/ immigration/default (accessed June 18, 2009).

178   *In addition to seeking changes in federal immigration laws*   Randel Johnson, "Labor and Immigration," Policy Positions and Activities, 2008, U.S. Chamber of Commerce (2008).

178   *The focus of EWIC*   American Immigration Law Foundation, 2005 Annual Report (2006).

178   *Compete America represents companies*   Compete America—The Alliance for a Competitive Workforce, http://www.competeamerica.org/ (accessed June 18, 2009).

179   *At a 2007 House subcommittee hearing*   "Comprehensive Immigration Reform: Business Community Perspectives," hearing before the Subcommittee on Immigration, Citizenship, Refugees, Border Security, and International Law of the Committee on the Judiciary, House of Representatives, 110th Cong., 1st sess., June 6, 2007.

179   *During the Bush administration, the push*   "Lobbying Spending Database Immigration," OpenSecrets, 2009, Center for Responsive Politics, http://www .opensecrets.org/lobby/issuesum.php?lname=Immigration&year= (accessed April 4, 2009).

180   *Universities and colleges lobbied*   Roberto G. Gonzales, "Young Lives on Hold: The College Dreams of Undocumented Students," College Board, April 2009.

180   *To business-minded advocates of immigration reform*   Eunice Moscoso, "Fashion Models Could Get More Visas," Cox News Service, June 18, 2008, Washington General News; Jennie Cohen and Radha Vij, "Models & Visas," http://www.nycinteractive .org/2008/issue1/visas/page.swf (accessed June 18, 2009); Jim Snyder, "Everyone Loves a Pretty Face, but Immigration Laws Are Blind," *Hill*, January 24, 2007, 14.

181   *Experts say there are about*   "Nursing Shortage Fact Sheet," American Association of Colleges of Nursing. April 6, 2009; Emergency Nursing Supply Relief Act, HR 2536, 111th Cong., 1st sess., *Congressional Record* (May 20, 2009), H5890; Nursing Relief Act of 2009, HR 1001, 111th Cong., 1st sess., *Congressional Record* (February 11, 2009), H1246; Rick Pollack, Jeanene Martin, and Catherine Sewell. Letter to Rep. Robert Wexler, May 16, 2008, http://www.aha.org/aha/ letter/2008/080516-let-aha-ashraa-wexler.pdf (accessed Oct. 12, 2009).

181   *"Although significant nurse recruitment initiatives have been adopted"*   "The Need for Green Cards for Highly Skilled Workers," Hearing of the Subcommittee on Immigration, Citizenship, Refugees, Border Security, and International Law of the House Committee on the Judiciary, June 12, 2008.

181   *President Obama has also expressed skepticism*   "Closing Remarks by the President at White House Forum on Health Reform, Followed by Q&A, 3/5/09," White House office of the press secretary. March 5, 2009, http://www.whitehouse .gov/the_press_office/Closing-Remarks-by-the-President-at-White-House-Forum- on-Health-Reform/ (accessed June 24, 2009).

182   *Similarly, U.S. computer programmers and engineers*   Senator Charles E. Grassley, "Senator Charles E. Grassley Holds a News Teleconference," ed. CQ Transcriptions, February 11, 2009.

182   *"America must compete in a global economy"*   "Another Harmful 'Stimulus' Provision," *Wall Street Journal*, March 10, 2009.

182   Forbes *writer Megha Bahree*   Megha Bahree, "Chuck Grassley Hurts America," *Forbes*, February 11, 2009.

182   *By the time President Obama signed the economic stimulus legislation*   U.S. Citizenship and Immigration Services, U.S. Department of Homeland Security, *Questions and Answers: Employ American Workers Act and Its Effect on H-1B Petitions* (2009).

182   *The compromise did little to stifle outrage*   "Fragomen—the Leading Provider of Corporate Immigration Services and Solutions." Del Rey Fragomen, Bernsen & Loewy. http://www.fragomen.com/about/about.shtml 9 (accessed April 9, 2009).

183   *"You are giving them a lot of new hoops to jump through"*   Matt Ackermann, "Stimulus Bill to Hamper Hiring of Foreign Experts," *American Banker*, February 18, 2009, 16.

183   *Microsoft Corporation, which has been a heavy user*   Brad Smith, "Appreciating Our Immigration System," http://microsoftontheissues.com/cs/blogs/mscorp/archive/2009/03/30/appreciating-our-immigration-system.aspx, April 1, 2009 (accessed April 9, 2009).

184   *Union organizers showed little regard*   "AFL Resolution Condemns Use of 'Wetbacks' in Farm Labor," *Daily Review*, September 17, 1951.

184   *In the early 1970s, the United Farm Workers union*   Loren Listiak, "UFW Has 'Wet Line' at Border to Discourage Illegal Aliens," *Yuma Daily Sun*, September 18, 1974, 1; Phoenix to Director, FBI, "United Farm Workers Demonstration, Sept. 9–10, Yuma, Arizona, Civil Unrest," memorandum, Oct. 11, 1974. Federal Bureau of Investigation, Communications Section. In Cesar Chavez and United Farm Workers, Federal Bureau of Investigation. http://foia.fbi.gov/foiaindex/chavez.htm (accessed Oct. 12, 2009).

183   *In 1979, Chávez complained that the Immigration and Naturalization Service*   "A Lettuce Strike Takes Unusual Turn," *U.S. News & World Report*, May 28, 1979, 60.

184   *In a turnaround*   "Immigration," AFL-CIO Executive Council, New Orleans, February 16, 2000, http://www.aflcio.org/aboutus/thisistheaflcio/ecouncil/ec0216200b.cfm (accessed June 20, 2009).

184   *In April 2009, the labor federation took yet another step*   "The Labor Movement's Framework for Comprehensive Immigration Reform, AFL-CIO and Change to Win," April 2009, http://www.aflcio.org/issues/civilrights/immigration/upload/immigration reform041409.pdf (accessed June 15, 2009).

185   *"The labor movement is not opposed to temporary workers"*   Comprehensive Immigration Reform in 2009: Can We Do It And How?," hearing of the Immigration, Refugees, and Border Security Subcommittee of the Senate Judiciary Committee, April 30, 2009.

187   *"The assault on lawmakers in Washington was relentless"*   Julia Preston and Randal C. Archibold, "Grass Roots Roared, and an Immigration Plan Fell," *New York Times*, June 10, 2007, 1.

188   *By the summer of 2009, it was clear*   "Statements on Introduced Bills and Joint Resolutions," *Congressional Record*, U.S. Senate, S5504, May 14, 2009; Christine Souza, "Feinstein Reintroduces AgJOBS Bill, *Ag Alert*, May 20, 2009, http://www

.cfbf.com/agalert/AgAlertStory.cfm?ID=1312&ck=F29B38F160F87AE86DF31C
EE1982066F (accessed July 18, 2009).

188   *The slight shift change in tone—away from current needs*   ImmigrationWorks
USA, "ImmigrationWorks USA Talking Points. Future Flow. What Employers
Need in a Bill," http://www.immigrationworksusa.org/uploaded/file/IW%20TALK
ING%20POINTS%20-%20future%20flow%206_3.pdf (accessed June 24, 2009);
Immigration press briefing, Reform Immigration for America. June 24, 2009;
Zuraya Tapia-Alfaro, "Weekly Update on Immigration: As the Economy
Dives, DHS Targets the 'Engine of Our Economy,'" New Democrat Network,
Washington, D.C., http://ndn.org/node/3124 (accessed June 24, 2009).

188   *President Obama's immigration policies*   "Remarks by the President at the
Esperanza National Hispanic Prayer Breakfast," the White House, office of the press
secretary, June 19, 2009, http://www.whitehouse.gov/the_press_office/Remarks-
by-the-President-at-the-Esperanza-National-Hispanic-Prayer-Breakfast/
(accessed June 20, 2009); Mark Hugo Lopez, "The Hispanic Vote in the 2008
Election," Pew Hispanic Center. November 7, 2008; "Immigration Prosecutions at
Record Levels in FY 2009," Transactional Records Access Clearinghouse, Syracuse
University, September 21, 2009. http://trac.syr.edu/immigration/reports/218/
(accessed October 13, 2009).

189   *But making progress on immigration reform*   "Convention 2008—Obama Addresses
the League of United Latin American Citizens (LULAC)," July 9, 2008, http://www
.lulac.org/events/convention/cpress08-2.html (accessed June 20, 2009); Stephen
Lemons, "Phoenix—Feathered Bastard—White House Staffer Disappoints Phoenix
Latino Leaders in Meeting at El Portal (w/Update)," *Phoenix New Times* blogs, June
5, 2009, http://blogs.phoenixnewtimes.com/bastard/2009/06/white_house_rep_
disappoints_ph.php (accessed June 20, 2009); Peter Wallsten, "Immigration Reform
to Get a Quiet Kickoff," *Los Angeles Times*, June 20, 2009; Press briefing by press
secretary Robert Gibbs, White House, office of the press secretary, June 19, 2009.

189   *Washington's long stalemate over immigration*   "2009 State Laws Related to
Immigrants and Immigration, January 1–November 20, 2009," Immigrant Policy
Project, National Conference of State Legislatures, December 1, 2009, http://www
.ncsl.org/default.aspx?tabid=19232 (accessed December 11, 2009).

190   *Face-offs over immigration became particularly intense in the Southwest*   Pat
Flynn, "Phoenix Hard-Nosed Sheriff; He Loves to Lock 'Em Up," *San Diego Union-
Tribune*, March 11, 1996; "Sheriff Arpaio Vows to Not Back Down on Illegal
Immigration Arrests," Maricopa County sheriff's office, March 25, 2009.

11. Southwest Showdowns

191   *It was a typically balmy February afternoon*   "History for Phoenix, AZ," http://www
.wunderground.com/history/airport/KPHX/2004/2/16/DailyHistory.html? (accessed
June 28, 2009).

191   *The Republican chairman, Philip J. Hanson*   Arizona State Legislature, Member
Page, Philip J. Hanson, http://www.azleg.gov/MembersPage.asp?Member_ID=54
&Legislature=46&Session_ID=76 (accessed December 10, 2009); Arizona State
Legislature, Commerce and Military Affairs, House of Representatives Standing
Committee, http://www.azleg.gov/CommitteeInfo.asp?Committee_ID=68 (accessed
May 6, 2008); Minutes of Meeting, Committee on Commerce and Military Affairs,

Arizona House of Representatives, 46th legis., 2nd reg. sess. (February 16, 2004), http://www.azleg.gov/FormatDocument.asp?inDoc=/legtext/46leg/2R/comm_min/House/021604CMA%2EDOC.htm (accessed May 6, 2008).

191   *For years, the political climate in Arizona*   "Arizona Fact Sheet," U.S. Census Bureau, http://factfinder.census.gov/servlet/SAFFFacts?_event =&geo_ id=04000US04 & _ geoContext=01000US%7C04000US04&_street =&_county=&_cityTown=&_ state= 04000US04&_zip=&_lang=en&_sse=on&ActiveGeoDiv=&_useEV=&pct xt=fph&pgsl=040&_submenuId=factsheet_1&ds_name=ACS_2006_SAFF&_ci_ nbr=null&qr_name=null&reg=null%3Anull&_keyword=&_industry=   (accessed May 6, 2008).

192   *While the white population grew by a remarkable 45 percent*   William H. Frey, "Census 2000 Reveals New Native-Born and Foreign-Born Shifts across U.S.," Population Studies Center at the Institute for Social Research, University of Michigan, report no. 02-520 (August 2002).

193   *Arizona's identity had long been shaped by tricultural influences*   "Best of Phoenix 1999," *Phoenix New Times)*, September 30, 1999; "Bank of America to Launch 'Cerca De Ti' Advertising Campaign," *Business Wire*, September 12, 1995.

193   *Along the borderlands of Cochise County*   "2000 LULAC Resolutions," League of United Latin American Citizens, July 1, 2000, http://www.lulac.org/advocacy/resolutions/resolve00.html (accessed May 26, 2008).

194   *Alarmed by the violence, in May 2000*   Joseph Garcia, "Kolbe Urges Clinton: Act Now to Calm U.S. Border," *Tucson Citizen*, May 30, 2000.

194   *At the podium, he enumerated the costs of illegal immigration*   "Brookings-Princeton 'Future of Children' Briefing, Policies for Children in Immigrant Families," Brookings Institution, December 16, 2004, http://www.brookings.edu/comm/events/20041216panel_1.pdf (accessed May 26, 2008); "2 Maricopa County Deputies Shot, Along with Suspect," Associated Press State and Local Wire, December 16, 2004.

195   *Within weeks of taking office in January 2001*   "Russell Pearce,"   Arizona state legislature,   http://www.azleg.gov/MembersPage.asp?Member_ID=109&Legislature=49#bio (accessed June 27, 2009).

195   *"When did it become open season on minorities?"*   "Open Season," *Arizona Daily Star*, January 28, 2003.

195   *"They come here and they're a burden on society"*   Paul Davenport, "Debate on Immigration Initiative Already Heating Up," Associated Press State and Local Wire, July 8, 2003; Marji Allred, "Racists 'Protecting' Arizona," *Arizona Republic*, July 14, 2003.

195   *"This invasion is destroying America," he wrote*   State representative Russell Pearce, "The Costs of Illegal Immigration Costs" (*sic*), *Arizona Conservative*, News and Analysis, 2003, http://www.azconservative.org/PearceOn200.htm (accessed May 26, 2008).

196   *Until that point, business had been restrained*   "HB 2448, Employment of Illegal Aliens," State of Arizona, House of Representatives, 46th legis., 2nd reg. sess. (2004).

196   *It was a serious threat*   Judith Gans, "Immigrants in Arizona: Fiscal and Economic Impacts," Udall Center for Studies in Public Policy, University of Arizona (June 2008).

196   *And while federal law makes it illegal*   "Immigration Enforcement: 'Weaknesses Hinder Employment Verification and Worksite Enforcement Efforts,'" U.S. Government Accountability Office, GAO-05-813 (August 31, 2005).

199   *In March 2004, the Arizona Chamber of Commerce*   "Immigration Policy: Principles and Recommendations," Arizona Chamber of Commerce (March 12, 2004).

199   *Arizona's November 2004 general election*   Christina Leonard, "Thomas Easily Defeats Dem Harris for Position," *Arizona Republic*, November 3, 2004; "State of Arizona Official Canvass, 2004 General Election—November 2, 2004," http://www .azsos.gov/election/2004/General/Canvass2004General.pdf (accessed June 25, 2009).

199   *Organized labor had contributed to the losing campaign*   "Campaign Finance Report, No on 200; Arizonans for Real Immigration Reform," http://www.azsos .gov/cfs/PublicReports/2004/07E6CBAE-FE46-406A-B1A2-79C0CA714028.pdf (accessed June 25, 2009).

199   *Over the next two years, Arizona legislators*   Governor Janet Napolitano to Jim Weiers, "Re: House Bill 2577: Immigration Law; Employment; Enforcement (June 6, 2006), http://www.azsos.gov/public_services/Chapter_Laws/2006/47th_ Legislature_2nd_Regular_Session/HB_2577.pdf (accessed June 25, 2009).

199   *Later that month at the annual awards luncheon*   Mary Jo Pitzl, "Chamber Honors 7 at Annual Awards," *Arizona Republic*, June 26, 2006.

200   *Frustrated by Washington's inaction on immigration*   Abe Levy, "Texas Governor Commits Money to Border Security Plan," Associated Press State and Local Wire, October 12, 2005; Cathy Booth Thomas, "Taking Aim at Immigration in Texas," *Time*, November 17, 2006.

200   *On the floor of the legislature, Anchía made his intentions clear*   Jaime Vasquez, "Regulating Immigration through Fiscal Policymaking: Reexamining Texas's New Margin Tax," *Houston Business and Tax Law Journal* 9, no. 1 (2008).

201   *The proposal sailed through the legislature*   April Castro, "Tax Measure Would Discourage Undocumented Workers," Associated Press State and Local Wire, April 26, 2006; Megan Headley, "How the Immigration Debate Left Texas," *Texas Observer*, March 23, 2007.

201   *"Immigration Issue Sparks Odd Alliance"*   Gary Scharrer, "Immigration Issue Sparks Odd Alliance," *San Antonio Express-News*, June 14, 2006.

201   *With the increasing prospect of immigration restrictionists*   Adams Insurance Service, http://www.adamsins.com/; Jerry Nevlud, "TxSIP Continues Education Effort on Immigration Reform," *Cornerstone* (Spring 2007).

202   *"There are simply too few American workers to fill the jobs we have"*   Texans for Sensible Immigration Policy, http://www.txsip.com/video (accessed June 25, 2009).

202   *While TSIP was producing its video, Hammond*   "The Texas Association of Business: Bill Hammond, President," http://www.txbiz.org/Staff/bio_bill_hammond .asp (accessed June 25, 2009). MALC—Mexican American Legislative Caucus— Texas, http://web.archive.org/web/20051225191354/www.malc.org/membership .html (accessed May 25, 2008).

202   *An early gesture of solidarity was "an unprecedented joint statement"*   "MALC and TAB Urge Defeat of Punitive and Hurtful Amendment," press release, June 27, 2006, http://www.malc.org/pdfs/PR-TAB-062706.pdf (accessed May 28, 2008).

202   *By the time negotiations between Hammond*   Gary Scharrer and Peggy Fikac, "Unity on Immigration Reforms: Hispanic Caucus and the State's Top Business Group See Common Goals," *Houston Chronicle*, August 24, 2006.

203   *In late August 2006, Hammond, Jacoby, and about half a dozen*   Patrick McGee, "Businessmen Promote Legal Immigrants," *Fort Worth Star-Telegram*, August 30, 2006, B4.

203   *Calling for a more robust temporary worker program*   Katherine Yung, "Group Calls for Immigration Overhaul: Texas Business Coalition Urges Guest Worker Program," *Dallas Morning News*, August 30, 2006.

203   *(If there were any question about Pilgrim's*   "Pilgrim's Pride Issues Statement in Response to U.S. Department of Homeland Security's Immigration and Customs Enforcement Action at Five Company Facilities" (April 16, 2008), http://phx .corporate-ir.net/phoenix.zhtml?c=68228&p=irol-newsArticle&ID=1130817& highlight= (accessed June 28, 2009).

204   *By January 9, 2007, when Texas lawmakers*   Juan Castillo, "Texas's Costs, Gains Tallied," *Austin American-Statesman*, December 8, 2006.

204   *The 2007 Texas legislative session promised to be a stormy one*   R. G. Ratcliffe, "Illegal Workers the Talk of Texas," *Houston Chronicle*, January 3, 2007; Dianne Solis, "Anchía Counters Immigration Bills: Plan Would Withhold Incentives to Firms Hiring Illegal Migrants," *Dallas Morning News*, February 3, 2007.

204   *Anchía was referring to a one-paragraph employer sanctions bill*   "An Act Relating to Prohibiting a Grant from the Texas Enterprise Fund to a Recipient who Employs an Undocumented Worker," H.B. no. 351, http://www.legis.state.tx.us/tlodocs/80R/ billtext/html/HB00351I.htm, February 1, 2007 (accessed June 25, 2009).

205   *"Diverse coalition pledge [sic] unity and civility on immigration debate"*   "Diverse coalition pledge [*sic*] unity and civility on immigration debate," Mexican American Legislative Caucus, February 15, 2007. http://www.malc.org/pdfs/Press_ Release_021507_Press_Conf.pdf (accessed June 28, 2009).

206   *Goldwater took a libertarian approach*   John W. Dean and Barry M. Goldwater Jr., *Pure Goldwater* (New York: Palgrave Macmillan, 2008).

206   *Those laissez-faire values toward illegal migrants*   Investigative Reporters and Editors, Inc., "Robert Goldwater Linked to Illegal Mexican Aliens," United Press International, March 21, 1977.

206   *Robert Goldwater and his business partner in the Goldmar Corporation*   Helen DeWar, "Employer Agrees to Aid 'Undocumented' Workers," *Washington Post*, January 31, 1979.

207   *Barry Goldwater Jr., a Republican businessman*   Barry Goldwater Jr., "Hysteria over Illegal Immigrants Must Stop," *Arizona Republic*, November 25, 2007.

208   *"Our conservative leaders today"*   Anne Denogean, "Migrant Debate Rhetoric Alarms Goldwater Jr.," *Tucson Citizen*, December 10, 2007, 1A.

208   *Things were certainly not looking good for Arizona businesses*   State of Arizona, House of Representatives, 48th legis., 1st reg. sess. (2007), chap. 279, House Bill 2779, http://www.azleg.gov/FormatDocument.asp?inDoc=/legtext/48leg/1r/laws/ 0279.htm.

208   *Arizona businesses got the message*   Pew Hispanic Center, "Arizona: Population and Labor Force Characteristics, 2000–2006," January 23, 2008, http://pewhispanic .org/files/factsheets/37.pdf (accessed June 28, 2009).

210   *On July 2, 2007*   "Governor Signs Employer Sanctions Bill." State of Arizona, Governor Janet Napolitano, news release. July 2, 2007.

211   *"I'll tell you what," Magruder amplified*   Wake,Up! Arizona kickoff press conference, July 17, 2007.

212   *Within weeks of the Arizona sanctions law enactment*   *Arizona Contractors Association et al v. Napolitano et al.*, U.S. District Court for the District of Arizona, CV- 07-1355-PHX-NVW.

213   *As business groups fought the employer sanctions law in Arizona*   "Immigration Works USA—Who We Are," ImmigrationWorks USA, http://www.immigration worksusa.org/index.php?p=20 (accessed April 7, 2009).

12. Fresh Blood and National Selection

214   *"U.S. immigration policy should encourage high-skill immigration"*   Robert Rector, House of Representatives Judiciary Subcommittee on Immigration, Citizenship, Refugees, Border Security, and International Law (May 17, 2007).

214   *Rector's viewpoint was echoed not only by the Bush administration*   "Immigration," White House, http://www.whitehouse.gov/issues/immigration (accessed June 6, 2009).

215   *Putting national economic interests in the forefront*   "Donor Lookup," OpenSecrets .Org,   http://www.opensecrets.org/indivs/donor_lookup.php?name=meissner,%20 doris (accessed June 6, 2009).

215   *"Perhaps the most broken element of the nation's immigration system"*   Karoun Demirjian, "Immigration: New Faces, Better Odds," *Congressional Quarterly Weekly*, May 30, 2009; U.S. Chamber of Commerce, "U.S. Chamber Resists Immigration Commission to Control Flow of Workers," States News Service, June 1, 2009; "ImmigrationWorks USA Talking Points, What Employers Need in a Bill," ImmigrationWorks USA, June 3, 2009, http://www.immigrationworksusa.org/ uploaded/file/IW%20TALKING%20POINTS%20-%20future%20flow%206_3.pdf (accessed June 23, 2009).

216   *Either way, the romantic "golden door" allusion offered by Emma Lazarus*   Philip L. Martin, "The United States: Benign Neglect Toward Immigration," in *Controlling Immigration: A Global Perspective*, ed. Wayne A. Cornelius, Philip L. Martin, and Frank Hollifield (Palo Alto, Calif.: Stanford University Press, 1994), 83–100.

216   *Even during the most restrictive periods of U.S. immigration policy*   Kitty Calavita, "Administrative Officials Apply the Law: Two Historical Examples: Collisions at the Intersection of Gender, Race, and Class: Enforcing the Chinese Exclusion Laws," *Law and Society Review* 40 (June 30, 2006); "President Orders Courtesy to Chinese," *New York Times*, June 26, 1905.

216   *Subsequent immigration measures*   Immigration Act of 1921, *United States Statutes at Large* 42 (1921): 5–7.

217   *Complex formulas and numerical ceilings*   Ruth Ellen Wasem, "U.S. Immigration Policy on Permanent Admissions," Congressional Research Service, Library of Congress, February 18, 2004; "Visa Bulletin for June 2009," U.S. Department of State 9, no. 9 (2009), http://travel.state.gov/visa/frvi/bulletin/bulletin_4497.html (accessed June 26, 2009).

217   *The U.S. government's immigration priority*   Kelly Jefferys and Randall Monger, "U.S. Legal Permanent Residents: 2007. Annual Flow Report, March 2008," Office of Immigration Statistics, Policy Directorate, U.S. Department of Homeland Security (March 2008).

217   *But there has been pressure to change the system*   Teresa Watanabe, "Businesses, Families Have a Lot Riding on Immigration Change," *Los Angeles Times*, May 21, 2007.

219   *But Mrs. Dello's apparent tolerance*   "Transatlantic Trends, Immigration 2009 Country Specific Results, United Kingdom," German Marshall Fund of the United States, December 9, 2009. http://www.gmfus.org/trends/immigration/doc/TTI2009-UK.doc (accessed December 12, 2009).

220   *In half a century, the size of Britain's*   "Country and Comparative Data," Migration Policy Institute, http://www.migrationinformation.org/DataHub/countrydata/data.cfm (accessed February 21, 2009).

220   *After World War II, until 1962*   Dhananjayan Sriskandarajah and Francesca Hopwood Road, "United Kingdom: Rising Numbers, Rising Anxieties," Migration Policy Institute (May 2005), http://www.migrationinformation.org/Profiles/display.cfm?ID=306 (accessed February 21, 2009); D. A. Coleman, "Ins and Outs of British Migration Policy," *Social Contract* (Summer 1994), http://www.thesocialcontract.com/artman2/publish/tsc0404/article_355.shtml (accessed February 21, 2009); Arriën Kruyt and Jan Niessen, "Integration," in *Immigrant Policy for a Multicultural Society. A Comparative Study of Integration, Language, and Religious Policy in Five Western European Countries*, ed. Hans Vermeulen (Brussels: Migration Policy Group, 1997), 37–38.

220   *Rising unemployment, racism, and the formation of immigrant neighborhoods* Enoch Powell, "Enoch Powell's 'Rivers of Blood' Speech." *Telegraph.co.uk* (November 6, 2007), http://www.telegraph.co.uk/comment/3643823/Enoch-Powell%27s-%27Rivers-of-Blood%27-speech.html (accessed February 21, 2009).

221   *The more recent adoption by the United Kingdom of a "managed migration"*   Demetrios G. Papademetriou, "Selecting Economic Stream Immigrants through Points Systems," Migration Policy Institute (May 18, 2007), http://www.migrationinformation.org/USfocus/display.cfm?ID=602 (accessed February 21, 2009).

221   *Under the British system, employers may import workers*   "U.K. Border Agency, About Us," http://www.ukba.homeoffice.gov.uk/aboutus/ (accessed February 21, 2009); "Skilled, Shortage, Sensible: The Recommended Shortage Occupation Lists for the United Kingdom and Scotland," United Kingdom Border Agency (September 9, 2008), http://www.ukba.homeoffice.gov.uk/sitecontent/documents/aboutus/workingwithus/mac/uklist (accessed February 21, 2009).

224   *The JCWI had urged the government*   *The Points-Based System: Can It Really Make Labour Migration Work for Britain?: A Critique of the PBS*, Joint Council for the Welfare of Immigrants (November 2006): 3.

226   *The careful migration management*   Marianne Slegers and Nathalie Vandystadt, "Immigration: Parliament Cautiously Backs Blue Card' Scheme," *Europolitique* (November 25, 2008).

227   *Poland became a part of a more or less borderless Europe*   "Internal Border Controls to Be Lifted between the New and Old Member States as of 31 December 2007 and 29 March 2008," Finland's European Union presidency (December 5, 2006), http://www.eu2006.fi/news_and_documents/press_releases/vko49/en_GB/177677/ (accessed February 22, 2009); "European Migration Policy Receives Funding," *Europaworld* (December 15, 2006), http://www.europaworld.org/week289/europeanmigration151206.html (accessed February 22, 2009).

228   *Between 2004 and 2006, Polish border authorities*   "Wladza Wdrazajaca Program Wspólpracy Przygranicznej," *Podstawa Prawna*, June 28, 2005, http://translate.google.com/translate?prev=_t&hl=en&ie=UTF-8&u=http%3A%2F%2Fwww.wwpe.gov.pl%2Findex.php&sl=auto&tl=en&history_state0= (accessed February 23, 2009).

228   *Ostrowski took me to see another European-financed*   Kinga Rodkiewicz, "Immigration Center Opens in Przemysl," *Krakow Post*, November 24, 2007; Caroline Brothers, "Obscurity and Confinement for Migrants in Europe," *International Herald Tribune*, December 30, 2007.

229   *An estimated forty thousand*   Aleksandra Grzymala-Kazlowska and Marek Okólski, "Influx and Integration of Migrants in Poland in the Early Twenty-first Century," Institute for Social Studies, Warsaw University (Fall 2003).

229   *One program is the E.U. Border Assistance Mission*   "EUBAM Press Pack," European Union (December 2007), http://www.eubam.org/files/300-399/323/press-pack-eng-jan 08.pdf (accessed February 21, 2009).

229   *Although ostensibly started as a result of requests*   "Political Outlook: E.U. Enlargement," *Economist* (December 12, 2008); Markus Euskirchen, Henrik Lebuhn, and Gene Ray, "From Borderline to Borderland: The Changing European Border Regime," *Monthly Review* (November 2007).

231   *Human rights groups criticized Morocco*   "Spain: Deportations to Morocco Put Migrants at Risk," Human Rights Watch (October 12, 2005), http://www.hrw .org/en/news/2005/10/12/spain-deportations-morocco-put-migrants-risk?print (accessed February, 23, 2009).

231   *In actuality, Morocco had received billions of dollars*   "European Neighborhood and Partnership Instrument," Morocco Strategy Paper 2007–2013," European Commission—External Relations (March 8, 2007), http://ec.europa.eu/world/enp/ pdf/country/enpi_csp_morocco_en.pdf (accessed February 23, 2009); "Morocco Urges E.U. to Abandon Policy of Repatriating Immigrants," BBC Worldwide Monitoring (July 9, 2008).

232   *In addition to cornering people*   "Canaries Migrant Death Toll Soars," BBC News (December 28, 2006).

232   *To try to stem the exodus*   "Finance," Frontex. http://www.frontex.europa.eu/ finance/; "Examples of Accomplished Operations," Frontex (September 16, 2007), http://www.frontex.europa.eu/examples_of_accomplished_operati/art5.html (accessed February 23, 2009).

233   *But as the U.S. immigration experience has shown* "All In the Same Boat: The Challenges of Mixed Migration," *UNHCR—Asylum and Migration*, UNHCR— the United Nations Refugee Agency, http://www.unhcr.org/pages/4a1d406060 .html (accessed June 6, 2009).

234   *Much of the equipment used by Senegal*   Alexandre Grosbois, "Spain, Senegal Seal Deals to Stem Wave of Illegal African Migration," Agence France Press, December 5, 2006.

235   *The Europeans also are aware that the demands*   "The Global Approach to Migration One Year On: Toward a Comprehensive European Migration Policy, Communication from the Commission to the Council and the European Parliament," Commission of the European Communities, Brussels (November 30, 2006), http://eur-lex.europa.eu/LexUriServ/site/en/com/2006/com2006_0735en01.pdf (accessed June 25, 2009).

236   *"The American people want their government"*   "Sen. Schumer Announces Principles for Comprehensive Immigration Reform Bill in Works in Senate," *U.S. Fed. News*, June 24, 2009.

236   *The message was identical to one*   "Emergency Preparedness and Immigration Reform," remarks by Secretary of Homeland Security Janet Napolitano at the National Hispanic Prayer Breakfast, Washington, D.C. (June 19, 2009).

237   *"the majestic quality of the law"*   Anatole France, *The Red Lily (Le Lys Rouge)* (New York: Current Literature, 1910), 87.

13. "Torn Apart for the Need to Survive"

238   *On Monday, January 5, 2009, with the economic downturn in full bore*   Paul Kane, Lori Montgomery, and Shailagh Murray, "Obama Pitches Stimulus Plan; GOP Asked to Help Design Bill; $300 Billion in Tax Cuts Sought," *Washington Post*, January 6, 2009; "Wall Street Pares Losses, Eyes Obama," Agence France Presse—English, January 5, 2009; Joseph Tartakoff, "Analyst Says 10% Staff Cuts at Microsoft Would Help Stock but Massive Layoffs Appear Unlikely," *Seattle Post-Intelligencer*, January 6, 2009; Chris in Paris, "Microsoft to Announce Job Cuts," *AMERICAblog*, January 5, 2009.

238   *The policy proposal came in the form of a posting*   Microsoft, "Microsoft—Developing, Attracting, and Retaining the World's Best and Brightest," Change .Gov, office of the President-elect, http://change.gov/open_government/entry/microsoft_developing_attracting_and_retaining_the_worlds_best_and_brightest/, January 5, 2009 (accessed June 26, 2009).

239   *Microsoft's long-term plan for more migrant employees*   "Microsoft Reports Second-Quarter Results," Microsoft Corporation, January 22, 2009, http://www.microsoft .com/presspass/press/2009/jan09/01-22fy09Q2earnings.mspx (accessed June 29, 2009).

239   *"There are only so many brains available"*   James Detar, "Europe Wants World's Brightest As America Keeps Limits Tight; with Plenty of Options, High-Skilled Foreigners Might Look Elsewhere," *Investor's Business Daily*, December 12, 2007.

240   *California landscape contractors*   Harry Funk, "Employing Immigrants: Legal Status, Not a Wall, Will Help Illegal Workers," *San Diego Union-Tribune*, February 9, 2006.

240   *"Europe is facing a demographic time-bomb"*   Graham Watson, "Mitigating Risk, Maximizing Benefit: Towards a Progressive Migration Policy for Europe," in *Making Migration Work for Europe*, ed. Christine Gilmore (Somerset, U.K.: Bagehot, 2008), 73.

241   *"Invasion from Mexico; It Just Keeps Growing"*   William L. Chaze, "Invasion from Mexico; It Just Keeps Growing," *U.S. News & World Report*, March 7, 1983; Alan L. Adler, "Even Beefed-Up Forces Can't Stem Rising Tide of Illegals," *Los Angeles Times*, June 1, 1986; Tom Morganthau, Gloria Borger, Nikki Finke Greenberg, Elaine Shannon, Renee Michael, Daniel Pedersen, et al., "Closing the Door?," *Newsweek*, June 25, 1984; George J. Church, Carolyn Lesh, and Richard Woodbury, "We Are Overwhelmed," *Time* June 25, 1984; John Dillin, "Illegal Immigration Surges in '89," *Christian Science Monitor*, December 27, 1989.

241   *In 1984, producing a public television documentary*   Jeffrey Kaye, "L.A.'s Tomorrow," KCET-TV, February 1984.

242   *In Poland, Border Guard major Marek Osetek*   Anna Mazurkiewicz, "Vietnamese Immigration to Poland," *Contemporary Perspectives on Immigration*, Immigration History Research Center, March 10, 2008, http://blog.lib.umn.edu/ihrc/immigration/2008/03/vietnameseimmigration_to_pola.html (accessed January 27, 2009).

242   *Those, of course, are among the tamer reactions*   Sarah Schafer, "Russia's Recession Squeezes Migrants," *Washington Post*, February 8, 2009.

243   *In Italy, in February 2009*   Leigh Phillips, "Italy Creates Anti-Immigrant Vigilante 'Patrols,'" EUobserver.com, February 18, 2009.

243   *And in England at about the same time*   David Brown, Richard Ford, and Fran Yeoman, "Volatile Mix of Jobs and Race Will Give Ministers the Jitters," *Times* of

London, February 12, 2009; John Mahoney, "Foreign Workers Flood Will Spark Riots, Warns Bishop," London *Daily Star*, February 27, 2009.

244   *It's a three-pronged attack, the 'Triple I'"* U.S. Department of Homeland Security, Office of Public Affairs, "Fact Sheet: The ICE 287(g) Program: A Law Enforcement Partnership," November 19, 2008.

245   *Not surprisingly, the American Civil Liberties Union* Ortega Melendres et al. v. Arpaio et al., first amended complaint, U.S. District Court, District of Arizona, July 16, 2008.

245   *In response to complaints, the federal government* Daniel González, "Arpaio to Be Investigated over Alleged Violations," *Arizona Republic*, March 11, 2009; Daniel González, Amy B. Wang, and Lisa Halverstadt, "Sweeps Led ICE to Limit Arpaio Power," *Arizona Republic*; October 17, 2009; Matt Bunk, "Poll Shows High Approval Rating for Maricopa County Sheriff Joe Arpaio," *Arizona Capitol Times*, October 28, 2009.

245   *Similar migration law enforcement issues have played out* "Local Immigration Teams to Be Introduced across the U.K. Home Office," Home Office, June 19 2008, http://www.bia.homeoffice.gov.uk/sitecontent/newsarticles/2008/localimmigration teamstobe (accessed February 28, 2009); Migrants Rights Network, *Migrants Rights News* 8 (July 2008), http://www.migrantsrights.org.uk/enews/2008/july .htm#crimepartenrship (accessed February 28, 2009).

246   *Another U.K. rights group* Jon Burnett, "PAFRAS Briefing Paper Number 7," in *Wage Exploitation and Undocumented Labour*, PAFRAS (Positive Action for Refugees and Asylum Seekers) (October 2008).

247   *On the international scene, debate about migration* International Convention on the Protection of the Rights of All Migrant Workers and Members of Their Families, office of the U.N. high commissioner for human rights (OHCHR), http://www2 .ohchr .org/english/bodies/cmw/cmw.htm (accessed June 30, 2009); U.N. Treaty Collection, http://treaties.un.org/Pages/ViewDetails.aspx?src=TREATY&mtdsg_ no=IV-13&chapter=4&lang=en (accessed June 30, 2009).

248   *There may be other ways to regulate migration* Jagdish Bhagwati, "Borders beyond Control," *Foreign Affairs* (January/February 2003); Peter Deselaers, "Population: Annan Calls for U.N. Migration Agency," IPS-Inter Press Service, November 22, 2003.

248   *The proposal for an agency that might rein in rich countries* "Nations Must Manage Migration, U.S. Official Says. Human Trafficking, Smuggling Result from Improper Controls," America.gov, March 29, 2005, http://www.america .gov/st/washfile-english/2005/March/20050329165204cmretrop0.5620233 .html#ixzz0JxhcyoDv&C (accessed June 30, 2009).

248   *The Geneva-based International Organization for Migration* "MC/INF/274—IOM Strategy: Current and Future Migration Realities and IOM's Role," International Organization for Migration (IOM), November 4, 2004, http://www.iom.int/jahia/ webdav/shared/shared/mainsite/about_iom/en/council/88/MC_INF_274.pdf (accessed June 30, 2009); "IOM—about IOM," http://www.iom.int/jahia/Jahia/ pid/2 (accessed June 30, 2009); "MC/2258—Programme and Budget for 2009" (October 3, 2008), http://www.iom.int/jahia/webdav/shared/shared/mainsite/about_ iom/en/council/96/MC2258.pdf (accessed June 30, 2009); "MC/INF/287—IOM Strategy," Organization for Migration (IOM), November 9, 2007, http://www.iom .int/jahia/webdav/shared/shared/mainsite/about_iom/docs/res1150_en.pdf (accessed June 30, 2009).

251   *"Despite massive increases in border enforcement"*   Douglas S. Massey, "Beyond the Border Buildup: Towards a New Approach to Mexico-U.S. Migration (the Second in a Two-Part Series on Rethinking Immigration)," *Immigration Policy in Focus* 4, no. 7 (2005): 8.

251   *In Europe the following year*   Stephen Castles, "Back to the Future? Can Europe Meet Its Labour Needs through Temporary Migration?," International Migration Institute, James Martin Twenty-first Century School, Oxford University (2006).

251   *Aerospace and defense companies*   "Fact Sheet: Fiscal Year 2008," Office of Public Affairs, U.S. Immigration and Customs Enforcement, U.S. Department of Homeland Security (December 28, 2007), http://www.ice.gov/doclib/pi/news/factsheets/2008budgetfactsheet.pdf (accessed July 1, 2009); "Federal Contracts from Bureau of Immigration and Customs Enforcement, FY 2008, summary," http://www.usaspending.gov/fpds/fpds.php??reptype=a&database=fpds&mod_agency=7012&program_source_agency_code=&program_source_account_code=&program_source_desc=&mod_fund_agency=&PIID=&psc_cat=&psc_sub=&contractor_type=&descriptionOfContractRequirement=&compete_cat=&typeOfContractPricing=&dollar_tot=&fiscal_year=2008&first_year_range=&last_year_range=&detail=-1&datype=T&email=&busn_indctr= (accessed July 1, 2009).

251   *From sophisticated biometrics, to aerial surveillance*   "Protecting Public Safety," Accenture, August 1, 2008, http://www.accenture.com/NR/rdonlyres/4DB31375-B1ED-4669-9988-A93BA7ABC246/0/ProtectingPublicSafety.pdf (accessed July 1, 2009); Henry W. Boesel "PowerPoint Presentation," October 27, 2008, http://www.eu-ru.info/index-Dateien/project/photonics/Project%20Presentation_Henry%20Boesel_Moscow.pdf (accessed July 1, 2009); "Alcatel-Lucent Deploys Advanced Electro-Optical Observation Tower System in Poland," *The A to Z of Optics* . . . AZoM.com, November 21, 2007, http://www.azooptics.com/Details.asp?NewsID=1125 (accessed July 1, 2009); "Home—Precise Biometrics—World-Leading Provider of Match-on-Card, Biometrics for Smart Cards," http://www.precisebiometrics.com/ (accessed July 2, 2009).

252   *With some 43 percent of the ICE budget*   Leslie Wayne, "Sikh Group Finds Calling in Homeland Security," *New York Times*, September 28, 2004; Maxim Kniazkov, "Peace, Love, and Sikhism; Hippies Choose New Path," *Washington Times*, February 23, 2007; Anne Constable, "Sikh Leader Yogi Bhajan Dies," *Santa Fe New Mexican*, October 8, 2004; "Interested in Working for Akal on One of Our Homeland Security Contracts for Immigration and Customs Enforcement (ICE)?," http://www.akalsecurity.com/ice (accessed July 1, 2009).

252   *A growing population of deportees*   Cornell Companies, Inc., Form 10K (filed March 6, 2009), http://www.sec.gov/Archives/edgar/data/1016152/0001104659090 15153/a09-1374_110k.htm (accessed July 1, 2009).

252   *Executives from the Florida-headquartered GEO Group*   "Q4 2008 the GEO Group Earnings Conference Call—Final," FD (Fair Disclosure) Wire, February 12, 2009.

253   *Many private prison firms have global reaches*   The GEO Group, Inc., Form 10K (filed February 18, 2009), http://www.sec.gov/Archives/edgar/data/923796/00009 5014409001411/0000950144-09-001411-index.idea.htm (accessed July 1, 2009); "Immigration Removal Centres" Home Office, U.K. Border Agency, http://www.ukba.homeoffice.gov.uk/managingborders/immigrationremovalcentres/ (accessed June 30, 2009); "Serco Signs AUS$370M Contract with Australian Government

to Transform Immigration Centres," press release, June 29, 2009, Serco Group plc, http://www.serco.com/media/pressreleases/2009/daic.asp (accessed July 1, 2009).

253 *Oxford University's Stephen Castles*   Castles, "Back to the Future?"

254 *Our conversations and debates about migration*   "European Pact on Immigration and Asylum," Council of the European Union, Brussels, September 24, 2008, http://register .consilium.europa.eu/pdf/en/08/st13/st13440.en08.pdf (accessed July 1, 2009).

254 *In Southern California, where I live*   "Turf Removal," http://www.socalwatersmart .com/index.php?option=com_content&view=article&id=77&Itemid=102 (accessed June 24, 2009); Jeffrey Kaye, "Water Recycling Efforts Spark Policy Debate in California," *NewsHour with Jim Lehrer*, PBS-TV, March 24, 2008.

255 *There are ample precedents for planning rewards and disincentives*   "Agricultural Policies in OECD Countries: At a Glance 2008," Organization for Economic Cooperation and Investment, http://www.oecd.org/document/47/0,3343,en_2649_ 33773_40900655_1_1_1_37401,00.html (accessed July 2, 2009).

255 *Perhaps a migration tax on recruiters*   Fely Marilyn E. Lorenzo, Jaime Galvez-Tan, Kriselle Icamina, and Lara Javier, "Nurse Migration from a Source Country Perspective: Philippine Country Case Study," *Health Services Research* 42, no. 3, pt. 2 (2007): 1406–1418; Annie Gorman, "Unbalanced Care: Nurse Migration in the Philippines," *Heinz School Review* 4, no. 4 (2007), http://journal.heinz.cmu .edu/articles/unbalanced-care/ (accessed June 25, 2009).

INDEX